So How's the Family?
and Other Essays

ALSO BY ARLIE HOCHSCHILD

So How's the Family?

AND OTHER ESSAYS

ARLIE RUSSELL HOCHSCHILD

UNIVERSITY OF CALIFORNIA PRESS
Berkeley   Los Angeles   London

University of California Press, one of the most distinguished university presses in the United States, enriches lives around the world by advancing scholarship in the humanities, social sciences, and natural sciences. Its activities are supported by the UC Press Foundation and by philanthropic contributions from individuals and institutions. For more information, visit www.ucpress.edu.

University of California Press
Berkeley and Los Angeles, California

University of California Press, Ltd.
London, England

Library of Congress Cataloging-in-Publication Data

Hochschild, Arlie Russell, 1940–
    So how's the family? : and other essays / Arlie Russell Hochschild.
        pages   cm.
    Includes bibliographical references and index.
    ISBN 978-0-520-27227-9 (cloth : alk. paper)
    ISBN 978-0-520-27228-6 (pbk. : alk. paper)
    1. Families—United States.   2. Women—Social conditions.
3. United States—Social conditions—1980–   I. Title.
    HQ536.H6324   2013
    306.850973—dc23   2013003818

Manufactured in the United States of America
22 21 20 19 18 17 16 15 14 13
10 9 8 7 6 5 4 3 2 1

In keeping with a commitment to support environmentally responsible and sustainable printing practices, UC Press has printed this book on Rolland Enviro100, a 100% post-consumer fiber paper that is FSC certified, deinked, processed chlorine-free, and manufactured with renewable biogas energy. It is acid-free and EcoLogo certified.

For Rosa and Sonia

To see what is in front of one's nose needs a constant struggle.

George Orwell

Contents

WOMEN ON THE GLOBAL BACKSTAGE

Acknowledgments

Many thanks to Naomi Schneider of the University of California Press, who shepherded these essays into print with such heartening enthusiasm and care, and to the artist who drew the picture on the cover of the book, her eight-year-old daughter. And thanks for an extremely careful job to Christopher Lura, production editor Brian Ostrander at Westchester Publishing Services, and copy editor Vickie West.

Thanks to the anonymous readers for the Press and to Neil Smelser and Rob Willer for their extremely helpful comments on the manuscript, especially on "Empathy Maps." A very special thanks to Allison Pugh for a bracing but fantastic tough-love read that rescued me from the idea that I was done. Warm thanks to Sarah Garrett, my gifted co-author on "The Personalized Market and the Marketized Self" and comrade-in-arms through the long process of updating statistics and integrating fresh readings into the text. To Bonnie Kwan, deep thanks for her help through every stage of production, her loyal friendship, and her delicious sense of the absurd. To Anita Garey and Karen Hansen, I give my deep thanks for our safely probing conversations during summer visits over the years, a precious gift to this book and to me. To Adam, my deepest gratitude for taking time from his own emerging book on the Spanish Civil War to patiently revisit long-discussed ideas, and for all that he does and is.

And to Rosa, 7, whose leprechaun trap sits waiting on our kitchen floor, and to Sonia, 5, who offered me her most precious box of colored sequins, I dedicate this book.

Introduction

Most of the essays in this book originated as scribbles and exclamation points on yellow, lined paper, and they were often a puzzle to decipher months later. From there, they grew into public lectures, which found their way into print mostly in the last decade, and here they are newly revised. Two essays, "So How's the Family?" and "Empathy Maps," I wrote expressly for this book, while one essay, "The Diplomat's Wife," is the very first one I wrote.

Re-reading that essay decades later, I recall a powerful split between two parts of myself—one geared to "doing" and the other to "figuring things out." The year was 1965. Movements of social justice were sweeping the nation as well as the University of California at Berkeley campus where I was a graduate student in sociology. The civil rights movement was on, and I was fresh from a stint teaching black history at Palmer

Institute in Sedalia, North Carolina, and work as a freedom school teacher in Vicksburg, Mississippi. Almost weekly, hundreds of Free Speech activists protesting a ban on students' rights to sit behind political activity tables in the central plaza were being bused to jail. Fourteen thousand students and others opposed to the Vietnam War marched from the campus to an Oakland army base, holding signs such as "Peace in Vietnam," "Return to the Geneva Convention," or in one case, simply "Why?" Barred from the base, students were tear-gassed, beaten, and jailed. The feminist movement was soon to emerge through hundreds of consciousness-raising groups and departmental caucuses. Berkeley was at the epi-center of the national ferment of the 1960s.

With these movements swirling about me, I set about the quiet, steady work of gathering intellectual tools with which to clearly understand what was going on. One day, while researching my first essay, I was poring through an arcane 1963 U.S. Department of State bulletin sent to protocol officers and others at diplomatic missions around the world. It was an etiquette book for diplomats. In what order should various officers and their wives enter and exit a diplomatic reception, it asked. Ambassador first, counselor second, economic officer third, on down in order of importance. How long should the wife of a junior officer stay for an initial courtesy visit to the ambassador's wife? ("Approximately 20 minutes unless strongly urged by the hostess to stay longer," although the pamphlet warned that "Must you go so soon?" does not mean she really wants you to stay.)[1]

Reading about such decorous ritual moments while tear gas canisters were flying outside seemed a little like walking in on Elizabeth Bennett having tea in Jane Austen's *Pride and Prejudice*, while Tom Paine pounded on the front door, the American Revolution astir behind him. Part of me wanted to march out the door behind Tom Paine, the other part wanted to hang out in the parlor with Austen, curious to see what was really going on there. I wanted to climb inside the mind of the protocol officer who penned that advice, the mannerly world of the diplomat, the confining place of women in that world, and perhaps, above all, the dilemma of my mother who had spent thirty years quietly trapped in it. I wanted to find a magic key to unlock her gilded cage, it occurs to me now, and I was scouring sociology in search of it. I could not find that particular key, it turned out, but I collected other great magic keys along the way.[2] And my search began to link the public trends astir at that time to the more private world of the family. Some keys unlocked the injustices that so stubbornly remained long after the parades had passed and the marchers gone home. Other keys helped me into the lives of time-stretched working families, online daters, migrant nannies, commercial surrogate mothers, and others, as I report in this book, a sequel to my 2003 collection of essays *The Commercialization of Intimate Life: Notes from Home and Work.*

Some essays reflect a historical approach. In chapter 7, Sarah Garrett and I explore the shifting cultural meaning of terms such as "brand" appearing in the pages of the *New York Times* in the periods 1899–1901, 1969–71, and 2003–2005. At the beginning of the twentieth century, "brand" was used mainly to refer to animals and slaves and was spoken of as a neutral or bad thing. By the end of the century, "brand" was used to describe colleges, museums, and human beings, often to make them seem good. Other essays reflect a cross-national approach. In chapter 4, for example, I compare the wealth gap in the United States to that within Sweden, Japan, and other democracies, and in chapters 10, 11, and 12, I describe nannies and surrogates caught in the great divide between the rich and poor nations of the world.

In all these essays, I use the term "family" broadly to refer to all who feel like family—heterosexual, gay, lesbian, bisexual, and transsexual couples, married or unmarried, with and without children. For I think of families as our most precious and emotionally powerful form of mutual commitment. Also, although I have tried hard to limit repetition across essays, and between these essays and my books, some remains. In some cases, I have drawn passages from my books (listed at the beginning of this one) to pursue new points. In other cases, I sketch a context in one essay in the way I do in another, so a reader can understand one without having to read the other. Revising these essays, I have felt as if I were crisscrossing the same mountain, so to speak, binoculars in hand, telling of streambed dwellers on one expedition, and mountaintop dwellers on another, always bearing in mind the whole habitat.

EMOTION AND THE AMERICAN SELF

Varied though they are, all these essays derive from my deepest belief that it is through emotion that we know the world.[3] Without emotion, the world loses color and meaning. This might seem an obvious thing to say if it did not fly in the face of our usual American understanding of self. For many of us hold to the idea that a rational self is an emotion-free self, and that emotion gets in the way of rational understanding.[4] But the more fundamentally we understand emotion, our own and that of others, the better we know the world around us, and the closer we come to being reasonable people; and the better we get at detecting fake rationality. For many deeply irrational events—conduct in the Nazi camps, the Soviet show trials, the Cambodian killing fields, the torture of political prisoners around the world—are achieved through apparently emotionless, orderly, mechanical acts by people who claim to be rational.

In addition to valuing a non-emotional self, Americans have historically revered the independent self. Being self-reliant, self-controlling, start-from-the-bottom, non-dependent—we admire these things. They fit our history as a democratic, immigrant-based, entrepreneurial culture, proudly free of feudal or totalitarian rule. Psychologists who study "locus of control" find American students more likely to endorse such statements as "My life is determined by my own actions" or "When I get what I want, it is usually because I worked hard for it" than their counterparts in East Asia, Central America, Europe, or Canada.[5] Male business students born in America had higher ratings on locus of control than male business students born in Mexico.[6]

But every "I" comes with a "we." We depend on others and stand ready to be depended upon. The idea of the independent self, separated from history and circumstance, is a fiction. I often remember a student's remark: "It sure takes a lot of people—parents, aunts, uncles, teachers, friends, specialists, strangers—to make one independent self." Indeed, if my essays could speak in chorus, they would say, "Through what we imagine and do, we are forever *relating to* others, and often more dependent on them than we'd like." As the Argentine novelist Jorge Luis Borges noted in *Brodie's Report*—a story focusing on one person named

Brodie—"in every story there are thousands of protagonists, visible and invisible, alive and dead."[7]

Not only do we depend on other people, we are also creatures of larger circumstance—a widening class gap, a crashing job market, a warming and more volatile climate that leads to such things as rising food prices, and new anxieties. One circumstance we do not control is the very culture of the era into which we are born, and its tacit rules of emotional control. As the German sociologist Norbert Elias has argued in *The History of Manners,* modern society obliges us to cultivate a modern—and more emotionally controlled—self. As clans became fiefdoms and fiefdoms became nations, he pointed out, people developed wider networks of social interdependence.[8] To sustain those needed relationships, people learned greater emotional self-control. We moderns mind our manners and manage our emotions far better, Elias said, than our counterparts in medieval times did, when quarrels more often flared into murder and the sight of flesh led to acts of rape.[9] As we come to appreciate the importance of emotion management, we will become a more civilized people.

So what is an emotion? Is it a matter of pure biology and thus pretty much the same for everyone? Or do aspects of emotion—sadness, joy, jealousy—vary from one culture to another? One premise underlying all these essays is that culture has found its way into emotion. For one thing, various cultures provide special inventories of prototypic feelings. Like differently tuned keys on a piano, each cultural prototype guides us in the act of discerning different inner notes. As I have written, the Tahitians have one word—sick—for what people in other cultures might call ennui, depression, grief, or sadness. According to the novelist Milan Kundera, the Czech word *litost* refers to an indefinable longing, mixed with remorse and grief, a term with no equivalent in any other language.[10]

We *listen for* feelings in different ways. A man I met on a recent trip to Rovaniemi, Finland, a town by the Arctic Circle, described walking alone in the snow: "You walk along in whiteness. Suddenly there is a startling flutter of wings, and you see a white snowbird, its two black eyes staring at you. After that, you listen to the snow differently." Many people listen *to*—and listen *for*—feelings the way this man listens to the snow. Perhaps the more inexpressive the culture, the more one tunes an ear to ever-so-slight shifts in tone.

We have ideas about what feelings *should* be. We say, "You should be thrilled at winning the prize," or "You should be furious at his insult." We appraise the fit between a feeling and a context in light of what I call "feeling rules." By these rules, we try to manage our feelings—to feel happy at a party or grief-stricken at a funeral.

When paid to do a job, we are often asked to abide by certain feeling rules; thus, the company edict that "the customer is always right" means we do not have the "right" to feel mad at a customer, even if we are. So we find ourselves doing emotional labor—the effort to *seem* to feel and to *try* to feel the right feeling for the job, and to try to induce the right feeling in certain others. A flight attendant, as I described in *The Managed Heart*, is trained to manage fear during turbulence, exasperation with cranky passengers, or anger at abusive ones.[11] A bill collector is often trained to inhibit compassion for debtors. A wedding planner may coax a once-divorced groom to "get excited" about planning his second wedding. According to the Japanese scholar Haruo Sakiyama, hospice workers make it okay for relatives of the dying to face the dying of their loved ones.[12] Not all jobs that deal with feelings call for emotional labor, and not all emotional labor is stressful (see chapter 2). But as services now make up the largest sector of the American economy, service workers—salespeople, grocery checkers, complaints clerks, nurses, nurses' aides, social workers, dog walkers, nannies, doulas, secretaries, personal assistants, life coaches, actors, teachers, hospice workers, funeral parlor directors, commercial surrogates, call-center workers, and wantologists, among others—all do it.[13]

Some jobs that call for emotional labor are done by Americans on American shores. Other jobs immigrant laborers do in America. Service workers have long migrated from one country to another, but today increasing numbers of care workers leave their young and old in the poor global South to take up jobs tending—and giving their hearts to—the young and old in the affluent North.[14] Such jobs often call on workers to manage grief, depression, and anguish vis-à-vis their own families back home, even as they genuinely feel—and try to feel—joyful attachment to the children, elderly, and sick they daily tend in the affluent North (see chapters 10 and 11).

Emotional labor crosses borders in the other direction as well. By e-mail and telephone, service providers in Bangalore, India, tutor California children in math, make long-distance purchases of personal gifts, and even scan responses on Internet dating sites to help busy First World professionals chose whom to invite to a romantic dinner. Commercial surrogate mothers in India "rent their wombs" to infertile couples from the global North as I describe in chapter 11. This service calls for the ultimate in emotional labor: the effort to detach from the babies they carry and give up.

So it is through our way of seeing reality—our dictionaries and rule books of feeling—and our ways of managing it, that emotion and feeling are partly social. This is true of our lives at home and at work, in the United States and elsewhere around the globe. If, as C. Wright Mills said, the sociologist's job is to trace links between private troubles and public issues, then emotion lies at the very heart of sociology.[15]

Many economic and social trends bear down on private troubles. Important among them, I believe, is the growing dominance of large corporations and their indirect effects on the culture of personal life. As Franklin D. Roosevelt observed in the 1940s, the major corporations have become kinds of "private government."[16] Among the world's hundred largest economic entities, forty-four are corporations.[17] Corporations have been granted the status of legal persons, and the fiduciary responsibility of boards of directors has been legally limited to serving stockholder interests. As the engines of prosperity, the growth of American corporations has been heralded as a largely unmixed blessing.

But as Bob Kuttner has argued in *Everything for Sale*, a former balance of power—between companies, government, and labor unions—has now tilted in favor of large companies.[18] For in the 1970s, American companies started to relocate their plants near cheaper labor pools around the world, undercutting labor unions at home and getting city, state, and national governments to compete in their offers of lower taxes and more lax regulation in order to entice capital investment. As companies have grown in power, so have they grown in cultural influence over areas of private life far removed from the boardroom. A market culture has come to the fore, proposing its own ideas of self and relationship, its own rules of emotional attachment to and detachment from others, its own demands for emotion management.[19]

Indeed, as I suggest in chapter 1, many of us find ourselves moving along a market frontier. On one side of this frontier, we see activities as simple things we do. On the other side, we see them as *rent-able* or *sale-able*. When we come to see an activity as being for rent or sale, we see it differently. Take friendship: normally we understand friendship as the offer of generosity, trust, faith, and the promise of a loving, long-term give and take between two people. But in the ads for a new commercial service enabling clients to find friends in their local neighborhood, a new language has crept in.[20] An ad for Girlfriendcircles.com, a for-pay friend-finding site, reassures readers that they can rest assured that fellow clients are serious about finding a friend. Why? Because they paid money for it. "We value what we invest in," they note. Under "What Is the Cost?," the Web site reads, "We want you to care enough about friendship to put a little [money] into it. . . . Some have said, 'It's wrong to pay for friends!' And we whole-heartedly disagree! We pay for shoes, movies, mochas and manicures—why not for one of the very things that research shows plays a gigantic role in our happiness, health, longevity, stress reduction and chances of success in our life goals?"[21] By describing how to *find* a friend in a spirit of such breezy, self-interested pragmatism, the entrepreneurs pry us away from the idea of *being* a friend.[22]

Our emotions tell us where to draw the line. We say to ourselves, "This feels right," or "This doesn't feel right." We experience an anxiety tipping-point which tells us "this is new but it's okay" or "this is weird and not okay." We may do nothing in response to the sense that "this is not okay." But far more often, as I describe in chapter 1, we react to that feeling by trying to *re-personalize* our world.

Behind every answer in this volume are a host of yet more important questions. In the title essay, I ask, "So How's the Family?" But following that, I ask: How's empathy? How's the way we look for joy? Where in our lives are those precious connections between the Thomas Paines of the world and the Jane Austens? I invite you on a journey through these questions in the faith that finding better answers will help us build a better world.

The Feel of Things

ONE Going on Attachment Alert

At her sister-in-law's parties, Grace Weaver, a lonely 49-year-old divorcee and mother of a 12-year-old child, was looking for a "man to grow old with." Other relatives and friends tried to fix her up, but no dice. For several years now, she had not found "that certain someone," and time was getting on. So she tried a new tack.

> I remember waking up the morning after going out to a New Year's Eve party. I felt disappointed I hadn't met any interesting men. I flipped on the television and watched a show on Internet dating. I'd always thought Internet dating would be tacky and leave me feeling icky, over-exposed, naked. But then this coach Evan Katz came on saying, "Come on, guys. There's nothing embarrassing about Internet dating." I jotted down his name and wondered if this shouldn't be my New Year's resolution: hire a coach, take control of my life.[1]

She signed up for Match.com for $17.99 a month.[2] She also hired Evan Katz, whose online name was E-Cyrano and whose Web site read: "I am a PERSONAL TRAINER for women who want to FALL IN LOVE." He offered her three coaching packages: Basic, Premium, and V.I.P. She chose the $1,500 Premium package. For this, Evan would write her pro-file for the online dating Web site, pick her headshot from LookBet-terOnline (a photo service for online daters), create an alluring user name, write a catchy subject line, and advise her further on what to talk about on and offline. The entire service consisted of friend-like conver-sations by phone and e-mail between Grace in New Jersey and Evan in Burbank, California.

In her selection of Evan's Premium package, Grace was deciding how much to put herself in Evan's hands and how much she would do her-self. To the extent that she put herself in Evan's hands, she also accepted his guidance about how to feel. He started with how to feel about the very act of hiring him: "Congratulations for hiring me," he said. "Don't feel ashamed." In a separate interview, Evan told me, "I'm everybody's dirty little secret."

Clients kept mum about hiring Evan, he thought, because they felt they should be able to find a romantic partner in a natural way—through friends, family, work, or church. He was right. When she told friends she had hired a love coach, they said, "You're hiring a *what?*" But Evan told her to feel good about taking matters into her own hands by hiring him. Evan was changing the rule on shame: do not feel it.

He also recommended that Grace be wary of trusting a sense of "fall-ing in love," of rushing into the idea that she had met her soul mate. "If you sense yourself feeling that," he suggested, "it's probably infatua-tion." Paradoxically, he even warned Grace against the messages in the ads of his fellow love coaches: "Find your soul mate. Find perfect chem-istry. Fall in love." "Soul mate" is a retrospective concept, Evan cautioned. "Only when you look back after twenty years together, do you say, 'We've been soul mates all along.'" So Evan invited Grace to reinterpret what she had once defined as "true love" as being "infatuation."

Eager clients project onto their on-screen suitors all the wonderful at-tributes they so hope to find. So he cautioned Grace: "Keep a check on your dreamboat fantasies. Go slow. Don't be too eager." Grace might wishfully fantasize that the man she sipped wine with by the fire in her brother's living room was "the one," Evan counseled, but this would be a bigger problem when Grace clicked her way through hundreds of profiles of online strangers. Her hopes could be wildly unrealistic, he explained:

> Women come into my office with long lists of characteristics they want: the man should be successful, tall, handsome, funny, kind, and family-oriented. Does he like to dance? Is he a film aficionado? A real reader? They want a charismatic guy who doesn't flirt, a successful C.E.O. who's home at 5:00 p.m. Some women price themselves out of the market, and they're very touchy about not wanting to settle for less than the complete list that they believe promises a soul mate and chemistry. Then a lot of people get discouraged and conclude it's impossible to find real love.

Grace could imagine she had experienced a magical moment shared with the man of her dreams, only to discover it was all an illusion. So she needed to work out new terms of emotional engagement. How emotionally attached to an on-screen man should she feel at that first exchange? On the first date? The second? The third? Evan advised her on how attached to let herself feel by comparing dating to work at a job. Dating as work? Okay, Grace said, "I'm an engineer, so it was easy for me to think of dating as work. Just get it done. I know that sounds unromantic, but that's okay so long as I get to my goal. Evan kept my nose to the grindstone."

We usually think of meeting a person to go on a date—a hike, a picnic, a restaurant dinner, a play— as a voluntary and pleasurable act. Indeed, we imagine pleasure as the very purpose of it. To compare dating a potential partner to the tedious turn of a grindstone is to say, in effect, "Don't expect this to be fun."

Others writing on Evan's online blog also approached dating as work: "I keep plugging away, TableForSix [a service that sets up dinners with other singles], poetry readings, volunteering, it's hard work." Others did not agree: "Looking for love is *not* like work," one wrote defiantly. But Evan told Grace that dating was work—and that she *should not resent it*.

Indeed, part of the emotion work Evan was asking Grace to do was to try feeling upbeat about the fact that dating was work:

> When you're unemployed, what do you do to find work? When you are single, what do you do to find love? I'm not telling clients to spend forty hours a week looking for love, but I tell them, "You can give it three. Do the numbers—and don't resent it."

Another way Evan prepared Grace for the online dating market was by asking her to think of herself as a brand:

> The Internet is the world's biggest love mall. To enter it, you have to brand yourself because you only have three seconds. When I help a client brand herself, I'm helping her put herself forward to catch that three-second glimpse, and I'm helping her footnote the rest. A profile could say, "I talk about myself a lot. I go through bouts of depression, and Zoloft usually works." That might be the truth, but it's not going into her brand.

Like an object for sale, Grace had a label, Evan explained, and it had to grab attention. About her online profile, he said, "Don't hide behind generalities like 'fun-loving' and 'musical.' Bring out your *real* self. Put *that* into your brand." At the same time, he felt it was important to set boundaries on this public "real self" in early e-mail conversations with men. When Grace suggested telling about a stint at a Buddhist monastery where she was asked to clean a bathroom with a toothbrush, Evan replied, "That's a little out there." Grace prepared to emotionally detach from possible responses to that "real Grace" *and* to put that real Grace out there. That was Evan's counsel: be interested, of course, but stay detached.

Then there were numbers. As Evan explained, even if Grace did not think of herself as, say, a "6" on a 0 to 10 scale, numbers still applied to her. She should know about them because she was in a market and they reflected her market worth:

> In the eyes of many men a "10" woman is 24 years old, never married, has a sexy 36-24-36 figure, Nicole Kidman face, warm personality, a

successful but flexible career, and a love of gourmet cooking. As a "10" she would score the highest number of male responses on Match.com.

Grace was very pretty and sexy, but she was 49 years old, divorced, and had little time for gourmet cooking. So, Evan surmised, maybe she was a "6." He added, "I see a lot of 5 men looking for 10 women, and that leaves the 4 and 5 women in the dust." So Grace had to try to detach her feelings of hurt pride from "Grace-as-6."

In all of this, Evan counseled Grace to think about her ROI—return on investment—of time, thought, and emotional involvement. If a man was not right for her, she needed to keep an eye on the clock and move on.

Dating as work, dating as branding, dating as becoming a 5 or 6 in the eyes of others, dating as calculating her ROI, this was the market perspective Evan invited Grace to adopt. It called on her capacity to detach feeling from the idea of herself as a brand and as an ROI collector as well as from any given suitor.

In a grocery store, certain tacit feeling rules apply while transacting business: be friendly and pleasant with the checkout clerk. In the time you have, you can talk about the weather, the Dodgers game, or the taste of a new pesto, but do not get deeply involved. The clerk is doing a job and so are you. If you care too much about the clerk, it hurts the transaction, becomes a problem, and makes you seem strange. The basic feeling rule governing market transactions is to stay fairly emotionally detached.

We cannot apply the cheerful detachment we feel for a checkout clerk to a lover, spouse, parent, or child, of course, without something being haywire. However ambivalently, to them we usually feel deeply attached. Between these two boundaries—one demarking "too much" feeling and the other "too little"—flow all our feelings as we encounter the situations of life.

After Grace had written her profile, posed for her photo, and written her subject line, she panicked. As she recounted, "It was hard to push the button. That was my photo, and there are 20,000,000 viewers who are going to see it. What if some creep downloads my photo? I work in a state office building. What if someone walks in and recognizes me? It made me squirm." She had placed herself before strangers, some of whom could pose a terrible danger. People she knew could recognize her and disparage her as "desperate." But Evan told her to plunge ahead. He was the pro, and she trusted him.

Once she began to correspond with potential suitors, Grace kept notes of how many responses she received daily. When she first got on Match .com she was 49 years old, and she was delighted to receive many responses. On her next birthday, she changed her online age to 50; to her horror, the responses plummeted. "It was like my stock price fell overnight. 'What happened?' I asked myself. 'I'm the same person I was a day ago, but my ratings fell by half.'"

Ratings fall in face-to-face encounters, too, of course. Grace might have been braced against a dismissive glance from a man she had met at her sister-in-law's party, but on Match.com Grace was in the "world's largest love mall," as Evan called it; the fall may have been more impersonal, but it was still hurtful. She needed to remain partially detached from any wishful fantasies she projected onto a string of e-mails from a suitor because he, too, was on the market. He might be lying about himself and declaring his undying love to five other women. Was she projecting? she had to ask herself. Evan told the followers of his Internet blog that they often took Internet dating rejections *too* personally, and they suffered accordingly. One woman, who described herself as "nice, average looking, intellectually fun and creative," wrote, "I am SO SICK of these men who are fives (or lower) who think they're going to wind up with supermodels." She felt over-entitled men were passing her over, and that made her mad. But anger violated Evan's feeling rule: be upbeat and mildly interested but basically detached.

So when was the coast clear to feel open hearted? Grace wondered. Evan said this:

> People get very confused. They want to know when a relationship is serious. A relationship isn't real until you have committed to being boyfriend or girlfriend. Everything prior to that—phoning, emailing, dating, preliminary sex—all that isn't real until you have each

committed. I've had clients devastated to realize that they've fallen in love with someone who is still looking online.

All of Evan's lessons about what, when, and how much to feel gave Grace a kind of user's guide to Internet dating, setting out new rules of emotional engagement. With the shrinking of what the German philosopher Jurgen Habermas calls "the life world" and the rise of the "system world" (which includes the market, state, technology, and media), people like Grace find themselves situated at the crossroads where the two meet—even as those spheres are themselves in flux.[3] Increasingly, people ask themselves, Should I prepare for a purely market transaction and emotionally detach? Or am I among friends, family, or community, in which case I should prepare myself to feel emotionally attached? What *mix* of market and personal should I prepare for, and what *measure* of attachment?

Grace saw Match.com as a means to an end. Alarm bells went off when she realized that, in the case of two suitors, one after the other, the means—the application of a market way of thinking—got stuck to the end: love. Before she met the man to whom she is now happily committed, Grace had had half-year relationships with two other suitors. Each had ended the relationship because he could not get along with her preteen daughter who disliked them both. As each one ended his relationship with Grace, he made the same parting remark.

> It was eerie. The first guy said, "I'm getting back on Match.com. It was so easy to find you, there must be others out there just like you." He came back three months later saying, "Oh my God! What did I do? There's no other you out there." I told him, "It's too late. I'm not dealing with someone who thinks people come in facsimiles." It was very weird, but the second guy said exactly the same thing as he left, "It was so easy to find you. I'll find another."

Both of them saw her "like a box of cereal on the shelf," she felt. "Just like me? What were they thinking?" It was as if one could exchange one "6" for any other "6."

A market way of relating to others is brilliantly suited to the purchase of a washing machine, a cell phone, or a hat. The idea of a 1 to 10 rating, a brand, and an ROI—all of these ideas are a good fit with the act of buying such things. But how do they fit romantic love? Grace wondered. Evan offered a market way of thinking as a *tool* for temporary use in finding a romantic partner, not as an end in itself. But what if some people keep using this tool long after the task has been accomplished? What if they apply ROI, branding, and 1-to-10 thinking to love itself? That was the problem.

Grace didn't want to get hurt but she didn't want to become heartless. So how attached did she dare to feel to a given suitor? To Evan? To herself? As with other Americans today, Grace was moving in a world of increasingly specialized market services—themselves set within a larger cultural remix of market and personal life (see chapter 7). She was calling on rules governing precisely how much or how little to care.[4] No one needed to care about a "6," but Grace wanted an open-hearted man to care about *her*.

GOING ON "ATTACHMENT ALERT"

At the most primal level, emotional engagement is a matter of attachment and, as such, a matter of survival. As the University of Chicago experimental psychologist John Cacioppo and his coauthor William Patrick show in their book, *Loneliness: Human Nature and the Need for Social Connection*, human beings share with nonhuman species strong responses to isolation or rejection.[5] According to their research, the more isolated people are, the less well they sleep, the higher their anxiety, the less well-functioning their immune system, and less well-regulated their glucocorticoid response. Isolated individuals show higher rates of sickness and, in older adults, higher rates of death. Not just isolation but loneliness creates a wear and tear on the body. Loneliness is as harmful to health, the authors report, as high blood pressure. It does twice as much harm to health as obesity and the same degree of harm as cigarette smoking. When Cacioppo hypnotized people once to feel lonely and once to feel among friends, big differences showed up in their physiological responses. When lonely, the subjects developed greater reactivity to stress and higher cortisol levels. And people are not the only ones:

when isolated from others of their kind, Cacioppo reported, even fruit flies die sooner.[6]

Within families, small children exhibit different kinds of attachment to their primary caregivers, as the researcher John Bowlby argued based on his study of World War II war orphans. And, like children, adults express different styles of attachment in their search for love.[7] But each style of attachment—say, the "anxious-preoccupied" or "dismissive-avoidant"—is not simply a state that we are inside or outside of. We continuously shape our attachments as we go along, sensing when we are "over-attached" or "under-attached." Such sensings send a signal: "anxiety and fear coming up" or "no worries here." If we become too detached, we fear sadness or depression. If we become too attached, we fear engulfment or loss of self. Our alarm system warns us to engage in some sort of restorative strategy in order to return to the degree of attachment to others that, as adults, we feel we need.[8]

For *The Outsourced Self* (2012), a book about clients' and practitioners' experiences of intimate services, I explored how people *draw lines,* at different moments and in different ways, between *themselves* and *symbols* of connection to others. It is as if people asked themselves, "Am I too detached from this symbol of connection to others? Or too attached?" Even apparently minor symbols of attachment seemed to matter. For example, one long-hours businessman hired a dog-walker to walk a beloved family dog on weekdays, but he raised his voice excitedly as he explained, "But not on Saturday or Sunday. If people go out and buy a dog and decide to care for it, I don't see how they could hire someone to walk it on Saturday. After all, it's their dog. Otherwise, why *have* a dog?" To him, walking the dog himself on Saturday, or seeing others do so, signaled attachment to the dog, and all the dog meant to him—a sense of home, belonging, warmth, devotion.

Another man, whose neighbors routinely hired birthday party planners to stage their children's parties, clung defiantly to the idea of *not* hiring one for his daughter's upcoming fifth birthday, and of instead planning it himself. He could afford to hire a service, but why do it? It was a powerful symbol, so he felt, of his attachment to his daughter and to the idea of himself as a "hands-on dad."

A third person drew the line on emotional detachment in the simple act of buying a gift for a colleague's new baby:

> The wife of a colleague had just given birth to a new baby. They had set up a gift registry at Babies "R" Us, so I went to my computer and clicked on the registry. There were about a dozen choices. I didn't want to pick the most expensive, since I don't know the couple that well. But I didn't want to be cheap, so I didn't choose the least expensive thing either. I aimed for something in the middle, gave my Visa details, and that was that. But then I felt strange. I hadn't visited the baby. I hadn't gotten in the car. I hadn't looked over toys or baby clothing. I hadn't wrapped the gift or written the card. I didn't deliver the gift. I hadn't even called to congratulate them on the birth! A month later I couldn't remember what the gift was, only how much it cost. So I bought some little plastic measuring spoons, got in the car, and paid the family a visit.

If she could not even remember what she had given, this woman wondered, had she really *given* a gift at all? For a warm-hearted person, that felt too cold. So she did things—bought the plastic spoons, paid a visit—to express the degree of warmth that seemed right to her. She sensed that she had been too detached from the colleague, the mother, the baby, and the very idea of herself as a loving person. So she made up for it.

People also guarded against over-attachment. One kindly woman who was coping with both a husband and son in ill health drew the line at taking on an ill niece. "I'm a show-up person," she declared, "but I can't worry about Lily now. I have to watch that I don't over-extend." She had overextended herself in the past:

> I was helping so many people, I felt like the old woman who lived in a shoe. Partly, it was a matter of timing; within one week, bad things happened to three people I love. But partly I just have to watch that I don't over-do, because I get exhausted and then resent it—which I hate because then I'm not helping anyone.

We each set up terms of emotional engagement. We listen for bells signaling an "attachment alert." In response, we extend our attachment here, decrease it there, to maintain those terms. Consciously or not, we try to avoid feelings of anxiety, fear, or sadness, which tell us when we have reached our symbolic limit. It is our desire to avoid those feelings that motivate us to work as hard as we do to set up the right degree of attachment to the world.

Most of the time, we do not notice what sets off our moments of attachment alert, nor could we coherently describe the exact terms of emotional engagement that these alerts help us maintain. It is only when we *cross over* one of the invisible boundaries between emotionally engaged enough and not enough that we find ourselves estranged—or, like Grace, in the company of others who are. An attachment alert goes off inside us not so much in response to what we are feeling as much as in response to *how much* we feel anything at all. As intimate life moves into the market, we continually ask just where, on the banks bordering this wide channel, it feels right. As the market frontier moves, so too does the language, the way of thinking and talking about relations, and the feeling rules that influence just what degree of attachment "feels right."

In recent years, we have seen a rapid growth in personal services such as that which Evan offered Grace. Childcare workers, potty trainers, closet organizers, photo album assemblers, personal shoppers, physical trainers, eldercare workers, and grave beautification services now do what families, friends, and neighbors used to do in many communities (or which might not have gotten done at all). Such services save time, provide skill, and often help. But they also separate us from the acts by which we used to say how much we care. They shake up our terms of emotional engagement. This shake-up can alienate us from ourselves and others, but more often it sets us to doing the strangely invisible work of shoring up our bonds, in order to keep our personal life personal.

TWO Can Emotional Labor Be Fun?

In his 1776 *An Inquiry into the Nature and Causes of the Wealth of Nations*, Adam Smith describes the hapless worker in a London pin factory standing for hours measuring pin after pin. In the 1867 first volume of *Das Capital*, Karl Marx takes us into the grueling twelve-hour day of a worker spinning, weaving, and dyeing wool in a Manchester cotton mill. For both authors, the iconic laborer was a man doing physical labor in a dreary factory. For Marx, the grim nineteenth-century factory— with its poor lighting, long hours, and low pay—oppressed the manual worker, whose focus on one tiny part of a larger process of production made him feel alienated from the things he made and from himself. For Smith, the pin-maker's tedious task was the downside of a division of labor that nonetheless benefited the whole world. The Highland sheep-herder, living far from city factories, mastered many more skills and more greatly enjoyed his work than the city pin-maker, Smith noted, but he lived in a poorer world.

Neither Smith, who extolled the virtues of capitalism, nor Marx, its most powerful critic, could have envisioned the new iconic worker: a female service worker doing emotional labor. Nanny, childcare worker, nursing home attendant, call center employee, waitress, teacher, nurse— all such workers maintain voice-to-voice or face-to-face contact with clients and, in the course of doing so, perform emotional labor. This is the work of trying to feel the appropriate feeling for a job either by evoking or suppressing feelings—a task we accomplish through bodily or mental acts.[1]

Service jobs vary. For the psychotherapist, emotional labor requires years of training, a formal degree, and is central to the job; for the hairdresser, manicurist, physical trainer, wedding planner, or bartender— emotional labor requires no training or degree and is largely optional.[2] One married mother of two in California told me in an interview I conducted for The Outsourced Self, "I have three mothers: my physical trainer, my masseuse and my psychotherapist. I'll be going to them all until I die or they do." In confessing a strong attraction to an older male colleague, she appealed to them all for advice: "My physical trainer is telling me, 'He's trying to seem cool because he's so into you.' My masseuse is telling me to take a vacation, and my therapist is helping me examine my marriage."[3]

Some workers are superb natural therapists, while others do it poorly. Some manage emotion workers (head nurses, for example), while others are those managed by them (the nurses under supervision). Some work in teams; others alone. But for all of them, the same question comes up: Can emotional labor be fun? Or in a deeper sense, can it be meaningful?[4]

One can enjoy emotional labor immensely, I think, provided one has an affinity for it and a workplace that supports that affinity. Of the American childcare and eldercare workers I've interviewed, most expressed an affinity for the work they did. One nanny told me, "I'm a kid person. I climb right into the sandbox. I couldn't handle working with the elderly." I also heard eldercare workers express a special affinity for work with the elderly. "The lady I take care of reminds me a lot of my grandma," one worker declared, "and I'm not one for kids." Other workers were first drawn to their job on pragmatic grounds—the pay, the commute, the hours, or the availability of work—but later came to enjoy it.

But by itself, affinity does not tell us how much a worker loves her job. That is because we bring to work a certain idea about what it would take to love the job. Contained in that idea is what aspect of ourselves we wish to have affirmed, and people differ in what that aspect is. One person may be most gratified by the ability to provide for her family (a pragmatic source of meaning), or to serve God (devotional), or to seek opportunity (entrepreneurial), to overcome challenges (self-challenging), to exhibit great skill (professional pride), or to demonstrate one's character as trustworthy, reliable, and helpful (to be a good person).[5] Most of all, many care workers feel gratified by the pleasure they give others.[6]

A meaningful job is one thing; an easy job is another. A child erupts in a wild tantrum. A patient glares in a flash of paranoia. A confused client delivers a slap in anger. In such cases, work is not easy. But skilled emotion workers develop the art of appraising unwelcome events and know when and how to detach themselves from the display while remaining attached to the client. Indeed, many take special pride in handling really tough clients. A tantrum winds down. A paranoid flash subsides. An elderly person is soothed. The caregiver feels gratified in accomplishing these ends.

Some discover a yet deeper source of gratification. In an eight-city study, the sociologist John Baugher asked hospice workers how they decided to work with the dying and what effect it had on them. They spoke of the surprising joy they found in the experience of dropping social convention. Little things—conversational pleasantries, the time of day, disarray on a bedside table—ceased to matter. In the presence of a dying person, they felt welcomed, accepted, and trusted. Rather than feeling strained, many workers—Christian, Buddhist, atheist—felt a sense of peace and awe that they had stood by a person's side at his or her passing. For them, emotional labor opened up a channel for the experience of awe in the face of the ultimate in human vulnerability.[7]

Satisfaction did not depend on having the perfect client. "A lot of my co-workers want to avoid Alzheimer's patients," one eldercare worker explained, "but I like working with them. I work with one man who doesn't remember a thing that happened yesterday. He lives in a just-now world. But when I fixed him a steak today, he loved it. I've learned to *enjoy* him in a *just-now way.*"

An emotion worker is obliged to attune herself to a client's needs, to empathize with the client, and to manage her *own* emotions in the course of doing so. She may get bad news from home: a child falls ill, a house is robbed. Or she may become aware of her client's unpleasant bodily odor, or be jarred by his or her erratic behavior. Often the care worker makes herself into what psychoanalyst Donald Winnicott has called "a holding environment"—an ambience sealed against disturbing leakage of anxiety, anger, envy, or sadness, for these might make the patient feel agitated, threatened, or unsafe.[8] Emotional labor implies directionality, intention, and effort; it is, in that sense, real *work.*[9] Just as a professional singer takes pride in her highly trained voice or an actor in a moving performance on stage, so the care worker often takes pride in cultivating warm, trusting, and resilient relationships with clients.

EMOTIONAL LABOR AND ITS DISCONTENTS

So what can get in the way of the gratifications of emotional labor? A number of things, first among them being low pay and low respect. In an age of public budget cuts, layoffs, high turnover, and public criticism of the public sector and its workers, it can be hard to enjoy doing emotional labor. As one California childcare center attendant told me,

> I love the two- and three-year-olds I work with. But we only get $8.50 an hour [in 2000]. So a lot of my coworkers are quitting to get paid more as secretaries or bank clerks. The kids get attached to one worker only to have her replaced by another and another. They get upset. One little boy, Matthew, is getting very anxious that I may leave. I can't live on $8.50 an hour, but I hate to leave him in the lurch.

In the United States, most eldercare is provided by lightly regulated, for-profit nursing homes, and many care workers are assigned too many patients. One study of for-profit nursing homes in western New York State found that 98 percent of them fell below the standard set by a federal study for the optimum patient-staff ratio of five to one.[10] In some homes, nurse's aides had to try to feed, wash, and assist thirty or more patients.[11] As Russell Reynolds, a former nursing aide at a for-profit suburban New York nursing home recounted, "Some nights we'd have four aides trying to take care of more than 300 people. . . . You might have to spend a half-hour helping somebody get to the bathroom. In that time, two other residents might fall down and need help."[12]

When a care system breaks down, one sign is that the three-way relationship between the manager, the emotional laborer, and the client becomes frayed. A manager overextends the idea of efficiency or profit making, trying to "get more work out" of workers. They cease to be a team. The worker rushes about. She skimps. She spends too much time with one patient and neglects another. She cannot give her best; she does a broken job. She may unconsciously side with the malfunctioning system against its patients, whom she sees as "too demanding." Or she may identify with the patients whom she feels she has failed, absorbing the shame of the system as her own: "I've been too callous. I've hurt the clients' feelings." Either way, the broken system has prevented her from feeling proud of her work. It has forced her to *manage her feelings about doing her job in a broken care system.*

HYPER-BUREAUCRATIZED, GLOBALIZED, AND DEVALUED CARE

Even when staff are well paid, have long-standing coworkers, and work in pleasant surroundings, the work may be rigidly rule bound or technology-driven. In one nursing home in Maine, in which my elderly aunt lived for a while, electrical cords were routinely attached to chairs in patients' rooms so that every time my aunt rose from her chair, a loud buzzer, audible down a long corridor, rang in the nursing station. It alerted an attendant to come help her walk to the bathroom. It prevented falls, broken hips, and lawsuits, but it greatly demoralized my aunt as well as the other residents who were seated in the same kind of chairs. The attendants themselves responded as if the buzzer, not the person, had called them.

At a Maine-based home-care agency, eldercare workers are forbidden from socializing with their clients outside of work hours. As one care worker recounted to me, "I work for an agency that sends me out to care for a variety of elderly people in their homes. I became fond of one lame man and would drop by to bring him flowers on my way home from work. Well, my supervisor found out and told me that was forbidden. They don't want clients hiring us directly, because then the agency would lose its cut of the money. I had to sneak behind the agency's back to bring him flowers."

Even if the hospital, nursing home, or childcare center is humanely run, a care system can be broken in a hidden place—at home. American nannies who put in shifts of nine, ten, and even twelve hours and return exhausted to their own neglected homes are working in broken care systems, too. But at least the children of such workers share residency with their mothers, unlike the children of immigrant caregivers who are cared for by relatives and local nannies back in Mexico, the Philippines, or elsewhere. Such immigrant working mothers suffer an accumulating sense of loss as the separation stretches to two, five, ten, or more years. And a higher proportion of migrant mothers are leaving their children behind than in the past; more that 80 percent of immigrant children now living in the United States had been separated from their parents prior to migration.[13] In her study of the children of female migrant workers left behind in the Philippines, Rhacel Parreñas found that such children were often abandoned by their fathers. Taking their wives' departure as a "divorce," some fathers left the care of their children in the hands of their ex-mother-in-law or aunt, moved away from the natal village, and moved in with a new woman to start a new family.[14]

Still, the strained economies of the South have sent an ever larger stream of young and middle-aged mothers to jobs in the Global North. They travel along one of several corridors. From Central and South

America to the United States and Canada, from Eastern Europe to Western Europe, from South Asia to the oil-rich Persian Gulf, from South Asia to the Asian north of Hong Kong and Japan, and from North Africa to Europe, emotional laborers travel from poor to rich countries.[15] However much a migrant worker wants to migrate, she often experiences a sense of loss and loneliness as she daily feeds, bathes, and plays with her client's children while living half a world away from her own (see chapters 10, 11, and 12).

Finally, child and eldercare workers often speak of feeling that they, like the nature of their work, are unseen and underappreciated, which makes it all the harder to do. Care work is a hot potato job. Many husbands turn over care of the young and old to their wives. Wives, if they can afford to, often turn it over to childcare and eldercare workers. In turn, many immigrant nannies hire nannies back home to help care for the children that they have left behind, forming a care chain.[16]

Underlying this gender/class/national transfer is the devaluation of care. This is based on the idea that care work is "easy," "natural," and—like parenting—not quite real work. Part of what makes care work invisible is that the people the worker cares for—children, the elderly, the disabled—are themselves somewhat invisible.[17] Strangers entering a room may tend to ignore or "talk over" the very young and old.

The childcare worker who loved to "jump in the sandbox" with her 3-year-old charges—and who had to comfort them when coworkers left for better-paying jobs—found that the value of her work was invisible even to her husband. As she explained, "My husband is a carpenter and has unsteady work. So some of the time we rely on my pay, which is low. One night he told me, 'Honey, why don't you quit childcare? The pay is lousy. We'll have our own kids—you can give your love to them. You could get a *real* job.'"[18]

This all means that many emotional laborers face a great paradox. Though they may come to work hoping to take pride in a job well done, low pay, understaffing, rigid rules, and devaluation can set up circumstances which prevent that. Sadly, their main job becomes protecting patients from the harm of life in a broken, globalized, over-bureaucratized, or profit-hungry system. A tragic cycle is set in motion. The more broken the system, the more disheartened its emotional laborers. The more disheartened they become, the more detached they are from their work, the higher the turnover rates, and the more broken the system.

The alternative to accepting this is to *fix the broken system.* That starts with recognizing the extraordinary emotional labor it takes to maintain a thriving childcare center, nursing home, hospital, or family. It would also call for a bold nationwide care movement to improve the conditions of care workers. If these efforts were successful, people would work in systems that were themselves well tended. In such a world, jobs requiring emotional labor could still be tough, but they would be meaningful— and even fun.

THREE Empathy Maps

The world is in a race, Jeremy Rifkin argues in his book *The Empathic Civilization*. On the "good" team are all the forces pressing each of us to feel empathy for all other people—and indeed all living creatures—on earth.[1] On the "bad" team are the forces that accelerate global warming and destabilize the ecosystem on which earthly life depends, causing strife, fear, and a search for enemies. Which team gets to the goal line first, he notes, is up to those alive today.

The market economy is a player in this race on both teams. On one hand, by setting up vast global networks of makers, sellers, and buyers, market growth encourages the development of a wide, thin layer of empathy—at least enough to ensure peace—in order to conduct business and increase wealth.[2] In this way, the market is on the "good" empathy-enhancing team. On the other hand, economic overdevelopment—with its gas-belching industrial smoke stacks, toxic waste, and accumulation of discarded goods—proceeds headlong, heedless of the welfare of future generations.[3] The market also creates gross inequalities both within nations and between them, inciting a sense of injustice, envy, and conflict.[4] In these ways, the market is also on the "bad" team.

How could we win this race? By extending lines of empathy between American industrialists and the worried residents of sinking Maldivian islands in the rising tide of global warming. By drawing links between the prosperous London businessman and the impoverished Soweto street vendor. By encouraging a mother to stand in the shoes of her children on the upper east side of Manhattan and also in the shoes of her Mexican nanny's children, left behind in Mexico when their mother left to work abroad. Empathy needs to go global, and perhaps even harder, it has to go local—three zip codes down the street, up or down the class ladder. It must cross the barriers of class, race, and gender.

HIDDEN EVIDENCE OF EMPATHY

To ground such sweeping talk of empathy in the daily lives of real people, though, we need to wonder about its complexity and explore the intricate hidden patterns it fits. We need to look at maps. But how?

Clues to patterns of empathy can be surprisingly indirect. For decades, researchers had been finding that more women than men said they were depressed, and two researchers, Ronald Kessler and Jane McLeod, wondered why.[5] The prevailing theory in the 1980s was that women were more "vulnerable to life-event effects" because of their poor "coping strategies."[6] But if this were the case, the researchers wondered, why would women cope better than men—as they do—with financial bad news, a spouse's death, or, after an initial period, with separation and divorce?[7]

Then the researchers found that when exposed to the same disturbing events in the lives of immediate family and friends—death, accident, illness, divorce or separation, or losses in love—women more than men talked about and responded strongly to these events. Although the men were just as aware of these events as the women, the researchers surmised, they did not discuss them as much or respond as strongly to them.

Women also participated in wider circles of support. More unhappy, lost, or ill people came to women than to men, and the women invited them to do so. When the respondents were asked to describe "who helped them during the last period in their life when they needed help with a serious problem . . . women [were] between 30 and 50 percent more likely than men to be mentioned as helpers."[8] More often than men, women reached out to others for support—usually to other women. So as friends and family sought out more women than men as confidants, especially in times of crisis, the women came to hold—to remain mindful of—more stories of distress.[9] To some people, holding a story of distress signals a readiness to help, I think, while for others, sharing painful news was *itself* the help.

Men were as upset as women by such events as death, accidents, or illnesses that occurred to their *spouses* and *children*. Yet when such events occurred to those beyond spouse and children, men reported less distress.[10] So women in this study of Americans of the 1980s were not just feeling down about their *own* bad news, or even their own husband's and children's bad news, but about the bad news of *others* in their larger circle of family and friends. There, they were the designated empathizers—the ones others relied on to stay tuned in.[11] They held in mind the sad news of these others. They charted larger family-and-friend empathy maps.

But why did the news of others depress women? Maybe it is because people have a greater need to share bad news than good, and bad news is harder to hold, so women who get more of it, feel more blue because of it. Or maybe women's depression has nothing to do with their wider circle of concern but with other matters—such as the possibility that everyone needs to feel mothered, and that many women feel less mothered by men than men feel by women. But whatever is going on with depression, the key discovery here is something else: the different shapes of men's and women's empathy maps.

A 2002 study of over 1,000 people—part of the General Social Survey, a large, nationally representative U.S. survey—casts a broader light on such maps. Compared with men, women more often described themselves as "soft-hearted," and reported themselves feeling touched by events that they saw happen. They found themselves feeling "tender, concerned feelings" for people less fortunate than they.[12] They also held more altruistic values than men, agreeing more strongly, for example, that "people should be willing to help others who are less fortunate." Studies show that in close personal situations, women are much more likely to focus on emotion, to offer and seek emotional support, and to use "highly person-centered comforting messages" to help people feel better.[13] The same was found in studies of young girls and boys.[14] Women make up some three-quarters of caregivers for older relatives and friends, and two-thirds of those caring for grandchildren. Women are somewhat more likely than men to donate their kidneys (58 percent of living donors versus men's 42 percent).[15] The Yad Vashem archive of data on non-Jews honored for rescuing Jews shows that although men and women helped in equal numbers, among unmarried people, more women helped.[16] At work, women predominate in the caring professions: they make up 98 percent of kindergarten teachers, 79 percent of social workers, and 92 percent of registered nurses.[17] Maybe because women can have babies, evolution gives them an empathy advantage, or maybe it is because the culture encourages empathy more in girls than boys, or maybe both.

But that does not mean men do not help other people. In fact, many other studies concluded that, without being asked, men perform more public altruistic *acts* than women.[18] They offer directions to the lost, give up their seats in the bus, and give money to strangers for the subway. Men received 91 percent of the Carnegie Hero Fund Commission awards given between 1904 and 2008, and 87 percent of the Medal of Bravery awards given out by the Canadian government.[19] So while men are not the biggest empathizers, they often save the day.

WORDS, MEANINGS, CAUSES OF EMPATHY

We say we "stand in another's shoes," but what are we *doing, feeling,* and *thinking* when we stand this way? We see through another's eyes. We feel interested. We come to feel as they do. We say to ourselves, "What has happened to you *could* happen to me." And as we imagine this, we are often doing such things as looking someone in the eyes and listening closely. We feel curious. Or we come to feel empathy for certain categories of stranger that we learn about by word of mouth or by newspaper, television, a film, a play, or a book.

Empathy differs from feeling, or being held as, responsible for another.[20] A nephew might pay a dutiful visit to a grumpy uncle but lack empathy for him. In *All Our Kin,* Carol Stack describes "kinscription," whereby some members of poor black families were delegated to care for others.[21] The child of an ill parent may be sent to live with a childless aunt. A neighborhood orphan is taken in by his grandmother's friend from church. A family looks after a lonely neighbor. One accepts the continual possibility of a kin assignment and empathy is expected to follow.

But empathy does not always follow, nor does it always lead to, rescue or care. A 27-year-old, single photographer I interviewed described his feelings upon learning that his dear friend had received a diagnosis of cancer. He was grief-stricken but did not feel it was his role to help. "I wasn't the first person Steven called," the photographer remembered. "That was his sister, and then a female friend of his, and then the two women competed over who could take the best care of him, and called on their families to help. I wasn't part of that." Maybe he would have done something if others had not, but as things stood he felt empathy, but no call to action.

So empathy is *related* to doing things, but it is not the doing of those things. We console a bereaved colleague. We talk over the day with a partner. We pet a dog tied up outside a coffee shop. We leave coins in a homeless man's cup. We pray for others. These are acts of kindness that usually *go with* empathy, but empathy itself is an act of *feeling for* another person.[22] Our hearts can go out to Sudanese war orphans or Congolese rape victims, but we may do nothing to help them. As the philosopher Joan Tronto points out, caring *about* a person differs from caring *for* a person (such as arranging for care of an elderly parent), which differs from taking care *of* a person (feeding and dressing the parent).[23]

How do we distinguish empathy from other things like "understanding," "projection," or "identification"? Empathy is less purely cognitive than *understanding*, because it requires imagining what another is feeling. We also sometimes *project* the idea of ourselves onto another person, mistaking the one for the other. A recently bereaved widow, for example, recounted a friend's well-meaning attempt to comfort her:

> I knew Adrianne loved me and wanted to comfort me. But I knew my loss reminded her of *her* loss. In the living room that afternoon, I felt the presence of my husband and was trying to absorb all the marvelous recollections friends had shared of him. But Adrianne began rubbing my hand back and forth as if she were sanding it, and told me she knew how upset I must be feeling. But that was her upset, not mine.

The good side of projection, of course, is that we take flight from ourselves; we do not remain aloof or uncaring.[24] The bad side of it is that we mistake ourselves for the other person. We see the other as like our generous mother, depressed sister, or judgmental colleague, when he or she is not any of these. Projection distorts empathy. Again, we may *identify* with another person and, over a long period of time, gradually incorporate him into our personality. (We say, the young boy laughs just like his dad.) Empathy does not have to stick like that.[25]

This is because empathy is an *art*. It is the art of the surveyor, the draftsman and the reader of the empathy map.[26] A surveyor gauges the height of the mountain, depth of a sea, expanse of the desert. She discovers a reality that exists in places where, generally, she is not. By means of aerial, radar and sonar testing the surveyor gathers information about where things are, climates, and the possibilities of life. She needs a steady hand to hold her surveying instruments. As the surveyor of an empathy map, one learns to hold "a steady hand"—that is, to manage to some degree the anxiety, outrage, grief, or other emotion that the misfortune of another might evoke, so that the empathizer stays tuned into what the other is *feeling*.

A draftsman carefully draws a map based on the surveyor's report, and the reader reads the draftsman's map. So all told, the empathizer develops the skill of noticing, remembering, and imaginatively reproducing the feelings of another, and accepts in her—or his—own heart the feelings evoked by all that was seen. Empathy maps are not given to us: we develop the art of making them.

Some maps are mere sketches. A recovering alcoholic I talked to explained the simple suggestion of empathy she received from a "buddy" through Alcoholics Anonymous. "They assigned me a buddy who had been through the same struggle that I face. He called me every day and told me a short story. I responded with a story. No questions were asked. I didn't get to know him really well, but he reminded me that I wasn't alone." Other maps can offer rich details of the topography of another person's self.

When we draw a map, we draw boundaries around high-empathy, low-empathy, and no-empathy *zones*. We feel deeply for the people within a high-empathy zone, and refuse empathy to those in the no-go zone. We imagine individuals or categories of people as *eligible* for empathy and others, not. To widen the criteria for entrance into an empathy zone, we try out empathy on a wide variety of people. So we come to know how it feels to be an abandoned baby, a prize-winning student, a heartless murderer. We know these things because we have cultivated the art of imagining ourselves into other people's minds.

Cultivating this art is to open channels and keep them open. We can feel spontaneous empathy for a person or even a group, as we shall see, and in such cases the art lies in countering the forces which would—also spontaneously—inhibit empathy.

FEELING RULES AND ZONES OF EMPATHY

For in empathizing with another, we are guided by various tacit moral rules governing our idea of the "right" sort of person to be—the stand-alone individual or the helper-cooperator. To some, it is shameful to depend "too much" on others; so at the slightest sign of dependency, one is quickly disparaged as "a clinging vine," "a perpetual child," or "a welfare bum." The moral rule carries with it a feeling rule: Do not feel sorry. Do not empathize.[27] Others hold different ideas about needs, feeling that it is natural to have them and good to seek help from others. So for them, the feeling rule is: Feel compassion. Empathize. Which moral rule we hold dear determines who we feel empathy for, and how hard we try to feel it.

Our social class, race, gender, sexual orientation, and cultural beliefs—and thus our experience—greatly alter our map. I began to think this over in light of interviews I conducted for *The Outsourced Self.*[28] For example, a personal assistant working for an immensely wealthy employer was trying to help her partner work off $50,000 worth of graduate student debt and to pay for a caregiver for her dying mother who lived 500 miles away. "Every time I walked by his million dollar awful art collection, I thought about my partner's school debt. I'd look at the ugliest piece and say to myself, 'That piece would buy my mother excellent care, and that piece over there would cancel my partner's debt.' I had a hard time empathizing with them over their malfunctioning hot tub, you know?"

Some moral rules get in the way of empathy. In the pre-Emancipation South, for example, black slaves were held to be private property, and it was deemed wrong to steal or free them. To be sure, Quakers, free blacks, some indentured servants in similar circumstances, and sympathizers such as those who ran the underground railroad proved to be exceptions. But at that time, the idea of racial equality was largely absent, a point central to Mark Twain's classic 1885 novel, *The Adventures of Huckleberry Finn.*[29]

Twain famously juxtaposes the rule against theft and Huck's great empathy for his beloved friend, Jim, a runaway slave. After a long raft trip down the Mississippi with Jim—"we a-floating along, talking and singing and laughing"—Huck wonders whether to abide by the values he was brought up to believe in by the Widow Douglas and return Jim to his owner "like I should," or protect Jim and "go to hell"?[30] Huck struggles with himself:

Well, I can tell you it made me all over trembly and feverish, too, to hear him, because I begun to get it through my head that he *was* most free—and who was to blame for it? Why, *me*. I couldn't get that out of my conscience, no how nor no way. It got to troubling me so I couldn't rest; I couldn't stay still in one place. It hadn't ever come home to me before, what this thing was that I was doing. But now it did; and it stayed with me, and scorched me more and more. I tried to make out to myself that *I* warn't to blame, because *I* didn't run Jim off from his rightful owner; but it warn't no use, conscience up and says, every time, "But you knowed he was running for his freedom, and you could a paddled ashore and told somebody." That was so—I couldn't get around that no way. . . . [I felt] bad and low, because I knowed very well I had done wrong.[31]

Holding the deed of ownership of Jim in his hand, Huck said, "I studied a minute . . . then says to myself: 'All right, then, I'll *go* to hell'—and tore it up."[32] Huck brought himself to trust his affection for Jim and tear up his society's empathy map.

In his searing account of his horrific torture at the hands of Japanese prisoner-of-war camp commanders during World War II in Kanburi, Thailand, Eric Lomax faced a more difficult challenge: trying to empathize with someone he hated. In his book *The Railway Man*, he describes a change of heart about the Japanese interpreter who had helped those who mercilessly tortured him.[33] Captured in Thailand, Lomax, a British Royal Signals officer specializing in railways, was found to have a forbidden map detailing the stations along the Thai-Burma rails. He was severely beaten, then locked into an oven-like cell with both arms broken. He was left thirsty and hungry, and as ants crawled over him he was forbidden to wash or visit a latrine. Later, water was forced into his nose and mouth until his belly swelled, and he was certain he would die.

Given all this, how could Lomax forgive the Japanese interpreter, a man named Nagase, who witnessed and aided his torturers with a mechanical voice "with almost no inflection of interest"?[34] As Lomax recalls,

Then [the non-commissioned officer (NCO)] picked up a big stick, a rough tree branch. Each question from the small man by my side was immediately followed by a terrible blow with the branch from above the height of the NCO's head on to my chest and stomach. . . . I used my splinted arms to try to protect my body and the branch smashed onto them again and again. . . . The interpreter was at my shoulder, "Lomax, you will tell us. Then it will stop."[35]

Fifty years later, having survived his ordeal and retired from the army, Lomax was overwhelmed by fury at his torturers. He received psychotherapy and married a highly sympathetic woman. He also discovered a book describing his ordeal written by Nagase, the Japanese interpreter, who was now a devout Buddhist pacifist and antiwar activist. Lomax's wife wrote to Nagase, who responded to her: "I will try to find out the way I can meet him if he agrees to see me. . . . The dagger of your letter thrusted me into my heart to the bottom."[36]

The two men met in Kanburi, Thailand, the very site of Lomax's torture. "He was kind enough to say that compared to my suffering his was nothing; and yet it was so obvious that he had suffered too," Lomax reflects. "In all the time I spent in Japan [as a guest of Nagase] I never felt a flash of the anger I had harbored against Nagase all those years. . . . As we walked and talked, I felt that my strange companion was a person who I would have been able to get on with long ago had we met under other circumstances. We had a lot in common: books, teaching, an interest in history."[37]

At the end of his visit, Lomax asked to sit alone with Nagase one last time, a plan that frightened Nagase's wife, who feared Lomax might finally seek revenge. But that was not to be. Sitting quietly alone with Nagase, Lomax "gave [him] the forgiveness he desired. . . . I told him that while I could not forget what happened in Kanburi in 1943," Lomax recalled, "I assured him of my total forgiveness. He was overcome with emotion again, and we spent some time in his room talking . . . without haste."[38]

Huck Finn empathized with Jim. He came to *trust* his empathy and muster the courage to act on it. Eric Lomax first prepared the way (through psychiatry, a sympathetic wife, and the passage of time) before *coming to* empathize with the transformed Mr. Nagase. Huck had Jim on his map; his challenge was to follow it. Lomax came to recognize Nagase as worthy of his empathy, and to redraw his map. Huck wanted to act on his love, Eric Lomax wanted to transcend his hatred.

GETTING THERE

So how do we expand the empathy zones on our maps? One way is via an *unexpected personalizing gesture*. Perhaps the most astonishing example is the famous World War I "Christmas truce" of 1914 on the Western Front. Huddled in deep trenches hundreds of yards—sometimes only fifty yards—apart, were British and German soldiers who had each undergone strict military training to despise and kill one another, and shared little by way of language or culture. But in the early hours of Christmas day, each side raised white flags of truce, climbed out of their trenches, exchanged cigarettes and other gifts, played football, and alternately sang Christmas songs. Some from each side even danced together. For this day, the truce extended along some half of the front line on the Western front and included a few officers up through lieutenant colonels. When generals on each side discovered this shocking breach of discipline, the practice was immediately stopped. But such a brave act of trust was based on some sense that "you guys must be feeling like we're feeling." Perhaps it was the daily touch with death; 9 million soldiers died in World War I, and many must have felt "What do we have to lose?" What had transpired, though, was a surprise attack of empathy.

Many also extend their empathy more gradually through the logic of the *exceptional person*. Some whites have one black friend about whom they say "he's not like the rest of them." Some Christians have one Muslim friend about whom they say "he's an exception." Some straight people have one gay friend, and so on. Such connections cross boundaries, but they also re-create them. For each person says to himself, in effect, "I can empathize with my friend because he's so different from others of his kind whom I can't empathize with." But in other cases, empathy for one person becomes a pathway to empathy for others within a forbidden social category.

We can also expand empathy by establishing some practical common ground with people we have been taught to disdain. Summertime "Children Create Peace" camps have brought together 8- to 12-year-old Israeli, Palestinian, and Christian children to share an interest in animals.[39] Coming from areas such as Ramallah, Jenin, Bethlehem, East Jerusalem, and Jericho, where residents are ever prepared for gun or missile fire, these children learn to share a fascination with giraffes and extend empathy to each other. Other versions of this experiment exist in different forms in many public schools and colleges. Focusing on children from kindergarten to eighth grade, Mary Gordon established in 1996 the "Roots of Empathy" program, a nonprofit organization with twelve sites in Canada and three in the United States. In it, a parent and baby pay a series of visits to a classroom (twenty-seven visits in all), and a trained empathy instructor helps the children recognize what the baby is feeling.[40] Even such time-limited exposures can lead many to begin to redraft their maps.

By whatever means we find to alter them, the maps themselves seem to vary according to our membership in given social categories—gender, race, national origin, and social class. Again the clues can be indirect. A series of studies show that the poor give more to others than the rich. Independent Sector, a nonprofit organization that researches charitable giving, reported that "poorer households ($25,000 and below annual income) gave away 4.2 percent of their incomes while richer ones ($75,000 and above) gave away 2.7 percent.[41] In another study, the social psychologist Paul K. Piff and his colleagues found that low-income people were more "generous, charitable . . . and helpful to others" than were the wealthy.[42] The rich who live in neighborhoods with many other wealthy people give away an even smaller share of their income than do rich people living in more economically diverse communities.[43] The vast majority of income the rich do give away, another study found, is not directed toward the poor but to such things as the opera, museums, and their alma maters, institutions that largely benefit people like themselves.[44]

So what is the link between a person's empathy and their generosity? In an experiment, Piff's group discovered that if higher-income people were shown a sympathy-eliciting video and instructed to imagine themselves as poor, they became more willing to help the poor. But the reverse was also true: when lower-income people were instructed to think of themselves as rich, they became less charitable.[45] Notwithstanding generous-hearted rich men such as Warren Buffet and Bill Gates, the desire to protect wealth can get in the way of empathizing with those who don't have it.

Ideas about our placement in the world alter the maps we draw. Among American college students, ideas conducive to empathy seem to be losing, not gaining, hold. In a meta-analysis of 13,737 students—some who entered college in the late 1970s to early 1980s, some in the 1990s, and some in the 2000s—a team of psychologists discovered a decline in what they called "empathic concern."[46] (This was indicated by answers to questions such as how well statements like "I often have tender, concerned feelings for people less fortunate than me" described the student.) Maybe students today are more preoccupied with their own uncertain futures than earlier students were. But if, as the national gap widens between the very rich and very poor, the young express less empathy than those their age used to, we may be heading for serious trouble.[47]

In the end, the world may indeed be in a race, with a "good" team pressing for more empathy with our fellow creatures on the earth and the "bad" team pressing against it. But to increase the odds for the good team, we will need to discover far more about the making of maps. How can circumstances—such as those of the surprising battlefront Christmas dance, or the summer camp for children of warring states—enable us to empathize better and more than we do? In empathy, women have taken the lead. But so too have many men, such as the great fictional Huck Finn and the extraordinary, forgiving Eric Lomax. By itself, more empathy will not solve all the world's problems; but more empathy would make it an entirely different world.

Families, Class Gaps, and Time

FOUR So How's the Family?

Over the last half-century, talk of family has often focused on the working mother—her hours, her wages, her commute, the sympathies of her boss, the culture at her workplace. In the 1960s and 1970s, it was the "mom is working, so how are the kids?" conversation. Later people spoke of "work-family balance," but still held to the question: if *she* is working, how are *they* doing?

Over time, talk moved to an array of changes that a working mother would need to raise thriving children—partners who share the second shift, state-of-the-art childcare, a shorter workday, a three-day weekend, flextime, or flexplace, for example. Although some called for public programs such as European-style parental leaves and federally funded childcare, such calls were gradually abandoned in America as being hopeless pipe dreams. In the hallway at conferences, conversations on work-family balance through the 1990s and 2000s seldom mentioned tax policies that exacerbated a growing class gap, or the deregulation of advertising to children. Such issues seemed far beyond the scope of "mom is working, so how are the kids?"

Meanwhile, a separate but parallel conversation arose linking a free market to family values.[1] Cuts to public services, deregulation, reduced corporate and individual taxes, privatization—such policies, its advocates claimed, strengthen both a free market and the family. In their talk of "family values," conservative commentators generally exclude gays, oppose a woman's right to abortion, and link the idea of a free market with that of a strong, loving home. The smaller and less active the civilian government, they propose, the stronger the family.

For the most part, these two conversations—"mom is working, so how are the kids?" and "free-market family values"—have moved along separate tracks. Even today, those who engage in the one do not engage in the other, or not at the same time. So what if we link the two conversations and ask: In an era of the working caregiver, how do free-market policies affect families? In search of the answer, we discover a surprisingly rich body of evidence.

But first a word about why this question matters. When American women moved en masse into the workforce, they were not alone. The female labor force participation rate increased 20 percent worldwide between 1993 and 2003, while the participation rate of men decreased in all regions but Southeast Asia.[2] Over 70 percent of working-age women in Denmark, Norway, Sweden, and Switzerland are now in paid work, as are 53 percent in Spain and 46 percent in Italy.[3] The United States, the United Kingdom, Germany, France, and most other states of the European Union fall in between.[4] So the rise of the working woman in America is part of a global trend which shows no sign of reversing itself.

And there are many stakeholders in this trend. As Klaus Schwab, the head of the World Economic Forum, wrote in the preface to the 2012 Global Gender Gap report:

> With talent shortages projected to become more severe in much of the developed and developing world, maximizing access to female talent is

a strategic imperative for business. The World Economic Forum has been among the institutions at the forefront of engaging leaders to close global gender gaps as a key element of our mission to improve the state of the world.[5]

Indeed, the World Economic Forum (WEF) report links each nation's ranking on an index of gender equality to its GDP and its score on the so-called Global Competitiveness Index.[6] If women were to perform paid work at the rate men do, the authors state, the American GDP would rise "by as much as 9 percent, the euro-zone G.D.P. by as much as 13 percent . . . [and] the Japanese G.D.P. by as much as 16 percent."[7] When women work they also earn, of course; as they consume more goods and services, they push up the GDP.[8]

State officials have still other interests in the employment of women. Especially in Europe, women are encouraged to earn money and contribute to social security to help bankroll the state pensions currently drawn by retirees in a "graying" Europe.[9] To sustain pension funds, some countries are raising the retirement age of public employees— from 65 to 67 years old in the United States, from 60 to 62 (and 67 for some workers) in France, and from 65 to 67 in Spain.[10] Meanwhile, 2.1 children per woman are considered necessary to maintain a country's population. But in some countries, the fertility rates have sunk lower— Italy and Greece are at 1.4, and the United Kingdom is at 1.9.[11] So women are urged both to work more and to have more children.

Women themselves take jobs for many personal reasons, of course—to pay family bills, to develop talents, to be more autonomous, and to contribute to society. With two parents working full time, then, the call turned to "work-family balance"—both a balance between the contribution of one partner and the other, and a balance between the demands of home and work. In *The Second Shift*, I found that comparing the paid and unpaid work of women to the paid and unpaid work of men, husbands (all fathers of children aged 6 years and under) enjoyed an extra month a year of leisure compared with their full-time working wives. But from 1980 to 2005, this leisure gap between the sexes narrowed to between a half and a third of what it had been.[12] At the same time, as the workday has lengthened for the middle class, jobs have become more insecure. So men, like women, are putting on shoes for a work-family shuffle that the comedian Tina Fey describes as a "tap dance recital in a minefield."[13]

A call has also gone out for a new workplace. With flextime, workers can work at the kitchen table, or a nearby hub-office, saving time, gas, and space on traffic-clogged freeways, and fetch the children from school. But only 16 percent of workers actually telecommute in any given year.[14] Job-sharing and good part-time work are also yet to become part of the normal scene. And in an era of insecure jobs, many workers are loath to ask too much of hidebound bosses who might lay them off. The "mom is working, so how are the kids?" and "work-family balance" conversations continue into the present, with less and less hopeful talk of help from the government.

FREE MARKETS AND FAMILY VALUES

Meanwhile, in a parallel conversation linking the free market to family values, proponents have called for a set of government policies: lower and less progressive taxes, privatization, deregulation of companies, and cuts to state services. These policies are said to free the market and, by so doing, to strengthen the family. Just as General Motors' CEO once argued that "what's good for General Motors is good for the American people," so free-market advocates argue that what is good for the free market is good for the family. Lower and more regressive taxes may widen the class gap, they note, but it will not harm families because wealth will "trickle down" from top to bottom. Deregulation will also help by allowing companies more freedom and—although this is a less explicit part of the argument—inducing them to invest in the United States.[15] Strong cuts in state services will make for a leaner, "less bloated" government, they say. Yet the U.S. government supports companies such as Wal-Mart, Boeing, and Target through offers of free or low-cost land, the building of free water and sewer lines, and low-cost financing and insurance. Companies also raise billions of dollars through tax-free bonds. So their call to reduce bloat refers only to cuts in public services, not to policies that benefit companies.[16] The more America pursues these policies, they say, the freer the market and the stronger the family.

But is this true? One way to approach this question is to compare children in nations that have embraced free-market policies with children in nations that have not. A 2007 UNICEF "Report Card 7" does just that.[17] Capitalist countries vary among themselves, of course. The United States, United Kingdom, and Australia, and some now include Portugal—so-called neo-liberal regimes—do not favor publicly funded services such as paid childcare or family leave.[18] They have weaker social safety nets for the poor, and they pursue tax policies permitting wider gaps between rich and poor. Thus, the Report Card scholars were able to compare countries that pursue free market policies more with those—such as Norway and Sweden—who pursue them less.

Conducted by an international team of scholars, the report draws from dozens of national surveys as well as from cross-national data gathered by the World Health Organization (WHO) and the World Bank. Focusing on the twenty-one richest countries in the world, and comparing the health, education, and material and emotional well-being of middle school children, the researchers asked such questions as whether the children had a quiet place to study, a dictionary, and schoolbooks. They asked them whether they had someone to talk to, and if they had had an accident within the last year.

The highest ratings of child well-being went to the Netherlands, Sweden, Norway, and Denmark—nations that, far more than the United States or United Kingdom, tax the rich, regulate commerce, and provide public services such as paid parental leave. The lowest overall ranks went to the nations most strongly pursuing a free-market agenda—the United States and United Kingdom, both of which ranked in the bottom third for five of the six key dimensions of child well-being. The United States ranked dead last among the twenty-one affluent countries in child poverty and ranked second to last in "family and peer relations" and "behaviors and risks." The likelihood of a child skipping breakfast, becoming fat, smoking pot, or getting pregnant—on all these measures the United States and United Kingdom ranked worse than nearly all the other nations. Indeed, American girls had the highest rate of teen pregnancy.[19]

When asked how often they eat their main meal of the day with their parents "around a table," nearly 80 percent of the children from the Organisation for Economic Co-operation and Development (OECD) countries reported "several times a week"—in contrast to 66 percent of American children. A smaller proportion of American children described their peers as "kind and helpful" (53 percent) than did OECD children overall (66 percent). Compared with their OECD counterparts, a smaller proportion of American children ate breakfast each morning or fruit every day, and more 13- to 15-year-old Americans were overweight (25 percent vs. 13 percent). A higher proportion of teens in the United States had smoked pot in the last year (31 percent) than had teens from the OECD countries that provided information on its use (21 percent). In addition, each child in the study was shown a picture of a ladder and was told the top of the ladder (10) is the "best possible life for you" and the bottom (0) "the worst possible life for you"; they were then asked where on the ladder they stood. In how far up they placed themselves, the U.S. children ranked a low 18 out of 21.[20]

A 2010 follow-up study, UNICEF Report Card 9, recounted the same bad news—the United States ranked 23 out of 24 nations in the proportion of its children in poverty, beating out Slovakia, which came last.[21] The United States ranked 19 out of 24 in education and 22 out of 24 in health.

What are we to make of these findings? Most of us assume that richer countries offer children better lives than do poorer countries. But by itself, a nation's wealth does not improve the average well-being of its children. Nor is a higher proportion of stay-at-home mothers correlated with higher ratings in the well-being of children. Norway has one of the highest proportion of women aged 15 years and over in paid work (62 percent), but it ranked 7 out of 21 in overall child well-being. The United States, with its lower proportion (57 percent) of women in paid work, ranked 20 out of 21 in the overall well-being of children.[22]

Many Americans I have spoken to about the UNICEF report have responded with one reason or another why the high-state-support model would not work for the United States. "You can pay for state supports for working parents in little Norway with its population of 5 million," one man told me, "but not in a country as big as the U.S."[23] Yet the sheer size of a nation's population does not correspond to its Report Card ranking. Germany, with its population of 82 million, won higher scores in child well-being than Austria with its 8 million. Gathered together, the children of the 500-million-strong European Union rank higher than those of the 312-million-strong United States.

Still others point to the high proportion of poor minorities in the United States. "It's easier for Europeans to earn higher *average* scores on child well-being than it is in America," one woman explained, "because the U.S. has more minorities and immigrants who pull down our scores."[24] Although it is hard to compare the United States with the European Union in numbers of minorities—official figures are not comparable—France and Germany are home to roughly the same proportion of immigrants as the United States, yet they still score higher in child well-being.[25]

On the heels of the UNICEF study, the British epidemiologists Richard Wilkinson and Kate Pickett offered in their landmark book *The Spirit Level: Why Greater Equality Makes Societies Stronger* the most comprehensive cross-national overview we have of studies on the well-being of adults.[26] Drawing on 400 scholarly studies, the authors compared twenty-three of the richest countries in the world, looking at such things as rates of obesity, violence, drug abuse, mental illness, teen births, suicide, levels of social trust, school performance, social mobility, infant mortality rates, and overall health and life expectancy. Using studies based on data gathered by the United Nations, the OECD, and WHO, among others, Wilkinson and Pickett divided nations not by their wealth or government support for working families but by the *gap* between each nation's richest and poorest 20 percent.[27] In nearly all measures of human well-being, the low-gap nations were far better off than the high-gap nations—namely, the United Kingdom, Portugal, and especially the United States.

People in high-gap societies, they reported, suffer a homicide rate ten times that of people in low-gap nations as well as eight times the per capita rate of teen births and three times the rate of mental illness. Populations in high-gap societies are more likely than those in low-gap societies to disagree with the statement "most people can be trusted." They worry more about muggings and rape, their children are exposed to more violence, and they live with larger prison systems. Again, it is not a nation's GDP that correlates with these problem rates but, along with other factors, the size of the gap between rich and poor.

It is not simply that unequal societies have more poor people and the poor are more distressed than the rich. Even *middle-class people in high-gap societies*, the authors found, suffer poorer health, more mental illness and obesity, and feel less safe in their communities than do the reasonably affluent in low-gap societies. Those earning household incomes of $60,000 in high-gap countries suffer higher rates of death from all causes than do the $60,000-income people living in low-gap countries.[28] Similarly, infant mortality is lower in low-gap Sweden than in high-gap England for families at every occupational level.[29] Within the United States, Wilkinson and Pickett also compared low-gap states such as Vermont, New Hampshire, Minnesota, and North Dakota with high-gap states such as Texas and Louisiana, where homicide, teen pregnancy, and high school dropout rates are higher.[30]

Evaluating Wilkinson and Pickett's research, some scholars have confirmed the authors' findings regarding different rates of distress but have pointed out inconsistencies, too. Claude Fischer notes that between 1970 and 2003, U.S. homicide rates dropped by 30 percent even while inequality rose. However, he also concludes that "even the skeptics . . . do not argue that inequality is good for anyone but those on the top of the pyramid."[31] Another critic has questioned why the authors analyzed drug use instead of alcoholism, which is a bigger problem in low-gap Scandinavia than in the high-gap United States.[32]

As the "good outcome" nations are nearly all Scandinavian and the "bad outcome" nations are Anglo-American, Fischer observed, we are comparing the culture of "Sven" to that of "Jack." Surely he is right that national culture matters. But if the political policies that result from Jack's approach hurt families, maybe Jack should take a cue from Sven.

Another study of change over time in the United States provides powerful support for Wilkerson and Pickett's thesis. In his book *Coming*

Apart: The State of White America 1960–2010, the conservative political scientist Charles Murray traces the move between 1960 and 2010, during which the U.S. *shifted* from being a low-gap society to a high-gap one.[33] Drawing on five decades of U.S. government data as well as a host of national attitude surveys, Murray compares the top 20 percent of non-Hispanic whites in the United States (those with bachelor's degrees or higher, who are employed as managers or professionals) with the bottom 30 percent (those with high school diplomas or none, employed in blue-collar or low-level white-collar jobs).

In 1960, he found, rich whites (in their 30s and 40s) fairly similar to poor ones. Most were married, went to church, took pride in their work, and felt attached to their communities. Children were born to married mothers, and most couples stayed married and raised their kids together.

A half century later, family life was pretty much the same at the top and drastically worse at the bottom. In 2010, prime-age whites at the top pretty much fit the profile of prime-age whites in 1960: married, working, and involved in the community. But life for their lower-class counterparts had greatly changed. The lower-class mother who was likely to be married in 1960 was very likely to be single in 2010. Three percent of upper-class children but 22 percent of lower-class ones in 2010 lived with their single moms.[34] Women in the bottom 20 percent have become less likely to go to church, to volunteer in their schools or communities, to trust their neighbors, or to say they were happy than were their counterparts in 1960. Men have come to work shorter hours. Unemployed men passed up low-wage jobs and became absent to their children. In their new leisure, they did not take classes, do things with their kids, or help around the home. Instead, white men in the bottom 30 percent did two things more than either their counterparts of 1960 or their upscale contemporaries of 2010: they slept longer, and watched more television.

Although such men say they want to work hard and have strong families, Murray argues that they have lost the moral values they would need to achieve those ends. But that leads us to wonder why the bottom fifth in *low-gap* societies such as Norway and Finland do not fit this picture of the slacker. And we can wonder why even the rich appear to suffer when they become so much richer than the poor. In 2010, Murray found that the poorest 20 percent had come to distrust other people more, and to feel less supported and less happy than their counterparts from when America was a more equal society. *But so, too, did people at the top.*[35] In the General Social Survey data Murray uses, rich as well as poor were asked, "Would you say that most of the time people try to be helpful, or that they are mostly just looking out for themselves?" "Do you think most people would try to take advantage of you if they got a chance, or would they try to be fair?" "Generally speaking, would you say that people can be trusted or that you can't be too careful in dealing with people?" In their answers, *both* rich and poor were more distrustful in the more unequal America of 2010 than in the more equal era of 1960. When trust breaks down, Murray observes, it does so "across the board."[36]

What Wilkerson and Pickett discovered in their cross-national survey, Murray confirmed for prime-age whites in America. While the two studies tell the same story, they propose very different remedies. The authors of the *Spirit Level* call on governments to do the progressive "Sven" thing and develop policies to reduce the troubling class gap. The author of *Coming Apart* accepts the widened class gap, rejects government solutions, and urges rich kids to get to know poor kids and to join the conservative Heritage Foundation.[37]

Missing from both accounts is the deeper emotional story of the prime-age, blue-collar man. Shorn of his way of life, at the bottom of the heap in the job and marriage markets, he has quietly sunk into a dead-end crisis. His sleep and his television watching suggest less a loss of morals than a loss of morale. What is he watching on television? Ads for high-end vacations, scuba diving in Belize, mountain climbing in Switzerland, and whizzing through the Arizona desert in a luxury car. The rich often isolate themselves from the poor, but the poor tune in on the lifestyles of the rich every day.

Unable to support a family on his own wage as his father and grandfather did, the blue-collar man finds himself at the bottom in a high-gap society. This descent is evocative of a story Valerie Walkerdine and Luis

Jiminez describe in their book *Gender, Work and Community after De-Industrialization*, in which the honor, pride, and identity of men evaporated when iron and steel left a small town in southern Wales. They describe men in this former mining town in a form of "collective grief," which passed from man to woman and father to son.[38]

The engines of much of this are American multinational companies that, faced with new competition for market share, have off-shored their assembly lines to cheaper labor pools in Mexico, China, and India.[39] That is the U.S. poor man's new competition. This economic shift has hit him harder—and earlier—than the middle-class Americans for whom this frightening trend is hitting now.[40] Indeed, the blue-collar man has taken the hit for everyone else in America—and so has his family.

THE DEREGULATION EFFECT

If a freer market is the answer, what policies would enhance it, and what impact would they have on the family? Deregulation, as those who link the free-market with family values hold, encourages business, creates jobs, raises the national GDP and the average family's income, and so strengthens families. Deregulation, the argument goes, helps families. But such a claim bears a closer look.

We can look at the television commercials for high-sugar, high-fat, high-salt foods—Cokes, candy bars, and chips—that target children and are unregulated in the United States. In her book *Born to Buy*, Juliet Schor documents the link between the troubles of American children and the "child industry," as she calls it, based on the wide and increasing exposure of American children to advertising.[41] Most advertising is still delivered to children through television, although television and the Internet are merging into a whole new interactive—and marketing—experience for youth. By the age of 6 years, Schor observes, the American child's viewing time is just over two hours a day, and for 8- to 13-year-olds it rises to three and a half hours a day; a fifth of television air time is devoted to commercials.[42] One study found that American children aged 3 to 5 years spent more time watching television (14 hours a week) than being in school (12 hours and 5 minutes), playing outdoors (37 minutes), or doing anything other than sleep.[43] In 2004, the total advertising and marketing expenditures directed at children reached $15 billion.[44] Such ads are aimed at children's own piggy banks. Children aged 4 to 12 spent $30 billion of their own money in 2002, and a full third of that went for candy, soft drinks, and other products high in fat and sugar.[45]

Researchers have linked such ads to the rise in childhood obesity,[46] which has, according to the Centers for Disease Control and Prevention, quadrupled for 6- to 11-year-olds and tripled for 2- to 5-year-olds since 1970.[47] Children grow obese mainly through what they eat, of course; what has changed since 1970 includes the rise of convenience foods at home, restaurant dining, and scheduled passive pursuits, and the decline in school recess time and free roaming around the neighborhoods. But the main thing that changed is the increase in money invested in television and Internet advertisements for junk food. And on such child-targeted ads, there is no regulation.

Indeed, the junk food industry has aggressively pursued many strategies to get children to buy its products. Some companies enlist children to serve as "brand representatives" to other children. Companies fund school books—Amazon.com sells at least forty of them—that teach math and science using branded foods: the *M&M's Brand Counting Book* or the *Kellogg's Froot Loops! Counting Fun Book*.[48] Some ads for junk food make it "cool" to be oppositional and defy parental advice about healthy eating. The restaurant and beverage companies founded and fund the Center for Consumer Freedom, which ridicules public health authorities who link obesity to disease and opposes efforts to curb childhood obesity as "anti-freedom."[49]

With cuts in public funding, cash-strapped U.S. public school districts increasingly accept money in return for giving for-profit companies the right to place ads on public school buses and to create programming—including an ad for Coke—shown on Channel One television during compulsory assemblies at school. Nine states now allow ads on the outside of school buses, and some schools allow ads inside them.[50] In return for corporate money, some school boards now also permit district school buses to carry radios that play ads. Other cash-strapped schools are exploring corporate sponsorship of school bands, sports teams, and the general fund. Some public schools have accepted corporate money to develop curricula such as the American Coal Foundation's "The United States of Energy," a fourth-grade curriculum favorable to coal, and Shell's "Energize your Future" curriculum, which imagines the oil industry as a leader in alternative fuel production.[51] Kohl's department store's "charitable" campaign offered $500,000 to the twenty schools with the most votes on Facebook; all voters were then placed on a Kohl's promotional mailing list.[52] As scholars at the National Education Policy Center argue, such curricula are prompted by a desire to boost company brands, not help kids think.[53]

Some nations permit more child-targeted advertising than others. One scholar, who analyzed twenty hours of commercial television aimed at children under the age of 12 in twelve nations, found that the United States showed television ads for 11 minutes per hour while Norway and Sweden showed ads for 1 minute per hour.[54] In response to the obesity crisis in 2006, fifty-three European governments adopted the European Charter on Counteracting Obesity, which included a call to regulate the commercial promotion of "energy-dense foods," particularly to children.[55] Countries responded to this call in different ways. The United Kingdom banned ads to children under 16 for foods high in fat, sugar, and salt. France required nutritional messages on all foods targeted to adults and children—a proposal to ban ads to children failed by one vote in 2009. Ireland banned the use of celebrities in children's food ads and requires warnings on fast foods.[56] The U.S. Congress appropriated money in 2009 to set up a Working Group on Food Marketing to Children, and called for voluntary pledges by the food industry to regulate itself.[57] In his survey of children in twelve rich nations, the sociologist Tim Kasser found that nations allowing advertisers the freest hand in targeting children scored the lowest on a UNICEF ranking of child well-being.[58]

The dark side of deregulation can be connected to a wide array of other problems that families absorb, too. With staff cuts in the Occupational Safety and Health Administration (OSHA) or looser workplace safety regulations, workers go to jobs in riskier workplaces: a nurse is stuck with an unsafe needle, a construction worker steps on an unsafe scaffolding, a miner enters an unsafe mine. A less-protected environment produces diseased plants, animals, and potentially contaminated food. Seen in one light, these are unavoidable problems of a free-market system that people must deal with, one by one. Seen in another light, they are the preventable fallout of an under-regulated economy that harms all families.

THE SERVICE-LOSS EFFECT

A final "free-market and family values" proposal is to make large cuts in public services. Medicaid, food stamps, subsidized housing for the disabled, public school lunches, and Head Start help families who are poor or have special needs. Public libraries and parks serve all families, especially middle-class ones who tend to be their heaviest users.[59] The Nurse-Family Partnership program offers monthly visits over three years for poor—and often young and unmarried—mothers. According to the Coalition for Evidence-based Policy, the program has reduced child abuse, neglect, and injuries by anywhere from 20 to 50 percent.[60] It also has reduced the number of subsequent births and has motivated mothers to go back to school or get jobs. According to a 2005 RAND study, the Nurse-Family Partnership program saves $5.70 for every dollar it spends.[61]

Similarly, Success for All, a school-wide program in high-poverty elementary schools, offers daily 90-minute reading classes and other reading help and improves reading performance by 25 to 30 percent of a grade level.[62] Career Academies, which set up learning communities that prepare students in urban, low-income high schools for jobs, have also had important success.[63] Head Start, which helps children improve their reading, writing, and vocabulary, aids in their emotional development as well, according to some studies.[64] Youth Opportunities Grants, before their defunding, also helped low-income youth.[65] Insofar as it is families that absorb the bad news of their members, such programs have greatly helped families.

The free-market family-values agenda creates a two-sided market squeeze. On one side, tax-induced inequality, deregulation, and service cuts put heavy strains on family life. On the other side, cuts in social services reduce the support for handling such strains. It is precisely this market squeeze that I believe accounts for the great difference between the United States and most of Europe in the well-being of families.

HOW TO MOVE FORWARD?

At the moment, the "mom is working, so how are the kids?" and the "work-family balance" folks are not thinking about taxes or deregulation, which seem to them far removed from family life. And the "free-market family values" conversation is turning a blind eye to the dark side of the free market. Meanwhile, we have become a far more unequal society—and, at least after the late 1990s boom, curiously more tolerant of it.[66]

So how do we move forward? By starting with the right premises. Added up, all this research suggests that families are creatures of their context. Those who link free-market policies to family values herald the importance of "free choice." To be sure, parents and children do make "free choices." But they do so within contexts which constrain those choices. Obesity, physical illness, mental illness, teen pregnancy, violence, and social distrust—all these involve individual choice. A small child watches TV ads for junk food, gains weight, and becomes diabetic. He may have chosen to eat three bags of M&Ms, but not to have become fat and ill.

Meanwhile, a child's individual choice becomes a family matter. His mother takes the morning off from work to take him to the doctor. She learns how to give him insulin shots, and now she worries about the medical bills. The child made an "individual choice" to eat the candy, but a powerful industry made its free choice to put billions of dollars into making him want to do that. Should we blame the child, the parents, or the industry?

A painter falls from a scaffolding. He is taken to the hospital with a broken back. The family cannot afford the medical bill, so his stay-at-home wife gets a low-paid job, but she cannot pay both the house note and hospital bill. We can ask whether the painter was careful enough as he walked out on the scaffolding, or we can ask when the safety inspector last checked it.

A family cancels a lakeside camping trip because a public park has closed. We can ask why Mom and Dad were not working hard enough to foot the bill for a week at the Holiday Inn, or we can ask why the public camping ground is not open.[67]

People live in families, and families live in contexts. For Americans today, an increasingly powerful context is the market: large and small companies in our version of a free-enterprise system. Companies offer us much of what is good and necessary in life, but as systems they are also inherently designed to uphold the values—and free choices—of stockholders, not the value of families. To expand the power of companies and contract the power of everything else (the government, non-profits, and community), as "free-market family values" advocates wish us to do, is to adopt a stockholder's view of family life.

Some conservative leaders even behold the family through stockholder eyes. In an astonishing speech on work-family balance given to Harvard Business School students, for example, a young Mitt Romney, the 2012 Republican candidate for U.S. president, spoke of children as investments. "Your children [will not show] any evidence of achievement for 20 years," Romney warned, but if parents do not invest enough time and energy, their families could end up as "dogs"—which is "consultant-speak," a *New York Times* reporter explained, for the unprofitable parts of a corporation, "sucking energy, time and happiness" from the family.[68]

So how's the family doing? In America, not so well. This is not because Mom and Dad are at the office, and it is not because Americans do not value families. It is because we have yet to open a third conversation, built on studies such as these, about what can help. Holding ourselves open to this evidence has everything to do with the "moral zoning" we apply to our empathy maps (chapter 3). These empathy maps will determine how many children—in the country or world—we think of as our own. When we set out to vote, we will need to ask what a good government would do and how to get ours to be a good one.[69] And we will need to work for more socially responsible corporations, more imaginative nonprofits, and more vital communities. In the end, Americans need not fly off to Norway in search of a better family life. We can find our own examples in the low-gap, higher-well-being states that Wilkinson and Pickett discovered right here in the United States. So the next time someone asks "How's the American family?" we can proudly answer "Couldn't be better."

FIVE

Time Strategies

An issue of the *New York Times Magazine* devoted to the ninety-nine most innovative ideas of 2002 described a service called Family360.[1] Designed by a management-consulting firm called LeaderWorks based in Monument, Colorado, the program offers "personalized family assessments" to executives at corporations such as General Motors, Honeywell, and DuPont. Based on Management 360, a widely used program for evaluating executives at the workplace, Family360 offered, for $1,000, to evaluate a client's performance as a parent and spouse at home.[2] The journalist Paul Tough described how the service works:

> The Family360 process starts with the executive's spouse, children and in some cases his parents and siblings filling out a detailed questionnaire in which they evaluate the subject both quantitatively—scoring

him from 1 to 7 on, say, how well he "helps create enjoyable family traditions" and "uses a kind voice when speaking"—and qualitatively listing "three to five positive attributes" and "two things you want this person to do less." The data are then analyzed by LeaderWorks, and the results are sent to the executive in a "growth summary" report that presents his family's concerns in the form of bar graphs and pie charts and identifies "focus areas" for such things as "paying attention to personal feelings," and "solving problems without getting angry."[3]

In essence, Family360 is offering its clients a "time strategy"—a way of managing the symbols of family-related meaning and fun when faced with an overstretched work day. Mostly workers come to their time strategies through personal intuition, but the time strategy recommended by Family360 comes as a ready-made commercial service. We might call it a strategy of *scene-resetting*, for it imports into a manager's home the language, sense of urgency, practicality, and calculation of life at his office.[4] Coaches meet with the family to create a "Development Plan to Strengthen Family Relationships." The company then provides, as Tough notes,

> an investment guide with hundreds of specific actions that let you connect with your family as efficiently as possible: buy a speakerphone for the home so you can join in on family game night when you're on the road; go for a walk with your child every day, even if it's only to the end of the driveway; create "communication opportunities" while doing the dishes with your spouse or waiting in line with your child at the store.[5]

The executive can be as efficient at home as he is at work, this odd but well-meaning service implies, with no loss to family life. The client is asked to answer such questions as, "If you have children, what specific actions have you taken to teach values, encourage contribution or create memories?" The client's scores are totaled up, and the evaluators appraise the impact of his (and as far as I can tell, it is always a *his*) desired "individual legacy" and "family legacy." As is done in the business world, the executive compares his "person practices" with those of others—in this case, with more hands-on dads.

The service is designed to improve family life for busy top executives. And it may actually help fathers, as one father I interviewed for *The Out-sourced Self* felt it had, if only because it transfers to the home the sense of urgency that such men associate with work.[6] But the very language of investment and high-leverage activities suggests to fathers that they are still at the office: it invites men to come home only to bring the market-place with them.

The transport of workplace to home is not altogether new. The 1950 film *Cheaper by the Dozen* was based on the biographical book of the same title by Frank Bunker Gilbreth, Jr. and Ernestine Gilbreth Carey, who described how their parents, two efficiency experts, raised their twelve children. Clipboards in hand, the parents recorded and managed the "micro-motions"—a term they coined—as the kids washed and folded clothes, set the table, washed the dishes, and did other daily chores on the family "production line." The movie was a hit; the audi-ence could safely laugh at the absurdity of it all, maybe because, after all, much of the time Mom and Dad were home. For their house in Mont-clair, New Jersey, had become "a sort of school for scientific manage-ment," the authors wrote. "Dad took moving pictures of us children washing dishes so he could figure out how we could . . . hurry through the task."[7]

In Family360, the client has precious little time at home. So he is ad-vised to be efficient and focus on "high-leverage activities." Such a focus elaborates on the common distinction that working parents make be-tween "quality time" and "quantity time" with their children. Coming into vogue in the 1970s when many mothers entered the labor force, the line between quality and quantity time was based on the reasonable idea that what matters to a child or spouse is not the amount of time a person spends with them but the quality of it. Family360 seems to divide the "quality" category into high-leverage quality and low-leverage qual-ity, a division that suggests the possibility of yet more distinctions— high, higher, highest leverage and so on. Dad never takes his watch off.

To the extent that Family360 addresses the client's feelings or those of his child, it also treats them and all else as instruments to some ultimate *end*. A father is not asked to talk with his son about whatever is on his son's mind; rather, he is encouraged to do something that his son will remember later. It is not the boy's feelings themselves which seem to count, but the byproduct of the father's efforts—the boy's memory.

The idea of a high-leverage activity may help a man get things done at work, but at home it helps him feel he is a good dad without sacrificing time. In this way, the Family360 client and his family become more tolerant of—and increasingly enable—a workplace *without family-friendly policies*.[8] Indeed, as a time strategy, it is corporate-friendly.[9]

TIME STRATEGIES: MATCHING TIME
TO SYMBOLS OF MEANING AND FUN

The working parents I interviewed for *The Second Shift* and especially *The Time Bind* were all trying to reconcile a time bind—a scarcity of time—with the powerful desire to create meaningful or fun times at home. Each person I talked to seemed to have arrived intuitively at some sort of time strategy.[10] What, people seemed to ask themselves, shall symbolize my love of my spouse, partner, or child? Given the scarcity of time, how can I *resymbolize* activities? Can I move a symbol of "fun together" from, say, cooking a Thanksgiving dinner together to the act of going to the store to purchase a fantastic meal together? Can I symbolically substitute a weekend getaway with a candlelit dinner, or replace a camping trip with a game of catch and end up feeling I've shared the same kind of good time? Time strategies can be used serially or combined, but mainly people seemed to stick to one as they figured out how connect the time-limited lives they led with the symbols of meaning and fun that they were seeking to reaffirm.

Endurers: "We're Getting Through"

Some workers of long hours simply endure. They do not think about what would be fun or have meaning. They suspend any expectation of having—or even *trying* to have—meaning and fun in what they are doing at work or at home. They focus on getting through the week. As one assembly-line worker on a rotating seven-day schedule—different hours each week plus several hours a week of involuntary overtime—put it:

I'm just getting through. The other day I was so tired that coming off the shift I bumped straight into my locker door. Last winter I was so tired driving home, I ran into a mailbox. I'm not having a great time with my wife and kids. My wife and kids aren't having a great time with me, especially not my wife. We're just getting through. A lot of guys feel the way I do. We joke about it over break. "Are we having fun yet . . . ?"

This man was not seeking meaningful times with his loved ones. His family was there, and he loved them dearly. But he was in a state of siege and putting his relationship with them on hold. Fun and meaning—for the time being, he was renouncing these. He did not walk to the end of the driveway and back as a place marker for good times to come. As one young father of two, a night shift worker, told me, "Who promised us a rose garden? Life isn't supposed to be like it is on *Lifestyles of the Rich and Famous*. The sooner a person recognizes that, the better off he is. I'll be happy not to have this headache." One common refrain was, "You don't have to enjoy your job. That's why they call it 'work.'"

Another factory worker kept a lowered expectation of family life by comparing his fortunes to those of others still less fortunate, which helped him endure in the meantime:

My wife is working overtime too, and we have the three kids between us. She has two from her first marriage, and I have the one, Jessica, from my first. And I'll square with you, it's a challenge. But we're not as bad off as my brother. He's working eight hours plus an hour commute each way, and my brother's wife has a half-hour commute. Theirs are older, mind you, but they've got five kids in the house. He has two and the three steps, and I don't think their marriage is going to last.

"Just getting through" often turns out to be a temporary state, but to workers *in* that state it feels as though it could go on forever. To the extent that they are able to detach themselves from the immediate pressures of work, drinking Cokes around the break-room table during a late night, they often joke darkly about it: "Just three more brick walls to bump into." But beneath this bravado and jousting, workers seem to be helping each other gear up for the sacrificial act of renouncing fun and meaning, sometimes even the imagining of it.

Deferrers: "We'll Have Fun Then"

While the endurers are renouncing the joy of meaningful or fun times, the deferrers are deferring them. Instead of telling themselves "this is a hassle, but this is life," they tell themselves "this is a hassle for now." For example, one up-and-coming junior accountant explained:

> Jennifer and I both dig in during the week, and right now I'm working right through weekends, too. But we're planners, and we make sure to get away once a month up to the lake. I always talk about that with my daughter, the fishing we'll do when we get up to the lake.[11]

Deferrers do not renounce fun and meaning, as the endurers do. Rather, they attach great meaning to future plans and draw gratification from those—whatever future time slots they pick to enact those plans. When the family has arrived at the anticipated date at last, the plans are sometimes spearheaded by the father himself, sometimes by the whole family, or sometimes by the kids who nag and prod. To defer is to create a promise, which is not on offer by the parents who simply endure their jobs. Children hold on to such promises, each in his or her way, waiting for it to come true, enjoying it; then wait for the next, living promise to promise.

The deferrer can defer his wish for various lengths of time. "Later" could be hours later ("We'll have quality time tonight") or a week later ("We'll go to the lake this weekend") or a production period later ("We'll relax after tax season"). Fun is something one is *going* to have. As research by Rakel Heidmarsdottir shows, a number of workers keep themselves going by imagining their "real life" after they retire.[12] Indeed, for the early exemplars of the Protestant ethic, as Max Weber noted, the moments imagined to bring people the greatest joy came upon entrance to Heaven after they die.

The Busy Bee: "We Had Fun, Didn't We?"

While both those who endured and deferred had given up the idea of having a fun or meaningful time in the near future, the "busy bee" did not. She (and it was often a *she*)—would locate meaning right where it is always supposed to be: in the daily activities of the home. But she squeezes those activities into smaller time slots. She does not renounce or postpone fun or meaning; rather, she enjoys it now, but in a busy, fast-paced way. Indeed, she takes pride in being a skilled, efficient, effective, type A artist in condensing fun and meaning. In essence, she absorbs the time bind into her personal identity. Thus, a company-propelled rationalization of time seems no problem because it fits her, and she fits it. She is a busy, fast-paced-type of *person*. Hurry itself is fun.

What the endurers and deferrers view as a hassle, the busy bee takes as a challenge. She is energized by pressure. For her, working under pressure is like a strenuous hike—hard but good for you, something you will later feel glad you did. She brings her image of family life close to the reality of it by saying, in effect, "We like it this way." She often persuades her children that hurry is fun for them, too. "Come on kids," she will say. "Let's see who'll get there first!" It becomes a game. It becomes fun.

In this respect, the busy bee differs from the Family360 man who has his eye on the family-memory creation scorecard. Such a man envisions the home as an office; he resets the scene. But the busy bee sees home *as* home, while applying to it an office-like sense of time. To do this, she keeps herself in a state of "up." She evokes it, and feels pleased when she does so. When she is tired, she also reacts in a unique way: more than the others, she yearns to not have to *plan* anything. The very act of matching fun to small amounts of time calls for a capacity to brace against a child's or adult's resistance and an inner desire to let go.

Delegators: "Did You Have Fun? Tell Me All about It!"

While the endurers renounced happy or meaningful time, and the deferrers deferred it and busy bees shrank it, the outsourcers hired someone else to enact part of the happy and meaningful times for them. To be sure, all the two-job parents I interviewed for *The Time Bind* outsourced domestic tasks to clear time for fun and meaningful times that they could enjoy at home themselves. They hired a daycare worker or nanny to look after their children while they worked, and a few, in the so-called sandwich generation, hired care workers to tend to elderly parents. Most wanted their children and elderly parents to receive excellent care from these care providers but to receive the most deeply meaningful love from they, themselves. In other words, these families wanted helpers, not substitutes.

But the delegators hired others in part to experience fun and meaning for them. They realized that having fun with their children was part of good care, so they moved over to let another person have a place in their child's heart. As one female top executive explained about a nanny who cared for her 2-year-old daughter:

> We looked very carefully before we hired Karina, and I'm very glad we did. She is a dream come true. She's a widow, and lives alone. Her children live in Canada now, and she has no grandchildren. So she's alone here, and she's fit right into our lives and really clicked with Emily. We include Karina at Thanksgiving and Christmas, just like family. And she loves Emily like a mother, even better.

For the sake of little Emily, this executive wanted Karina to experience her own feelings of fun and meaning with two-year-old Emily. "I'm not competing with Karina," she explained. "The more good times Emily has, the better."

Downshifters, Innovators, and Exiters

Unlike deferrers and busy bees, who tended to be found at the top of the hierarchy—the successful examples of work-family balance despite intense work pressure—I found "downshifters" were scattered through the ranks of Amerco, a Fortune 500 corporation that I describe in *The Time Bind*. Instead of adapting to grueling schedules, these workers altered—or dreamed of altering—the schedule itself. As one mother of a 9-year-old girl described:

> I work 80 percent, and for now this is just right. Like this afternoon I went out with Cheryl's Brownie troop [a girl's activity club] on the bus.

We were laughing at a dress I'd tried to make her that just didn't come out any which way. The sleeves were uneven, the neck was too small, the skirt was too long. It was hilarious. And we were laughing, Cheryl and a bunch of her friends and me. A year ago, I would have tried to make one Brownie meeting a month, sneaking a look at my BlackBerry the whole time, not letting myself really relax and enjoy the occasion. It was a big deal for me just to let myself relax and enjoy it. I told my husband about it. Now I want him to get the same sort of into-it feeling.[13]

A number of creative company managers conceived of entirely new ways of reducing workloads. Although he had not considered how to implement it, one top manager thought that all American mothers should be granted two or three years of maternity leave, like military duty for men, and then they could return to the workforce full steam ahead. Another director of a plant in which 200 full-time assembly-line workers manufactured catalytic converters said, "I could manage a workforce of half- or three-quarter time workers. I really only need 10 percent to work full- or more than full-time to supervise the work flow." Yet another manager, head of the administrative center responsible for the company's payroll, described how his employees had created the solutions they needed:

The women have formed themselves work teams and manage themselves. If one woman has to take her kid to the dentist during the
afternoon, she gets another to cover for her and pays her back in work
time later on. It works beautifully. My secret is that I trust them to be
more creative managers than I am. And they are.

Finally, some people's strategy was to remove themselves from the time crunch entirely. I talked to workers who had quit Amerco, a company whose overall ethos of "hard work" meant long hours for employees. As one outplacement official described:

I had one father of three, married to a school-teacher, and while he loved
the company, they both hated the pressure. So he quit, and now they're
running a B&B in the country, and it's just the life they want.

THE FEELING SIDE OF TIME STRATEGIES

All these time strategies—scene-resetting, enduring, deferring, being a busy bee, delegating, downshifting, innovating, exiting—involved managing feeling and often seemed to go with a resetting of emergent symbols that affirmed ideas like "we're a loving family" or "I love you" or "we'll never forget them." And each puts the individual in a particular relationship to the corporation.

The Family360 strategy of resetting the scene at home as like that at work fits the demands of the corporation four-square. Its coaches invite clients to focus on "person practices" that one can measure, count and reward, and not on feelings which more often evade measure. A father might notice his small child's bottom lip tremble and eye glisten, but there was little in Family360 to help him understand the child's feeling. Yet at its best, much of parenthood is a series of efforts to attune oneself to and understand what a child is feeling and to help the child understand that, too.

Those who simply endured their long hours were, needless to say, the least happy. They tried to accept the necessity for unhappiness and made a virtue out of their capacity to do so. This very capacity to manage, to endure, symbolized their devotion to family: "I love my family so much I put up with this hell." Sometimes this symbolic message was passed onto the children but sometimes, sadly, it got lost.[14]

The busy bee and deferrer, on the other hand—generally the women and men of management—adapted to their long-hour schedules. They did not have much time at home, but they tried hard to keep the symbols of fun and meaning alive—the busy bee by hypersymbolizing small acts, and the deferrer by talking up future events. Some deferrers and busy bees also seemed to be using overbusyness as a way of suppressing feelings of discouragement, anger, discontent, or erotic interest. In the age of the time bind, we might even say that, next to television or online social networking, constant busyness is the most common way of suppressing feelings and, with them, ideas that might challenge the status quo. But all told, it was for the busy bee and deferrer that market culture most offered itself as a blessed solution to their problems—and not as a problem itself.

Such forms of emotion management are inner ways of dealing with outer issues—the fierce ongoing struggle between the unregulated demands of the market and the needs of families. Each struggle determines whether market culture will move into the family or stay in the market. Downshifters, innovators, and exiters removed themselves from market pressures. They resisted the cult of efficiency, the giving up on work-family balance, and all that this means for human feeling.

Whether we are scene-resetters, endurers, busy bees, deferrers, or something else, the basic question is whether we are guarding enough the critical space to ask, "How are we keeping our symbols of meaning and fun alive and well?" How much is market culture intruding on that? Those of us who cannot crack a smile at the Family360's "memory creation scale" may have lost that critical space. In the meantime, the Family360 client may try to increase the behaviors that get him a top memory score. But looking back years later, his children's most vivid memory of him may be those meetings around the dining room table, pencils in hand, when the Family360 experts tried to help Dad love them in a way that saves time.

SIX

The Diplomat's Wife

The wife of the Mauritanian ambassador gave a tea last Thursday for the diplomatic corps wives. The Red Chinese came—as usual there were three of them—and shook hands with me and found the Yugoslav. The Pakistani kissed the Red Chinese on the cheek, while the Indonesian, formerly the Chinese's best friend, turned her back and sat down with the Swede and the South Vietnamese.[1]

As an unofficial representative of the American government and people, the ambassador's wife has a full-time job helping her husband do his. Because she has no official role, she actually specializes in the more purely symbolic aspects of diplomatic life and in communicating political messages through nonofficial channels. She tunes an ear to a political Morse code woven into nearly every detail of her daily life.

She holds tea parties, which seem to most people like a public symbol of triviality. When Lenore Romney, the mother of the 2012 Republican candidate for U.S. president, ran for Senate herself, she told *Time* magazine that, as Michigan's representative, she would not "expect to . . . [hold] a series of meaningless teas."[2] Later, Hillary Clinton, the nation's First Lady from 1993 to 2001—and later the U.S. secretary of state—famously said, "I suppose I could have stayed home and baked cookies and had teas."[3] Former Secretary of State Madeleine Albright was reputed to have joked that the only way a woman could make her foreign policy views felt was "by marrying a diplomat and then pouring tea on the offending ambassador's lap."[4] Where others saw silliness, Albright saw the importance of indirection. The lift of a cup, the stir of a spoon, the half-bite of a cookie, an imagined spill—all such minor gestures offer hints about links between Washington and Karachi, China and the Czech Republic, Japan and South Vietnam.

Indeed, François de Callières, author of the 1716 book *On the Manner of Negotiating with Princes: On the Uses of Diplomacy, the Choice of Ministers and Envoys, and the Personal Qualities Necessary for Success in Missions Abroad,* wrote that "if the custom of the country in which he serves permits freedom of conversation with the ladies of the court, he must on no account neglect any opportunity of placing himself and his master in a favorable light in the eyes of these ladies, for it is well known that the power of feminine charm extends to cover the weightiest resolutions of state."[5] De Callières addressed his advice to a small eighteenth-century circle of European envoys, but much of his advice is astonishingly timely, for it tells us something about the influence of one person's reputation upon another.

In my own study of diplomats' wives, I began by taking systematic notes of my observations when I lived with an ambassador and his wife for a period of six months in the summer of 1963. I attended diplomatic luncheons, dinners, teas, and cocktail parties given by other diplomats and foreign officials, and observed preparations for similar functions in the home of my host.[6] I also sent open-ended questionnaires to wives at 116 chief of mission posts (ambassadors or their temporary representatives) in foreign capitals around the world.[7] Of the thirty questionnaires returned, most were from wives stationed in Europe and Latin America; the rest were evenly distributed between wives at posts in the Far East, Near East, and Africa.[8]

But over time, the role of the diplomat's wife—like that of most American women—has drastically changed. In 1969, diplomatic wives received no money for what informally constituted a full-time job. A decade later, women became eligible to receive stipends for work entertaining foreign guests, though not salaries. (At least one diplomat's wife was offended at the idea of pay to do what she considered her patriotic duty.) In 1974, the State Department removed the rule against wives of diplomats holding their own jobs, so long as their position created no conflict of interest. Today, nearly one-third of all ambassadors are women.[9]

So what can we learn today from a mid-century diplomat's wife? We can see in it, I believe, an extreme case of that which affects us all: *reputational reach*. In the culture of the 1950s, an ambassador's wife was legally barred from holding a profession of her own and lived far from her family and community, so she saw herself and was seen by others mainly as her husband's wife. She carried his reputation. And from that flowed two facts: she had a full-time job helping him build that reputation, and her life was deeply influenced by living under it. Indeed, her life provides an extreme example of a form of connection we all know.

Most of us do not work as hard at building the reputations of others, but we may be influenced by living under them more than we think. The action of a child reflects honor or shame on a parent, as does that of a parent reflect on the child. The same holds true with a spouse or partner. Similarly, a teacher reflects well on his school and a doctor on her hospital. In the realm of reputation, we are not free-standing individuals, we carry and lend reputations. Carrying—or struggling against carrying—someone else's reputation becomes part of who we are. The less recognized by others we are, the more we borrow or carry the reputation of others.[10] In its more elaborate form, reputational reach can form part of what Hannah Papanek calls a "two-person career."[11] With diplomatic couples, two people work full-time every day under the reputational umbrella of one, and do the job of one—the husband. Many spouses of corporate executives, professionals, and church leaders fit this pattern, as do spouses of candidates for U.S. president, whose gestures, dress, and off-camera remarks are closely inspected for clues to the person from whom the reputation emanates. We can respond to a reputational reach in any number of ways—by trying to hide it, ignore it, defy it, sabotage it, minimize it or, as in the case of the ambassador's wives I describe here, elaborate it.

The reputational carryover of a diplomat to his wife is greater than that of a dentist, lawyer, or shopkeeper. This is partly because the role of the diplomat is more diffuse; what does and does not contribute to good relations between countries is not as clearly defined as what does and does not contribute to a well-executed root canal or expertly kept shop inventory. Official life blurs into nonofficial life and public life into private.

A logic of power is often at work. In the case of the ambassador's wife, this logic begins with the U.S. president, who wields the most power. The ambassador is his "royal messenger," wielding the power attached to that task and carrying his portion of reputational reach. In turn, the ambassador's wife helps with the task assigned him. So just as people glean clues from an ambassador as to what the president "really thinks," they glean clues from the ambassador's wife as to what her husband really thinks. Each is dealing with a different link in the chain of reputational reach.

The ambassador's wife of the 1960s held frequent lunches, teas, and dinners that were not optional. One wife reported, "At this small post I average 14 'must' social functions a week, not counting entertaining an average of 40 people a week, large receptions excluded." Eighty percent of the ambassadors' wives reported either giving or going to ten or more dinners, luncheons, or receptions a week, and the average wife attended at least one function a day in someone else's home.

Officially, the role of the ambassador's wife is not a job. It is not mentioned in the *Dictionary of Occupational Titles,* and she receives no pay. She has no direct say in diplomatic negotiations. Indeed, she is instructed *not* to discuss official diplomatic business because she is not supposed to be told diplomatic secrets and her word could be mistakenly taken as official. At the same time, she deals continually with politics indirectly. Were she married to a poet or carpenter, she would not be holding innumerable receptions, riding in a diplomatic car, living in an embassy residence, or carrying a diplomatic passport.[12]

In addition to his wife, the ambassador's secretary, chauffeur, and maid reflect on the country the ambassador represents. In general, the closer the association and the more equal to him in status, the more carryover of the ambassador's representative function to them. For example, if his personal secretary has an illicit affair, this indirectly affects his reputation, but if his wife has the affair it affects it far more. Similarly, if his chauffeur is unfriendly to the chauffeurs of other diplomats, the ambassador's reputation is affected, but if his wife refuses invitations from the wives of other ambassadors, it is affected far more. This is the shape, then, of what we could call reputational reach—or sometimes glow—which varies by occupation, gender, and national culture.

The wife's training seemed to become more important with the decline of nineteenth-century "secret diplomacy" and the rise in "grassroots"—or people-to-people—diplomacy.[13] Accordingly, in the 1960s, the Foreign Service Institute began to offer briefing sessions for wives, including lectures on American culture, history, and foreign policy, guided tours to art museums, and language courses in both major languages such as Russian and local dialects such as the Ghanaian *Twi*. A bibliography was given out which included Emily Post's *Etiquette: The Blue Book of Social Usage*, Sir Ernest Satow's *A Guide to Diplomatic Practice*—now in its sixth edition—and the U.S. State Department's *Social Usage Abroad: A Guide for American Officials and Their Families*.[14] Included, too—this in the 1960s—were three books on communism, including J. Edgar Hoover's *A Study of Communism*, two books on American history, and only two on the nature of the non-Western world.[15] Some knowledge of the local language, American history and culture, and international etiquette were considered a minimal requirement. But many wives went beyond their husbands in representing America. The wife of the head of the Foreign Service Institute advocated that ambassadors' wives hold classes on "the American way of life" for local officials, conducting them to different rooms in her home, explaining different objects in each room, and serving American-style food while teaching their guests about U.S. eating habits and customs.[16]

Indeed, a wife was advised to think of her publicly visible life as a "class" for others on America. As a writer in the *Department of State Newsletter* noted, "We begin by remembering what all Foreign Service wives learn early in their careers: that the behavior of any American living abroad will invariably be considered typical of most Americans— our attitudes, our cultural values, our personalities and sensitivities."[17] Her sensitivity should extend to local customs as well: "Scrupulous observance of local laws . . . and careful attention not to offend local customs are urged. [But] 'going native' is as unwelcome in most countries as aggressive Americanism."[18]

Her husband's role also impacts what a diplomatic wife should do and not do. As mentioned, before 1974, diplomatic wives could not hold a paid job. As one wife explained, "A profession such as a lawyer, doctor, or work in any commercial field would be well nigh impossible, for your official position would prejudice any action and would cause resentment and criticism."[19] Only those professions removed from public life—those of an artist or musician, for example—were exempt. The same held for joining any group. As one official warned, "Caution is urged when joining new organizations; sometimes groups seek both the prestige and the cover afforded by participation of wives of American officials, so it is suggested that Embassy officials be consulted before joining unknown groups, signing petitions, or taking part in programs which involve innocent Americans in international political activities."[20]

When inviting people over, a wife was also advised to "confine the guest list to those whom your husband should know and with whom he works." She could pick people she wanted to see, but that wasn't the main purpose of her socializing.[21] As the wife of the ambassador to a small European country noted, "Naturally it is difficult to be closer to the wife of the French ambassador than to the wife of the British ambassador—or to spend more time with the Russian wife than the Italian wife; we must be 'diplomatic.'" As she also noted, "Remember . . . when you are invited to a party given by other than Americans, it is usually because of your husband's position in the embassy and his work. Therefore look upon yourselves as representatives of the United States *even when your hosts are good friends*."[22]

If her obligations were vicarious, so too were her honors—being given a seat of honor at dinner parties, having the American wives of lower ranking officials stand when she entered a room, and receiving near unanimous acceptance of invitations from embassy personnel. She enjoyed diplomatic immunity from legal prosecution, parking tickets, and travel-related customs inspections. Her house, servants, and chauffeured car also reflected a lavish standard of living through which she got to, and had to, express what Thorstein Veblen in *Theory of the Leisure Class* called "vicarious conspicuous consumption."[23] Her furs and limousine were symbols of the reputational reach of her husband, even as his work upheld the reputation of the U.S. president.[24]

HIDDEN IN PLAIN SIGHT: A MORSE CODE

According to Harold Nicolson, "the expression 'diplomatic language' is used to describe that guarded understatement which enables diplomatists and ministers to say sharp things to each other without becoming provocative or impolite."[25] Diplomatic terms describing breaches of understanding rise, like keys on a piano, from "unfortunate" to "regrettable" to "troubling" on up to "inexcusable." On both sides of a communication, a statement can be understood as an *under*statement. So, like the ambassador, his wife tunes a keen ear to mild statements and small gestures without becoming—or seeming—oversensitive. As de Callières pointed out, "The negotiator must possess that penetration which enables him to discover the thoughts of men and to know by the least movement of their countenances what passions are stirring within, for such movements are often betrayed even by the most practiced negotiator."[26]

There are two main covert message systems—a *political* message system links to her capacity as unofficial government representative, and a *social* message system attaches to her role as chief of the embassy wives. She sends and receives messages in both.[27]

Did the Yugoslav ambassador come to our Fourth of July party or not? If he was a no-show, was that because he had received a recent communiqué from his government to take a harder line against the war in

Vietnam? Or did he leave early without having another function to attend?[28] Or, then again, did he send a junior officer instead of showing up himself? Was he unusually friendly tonight, and did he snub the Russian official? Such minor moves might mean "Thanks for stepping up aid to Yugoslavia."

Why does not the Yugoslav diplomat or his wife just say, "I don't like your policy in Vietnam, and I am expressing this by not showing up at your party tomorrow night?" Or why not say, "My government opposes your government's policy in Vietnam, but I like you as a friend and will come to your party"? Because ambiguity is useful: it leaves room for multiple interpretations, and so for doubt. Should the political winds shift, it leaves a way out. The diplomat who shakes loose of such ambiguity is viewed as naïve, devious, or ill-suited to this line of work.

In the diplomatic world, as well as outside it, actions function as words. Just as there is a standard of grammatical correctness in language, so too is there a standard for behavior through diplomatic protocol. Much of this standard was originally set down in the Congress of Vienna in 1815, was revised in 1961 by a meeting of plenipotentiaries from eighty countries convened under the auspices of the United Nations, and was last updated in 2009.[29] Other books based on it became user guides. As one ambassador's wife explained in a speech,

> "Protocol" is a set of rules of the game—the game of diplomatic life where you meet people of different cultures, backgrounds and so on. If we all acted the way we did in our home towns, it might not be completely understood in Bangkok or Leopoldville or Lima or Paris. So there is "protocol" which tells us the right international way for an ambassador to present his credentials, to meet a visiting Royalty or a President, to arrange conferences and in what order to rank officials of countries, big or little.[30]

Large embassies have protocol officers whose job it is to ensure that "everything goes according to protocol." Who should precede whom into the dining room? (The guest of honor goes first.) What is the place of honor for male guests? (The right of the hostess.) The highest ranking lady at the dinner table? (The right of the host.) Protocol spells out the seating on down to the middle of the table.[31]

Social Usage, the official State Department document of protocol, instructs junior diplomats' spouses, for example, on how to pay a call on the ambassador's spouse:

> One stays for approximately 20 minutes, unless strongly urged by the hostess to stay longer . . . or if refreshments are served, and on leaving one shakes hands with and thanks the hostess. If no appointment has been made, one asks at the door if Mrs. X is "at home" or "receiving." . . . If not, upon departure, leave the proper number of cards to the individual who answers the door. . . . Cards must not be handed to the person on whom one is calling. Turning down either upper corner of cards indicates a personal call.[32]

If the hostess says, "Must you go now?" she does not mean "please stay." She is being polite. Because the boundaries of behavior are so clearly marked, even to the permissible deviation, "there is never any doubt in anybody's mind," Edward Hall writes, "that, as long as he does what is expected, he knows what to expect from others."[33]

So protocol provides a behavioral Esperanto. It sets out the correct way to greet a person, take a coat, or assign a seat. It gives diplomats a way to understand the *breaking* of protocol as a way to send and receive messages.[34] Was the newly arrived envoy from China not seated to the right of the hostess? Why might that be? Omissions from and additions to guest lists, accepting, rejecting or giving gifts, dressing up or down, turning music on or off, staying late or leaving early—all such details are a form of talk between states.[35]

Paradoxically, those living in highly formal cultures, Hall suggests, are more relaxed. That may be because they do not have to figure out what things mean; all they have to do is know the Morse code.[36] Protocol does it for them, and so reduces anxiety. Still, the continual premium on avoiding unintentional offense means that diplomats and their wives become good, as firemen are, at maintaining the strange state of being relaxed while also staying on the alert.

Can a diplomat's wife make real friends? Yes, but carefully. As the wife of a Consul-General remarked, "The moment one's husband is in charge, both Americans and local residents do not feel so free to drop in or to invite one for informal activities on the spur of the moment." Another obstacle to making real friends is the sheer number of people it is her job to know. This could become both a source of friends and a protection against intimacy. "You have so many friends and acquaintances that you find yourself spread too thin," one woman observed, "even if you enjoy people." Or, as yet another put it, "Your husband's position, and responsibilities connected [to it], don't leave you much time to cultivate close friends."

Of the ambassadors' wives I sampled, a third spent "most of their time" with other Americans (of that, 23 percent with other American embassy wives), 12 percent with foreigners not from the assigned country (mostly diplomats from other embassies), and 52 percent with locals.[37] Most diplomatic families are on two- to four-year tours of duty, so a wife might arrive at a post just as someone she likes is leaving. According to one wife, "It depends on the post. In one post I made extremely close friends. In Paris it was harder for the social life was so extremely active and Americans were passing through all the time." In addition to the continual stream of foreign visitors, local government officials get promoted, demoted, transferred, and replaced. A third of the time, the person at the front door is a new face.

Then there is age. The ambassador's wife and her husband are at the pinnacle of a small hierarchy, and, as one wife explained, "Ambassadors' wives, having gone up the ladder, are usually older and find few at the same stage of life." Also, in a young, developing nation where the political elite are young, many top officials and their wives will be twenty or thirty years younger.[38]

The number of people and their transience, age, and social position all tend to inhibit the development of personal bonds—even during so-called personal time. But personal time blends into work time. The weekend is not set off from Monday to Friday, and in going to church, playing golf, tennis, or—in countries such as England, Australia, or New Zealand—going to the races, one is also on the job.

CHIEF OF EMBASSY WIVES

When the ambassador's wife is alone with other officers' wives, the *political* symbolism of her role tends to disappear even as the *social* message system comes into play. In the company of foreign guests, the social distance between wives of differently ranked husbands tends to fade as does the salience of its Morse code. For example, *Social Usage* suggests that Americans in the company of foreign dinner guests "should forget precedence among themselves and be prepared to be seated in any way which will make conversation easier and which will take into account language qualifications."[39]

In the world of the 1960s, American officials and their wives often stood in receiving lines at diplomatic functions: the ambassador and his wife first, the political counselor and his wife next, then the economic counselor, the administrative counselor, and the junior officers and their wives.[40] Wives stood in the order of their husband's importance. Most embassies set up an American women's club to which all embassy wives were required to belong, and the ambassador's wife was its automatic—functioning or honorary—chair.[41]

In most embassies, wives referred to themselves as a "team" or as "one big family." "To be in a foreign post is to be a member of a large family, and the differences of interests between me and my old friends [in the United States] who do not belong to it," one wife reflected, "make a large gap in our relationship." The smaller the embassy, generally, the greater the team spirit.[42]

But given the hierarchical relations between the ambassador—whose evaluation matters in getting a promotion—and his subordinates, some social distance is required not only between an ambassador and a man working for him, but between their wives. The wife of a junior officer might be tempted to befriend the ambassador's wife in order to praise her husband to his boss's wife, but the other junior wives would bitterly resent and censure such a wife for "currying favor."[43] Three-fourths of the wives surveyed mentioned barriers between themselves and junior wives.[44] Of the half who said that most of their best friends were in the American diplomatic service, only 5 percent said their best American friend was at the same post.

Friendships, when they developed, were with foreign nationals or among social equals. As one ambassador's wife put it, "One's position of authority with other Americans precludes closeness. One shouldn't have 'favorites' although inevitably they exist. *The incentive to having friends . . . among the locals is higher.* It is your profession to develop friends. If you fail, you're sent home."[45] Another wife noted, "In general, one makes friends but not close ones." It is, much of the time, a lonely job.[46]

HOSTESS TO FOREIGN NATIONALS

The ambassador's wife entertains many people. One recommended keeping a file on all guests: "A card file, with a thumbnail sketch of the person being documented, his language abilities and general interests on one side, and on the other side, the dates and functions at the Embassy to which he has been invited, as well as the invitations accepted from him, has been of the greatest use to me."[47] Another official suggested notes on whom each had been invited *with* "in order to avoid duplication."[48] Conversely, the ambassador's wife is on comparable lists kept for the same reason by those who invited her to their occasions. One wife reported difficulty getting on the right list: "There is a problem in this country, since they are neutralist, and do not want to be tagged as Pro-American."

Because the ambassador's wife is either on her "turf" or on someone else's, there is not much time for walking around in public.[49] Rather, at home she is in public. She entertains at "the residence," a large house that looks like a public building and is literally owned, as it were, by the role, not the occupant. Furnishings such as chairs, rugs, and curtains are provided by the State Department, and the United States seal appears on all the glasses and plates.[50] Often one or two rooms in the mansion are "home rooms," furnished with familiar personal objects and pictures, and kept out of public view. The rest of the house is explicitly designed for formal entertaining, with large hallways for overflow crowds, closets large enough to hold dozens of coats, and large doorways and quarters to house servants who often come with the house.

Entertaining is mostly formal, and the higher one's husband's rank the more so.[51] It takes place at designated times and is tightly scheduled. One woman commented, "Local residents . . . feel that a diplomat's wife is always busy, and [they] are embarrassed if they drop in and find guests at the residence." Servants add to the air of formality since, unless they are known to speak no English, they can overhear.

The general purpose of the diplomatic function, as de Callières put it, is to help "to conduct the affairs of [the diplomat's] master to a prosperous issue, and to spare no pains to discover the designs of others."[52] Indeed, "if people of this kind [deputies in a democratic state] have a freedom of entree to the ambassador, a good table will greatly assist in the discovery of all that is going on."[53]

Conversation takes a certain form. Usually the hostess' conversation steers a middle course between serious and light,[54] but either way it is seldom carefree. As one ambassador's wife remarked, "Most of my friends are among the local wives, but there too I must be extremely careful of carefree conversation which can always be misinterpreted. An innocent remark can be carried (equally innocently) by my friend to her husband—and therein hangs many a diplomatic blunder." Thus, the ambassador's wife often talks to politically relevant people on politically nonsignificant subjects. Even if the wife of a local official is not consciously scouring the conversation for information useful to her husband, the result is often the same as if she were. One wife reported:

> You must avoid politically sensitive areas as your words will be taken as government policy in spite of the fact you never see the telegrams or are privy to secret information. If you slip once, or god forbid, twice on secret information your husband has confided in you, his job is at stake, and worse—he watches every word he says to you thereafter.

Ironically, formal entertaining often calls for the hostess to "take off" some of the formality. If a guest arrives at the front door, for example, she might open the door and greet the guest herself. In this way, she silently conveys the idea that "My servant answers the door for others, but you are special, so I answered it myself." She might make light of protocol but usually without deviating too much from it. At one dinner party, the ambassador's wife playfully complained, "I don't know where people sit here," although neatly printed name cards stood by each guest's plate; she thus ensured that guests would sit where they should, but in a genuine and friendly spirit—the ideal diplomatic combination.

The formal setting itself offers an ambassador's wife the choice as to whether to be as formal as her surroundings (keeping the ice) or informal (breaking the ice). As de Callières recommended to eighteenth-century diplomats, "The diplomatist will readily understand that at certain times he can win the good grace of those around him by living in an easy, affable and familiar manner among his friends. To wrap oneself in official dignity at all times is mere preposterous arrogance, and the diplomatists who behave thus will repel rather than attract."[55]

Because most entertaining involves feeding large numbers of people, a hostess shares many techniques in common with a restaurant manager, such as appreciating the foibles of one's staff.[56] One diplomat's wife posted in India noted an understanding she had come to with her servant:

> It was a different matter if guests were present. A plate of food might be spilled on the floor. The bearer would see it, might put a stool in front of it so that guests wouldn't stumble onto it but he would walk with dignity out of the room to get the sweeper to come and clear it away. He wouldn't embarrass me in front of my guests by behaving as if he didn't know the proper way for a respectful Hindu man to act. If there were guests, I wouldn't embarrass the butler by doing the job myself as any American housewife would be inclined to do.[57]

Many tire of the impersonality of diplomatic protocol, but at the same time, it helps them guard their inner selves from the encroachment of a highly impersonal order. Within the rule-based, message-conveying cocoons in which they live, diplomats' wives often develop close bonds with their husbands and a few friends with whom they draw very near. As one wife put it, "One makes hundreds of 'friends' and few close friends, but my close friends mean a lot to me."[58] Divorce seemed exceedingly rare.[59]

When asked what they felt about their role, most wives said they enjoyed it. Less than one out of ten said that if they could have chosen their husband's profession, they would have chosen a different one. All things considered—the travel, the variety, the style of life—most wives liked it, and that despite a certain "pinch." That is, the husband picked a role that fit his personality, so the one did not pinch the other; but his wife picked the man, not the role, so she was more likely to feel that pinch.[60]

In the daily life of the diplomat's wife, we glimpse an extreme case of something that affects us all. For other people's reputations often stick to us like burs, as ours do to the identity of others. Cultures set up different rules of reputational reach. The Taliban father gauges his honor by his daughter's sexual conduct and obedience to him, while the Western father gauges his honor more by the college she enters and profession she pursues. Honor goes beyond family too. The abusive priest dishonors his church, the pilfering businessman discredits his firm, while the heroic policewoman brings glory to her department, and the spelling bee winner bestows honor on his school and state.

Good reputations radiate an enjoyable glow and bad ones break hearts. We blissfully bask in the glory of another or anxiously fend off dishonor others cast upon us. And we stand vulnerable to being linked, in the minds of bystanders, to stereotyped ideas about some characteristic—such as creed, race, or nationality—that we may share as next-of-kin, neighbor, or friend to scoundrel or saint. Whether we whirl in the orbit of a fine reputation or knock about in the orbit of a bad one, we are managing our feelings about it. For in the end, we may think of jobs as clearly bounded and people as "individuals," but much of the time, we represent others and others represent us. And, without title, role, badge, or crown, we quietly act as diplomats of everyday life.

Boundaries and Blurs,
Market and Home

SEVEN

The Personalized Market
and the Marketized Self

WITH SARAH GARRETT

Central to the American experience in each era of the nation's history has been an encounter between the market and personal life. Observing early nineteenth-century America, Alexis de Tocqueville was struck by our materialism—our desire to buy and own things.

Looking at the United States in the late twentieth-century, Robert Bellah and his coauthors noticed a rising contractualism: we think in a buy-and-sell way about personal bonds. We do not simply buy things from the market, the authors argued; we turn to the market as a model for how to think about friendship and marriage. Both Tocqueville and Bellah and colleagues give us highly useful ways to look at the market-life we encounter today. Yet neither of them anticipated a new market/self blur that has gelled as corporations increasingly attach emotion to their brands, even as real people look to brand themselves in an uncertain world of work and love.[1]

During a nine-month voyage in 1833, Alexis de Tocqueville became an enthusiastic admirer of the new America—its can-do spirit, its relative equality, and the boldness of its women. A man of aristocratic bearing, with a trim brown beard framing a thoughtful face, Tocqueville was only 28 years old at the time, but he carried from his native France a penetrating curiosity and formidable acumen which he applied to two American traits that especially struck him: individualism and materialism. In the second volume of *Democracy in America*, he described individualism as "a mature and calm feeling which disposes each member of the community to sever himself from the mass of his fellows and to draw apart with his family and his friends so that he has thus formed a little circle of his own, he willingly leaves society at large to itself."[2] It was hard to interest an American in the "destiny of the state," Tocqueville thought:

> [He] does not clearly understand what influence the destiny of the state can have upon his own lot. . . . [Americans feel] they owe nothing to any man, they expect nothing from any man; they acquire the habit of always considering themselves as standing alone, and they are apt to imagine that their whole destiny is in their own hands.[3]

What Tocqueville called "individualism," we might today call "privatism"—a retreat into one's immediate circle of family and friends. Were these little circles even there? he also wondered. Or were Americans like a collection of marbles, each going its own way? He reflected, "Not only does [American] democracy make every man forget his ancestors, but it hides his descendants and separates his contemporaries from him; it throws him back forever upon himself alone and threatens in the end to confine him entirely within the solitude of his own heart."[4]

Free of the yoke of feudalism, Americans were unbound from ties that had long linked European serf to lord, and that, Tocqueville thought, was a good thing. But he also wondered what could replace those ties as the basis on which to pin a sense of obligation. In the absence of other sources of social glue, he feared America would devolve into a nation of self-sufficient Robinson Crusoes. Missing were the strong community-supporting "moral sentiments," as Adam Smith had much earlier called them: loyalty, trust, sacrifice, and gratitude. Such sentiments formed the emotional bedrock for a shared purpose and guided acts that reaffirmed the bonds of family, neighborhood, and nation.[5] If Americans were too individualistic, if they devalued moral sentiments, Tocqueville feared they would turn to materialism. Individualism arising from relative equality, he observed, "lays open the soul to an inordinate love of material gratification."[6]

Was Tocqueville right that Americans of the 1830s were a solitary lot, inclined to a love of things? If so, how are they faring today? The most important latter-day answer to that question is found in *Habits of the Heart*—a phrase borrowed from Tocqueville—the 1985 book by Robert Bellah and his coauthors, who noted:

> Individualism is deeply rooted in America's social history . . . the bondservant became free, the tenant became a small landowner, and what Benjamin Franklin called the self-respecting "middling" condition of men became the norm. Yet the incipient "independent citizen" of colonial times found himself in a cohesive community, the "peaceable kingdoms" that were colonial towns, where ties to family and church and respect for the "natural leaders" of the community were still strong. Individualism was so embedded in the civic and religious structures of colonial life that it had not yet found a name. . . . It took the geographical and economic expansion of the new nation . . . to produce the restless quest for material betterment that led Tocqueville to use the word "individualism" to describe what he saw.[7]

Tocqueville worried about the American love of things, but Bellah and his coauthors feared something deeper—the transfer of a contractual model of human bonds from "board room to bedroom and back again."[8] Less and less did Americans honor sacrifice, loyalty, and gratitude among loved ones, the authors felt, and more and more did they pursue a biz-speak search for a "reasonable return on investment" in their personal ties.[9] Especially from the late 1970s on, an increasing number of Americans began to believe in the virtues of a larger, freer market. What held Americans together as a people was not a commonly held set of values, Tocqueville thought, but their common role as consumers.[10] This view undermined community, Bellah and coauthors argued, by not according value to the moral qualities that sustain it. Their story of change in America still resonates, but it does not tip us off to the strange new convergence between corporations that now market their commodities in more personal ways, and people who have begun to think of themselves more as commodities.

Both Tocqueville's and Bellah's big-picture studies speak of habits of the heart. But for a habit to have a heart, it needs feeling rules, and ways of managing feeling so as to abide by them, and enough time to pass so that a way of thinking about these feelings becomes a habit. So what have been our habits of the heart? Where would we look to find out?

In method and approach, Sarah Garrett and I were inspired by a study devised by the Norwegian social psychologist Hilde Nafstad and her co-authors at the University of Oslo. In their 2009 essay "Globalization, Neo-Liberalism, and Community Psychology," the authors tracked two sets of values in Norway—one reinforcing market ties (competition, self-interest) and a second reinforcing community (duty, belongingness, thoughtful-ness).[11] Tracking the appearance of such words in Norway's most widely read newspaper, the *Aftenposten*, between 1984 and 2005, the Nafstad team discovered an "unequivocal decline" in most terms denoting the virtues of community. They also documented a rise in words referring to individual rights and the market, such as *shop, consumer power, greedy,* and *exposure to competition*. While such words as *we* and *us* held steady through this period, the authors found increasing mention of *I* and *me*. In this they saw a "collective forgetfulness" of community values.

Could the United States be facing a similar shift in discourse? Has talk of duty, trust, and thoughtfulness become less salient because we get more and more of our needs met by buying things and hiring experts instead of relying on neighbors and friends? Or are these qualities just as important today but expressed in different ways? Or is something else going on?

THE INDIVIDUAL ACROSS THE TWENTIETH CENTURY: CHURCH SERMONS, ARMY POSTERS, AND THE *NEW YORK TIMES*

To pursue our line of questioning, we sought clues in three rich archival sources: two, going back over a century and now available on the

Internet, bring us word from the journalist's desk and the pulpit; and the other, gathered from various electronic sources, brings us word from the military recruiter's office. Together, these sources reflect public discourse in civic, religious, and military life for the generations between 1900 and 2007. When we speak in shorthand of the decline of *duty* or *sympathy*, we refer to words that Americans of a certain time saw or heard day to day in a newspaper, on a billboard, or in a sermon. To this we have added evidence from our ongoing research of other surveys and modern-day advice books. From word counts and sermon titles we can find clues to shifts in public rhetoric, and infer changes in tacit public rules about what seems acceptable to feel. Together, these sources offer insights into what qualities Americans felt to be salient to their lives.

We focused first on the largest, best-known, and most-quoted newspaper in the United States—the *New York Times*—from the turn of the twentieth century to the beginning of the twenty-first, using search techniques that enabled us to spot trends independent of the changing size of the publication.[12] Using the Internet search tool ProQuest Historical Newspapers, we scanned thousands of pages, searching both for single words (for example, *brand*) and for words found in tandem with other words (for example, *brand* and *my* appearing within five words of each other). To get some sense of changes over the century, we conducted these analyses in three time periods, which we abbreviate here as "1900" (1899–1901), "1970" (1969–1971), and "2004" (2003–2005). For trends in community, we explored such words as *duty, trust,* and *sacrifice,* and for market, words such as *market, buy, sell,* and *profit.* In this way, we traced each family of terms as they traveled varying paths across the pages turned by readers between 1900 and 2004.

The same archive yielded riches of words from pulpit to parishioner as well. Compared with Europe, more Americans say they believe in God and claim to attend religious services weekly. That was true in Tocqueville's day and remains true today.[13] The scriptures, the congregation, the offerings and prayer—all drew the believer out of the "solitude of his own heart," Tocqueville and Bellah's group argued. The church acted as a *brake* on individualism and on the market, both reasoned. But could it also be—as the authors of *Habits* also suggest—a vehicle for their expression?[14] To find out, we analyzed the content of religious announcements as they appeared in the *New York Times*, the *Chicago Tribune*, and the *Los Angeles Times* during the first two weeks of February in 1900, 1970, and 2007.

At first, the guiding missions of the church and military would seem worlds apart—the church calling for peace, and the army mobilizing for war. But despite such differences in mission, each institution fosters a powerful sense of community—among members of congregations and buddies in the squadron. Both seek to draw Tocqueville's solitary soul into communion with a larger whole. But to what motives—national pride? duty? self-interest?—did army recruitment posters appeal over time? Drawing clues from newspapers, churches, and recruiting offices, we set out to check the observations of Tocqueville and Bellah's group, and to explore whether something more was also going on.

The Individual on the Rise

Nafstad and her coauthors discovered increasing mentions, over recent decades in the major Norwegian newspaper, of such words as *I* and *me*.[15] A study of the lyrics from the top ten American pop tunes for every year between 1980 to 2007 reported a similar rise in the appearance of *I* and *me*, and a decline in references to *we*.[16] So both recent American pop lyrics and the newspapers of a contemporary social democratic country suggest the rising salience, if not value, of the individual.

References to the individual in words such as *you*—as in "Your Free Spirit," "Your Spiritual Journey," and "Your Name Is Written in Heaven"[17]—appeared more often in the sermon titles of 2000 (one in every five) than in those of 1900 (one in every twenty). Modern sermons also focused more on what we could call self-help; nearly a third had titles about working on one's emotional, physical, or spiritual well-being, such as "Release the Energy" and "Healing Is a Decision."[18] Early sermons—with such titles as "Healing for Your Deepest Hurts" and "Never Feel Unwanted Again"—made more mention of God's needs and society's needs.[19] Later sermons appealed more to individual needs or desires (2 percent in the early ads versus 16 percent in the later ones).

A parallel shift appeared in military rhetoric. Most striking in the seventy-three posters calling young men to World War I was the clarion call to duty: "Our country needs you now." "Our first line of defense." "Uncle Sam's looking for every fit man. Are you fit?" "Do Your Duty." "Your Country Calls; Enlist." Other posters of that period appealed to pride in the United States and its forces: "US Marines; First to Fight for Democracy." Still others appealed to the nation's specific needs: "Wanted! 500 bakers for the US Army." "A Call for Volunteers! Aid the National Army, Men." "20,000 are needed and the recruiting stations are again enlisting soldiers of the sea." All told, more than four out of every ten World War I posters appealed to duty toward, pride in, or the needs of the nation. About 17 percent appealed to self-interest (for example, "US Marines: Good pay, foreign travel, congenial employment"). During World War II, the posters focused even more on the nation (close to half), and 14 percent focused on the recruit's self-interest.

But with the post-Vietnam War shift to an all-volunteer army and the more recent shift to private contractors, in the 2000s the proportion of ads appealing to self-interest rose to over 25 percent. For every two recruitment ads that appealed to national duty, pride, or need, there was now one that highlighted what the individual would get out of enlisting: travel, money, health insurance, or marketable skills, for example.[20] These contemporary notices feature messages such as "Need a College Scholarship? Get UP to $135,000 to launch your career!"; "Navy Dental Corps . . . Be Sure to Ask about the $30,000 Bonus"; and "Have something to REALLY talk about at your class reunion." The lead army recruiting slogan of the 1980s and 1990s, "Be All You Can Be," was replaced in 2001–2006 by the infamous Rambo-type paean to the self-sufficient, lone-star hero—"An Army of One."

To be sure, national pride, duty, and need still shined through in just over half of the messages. But the long American history of newspaper accounts, church notices, and military appeals suggests that the individualism Tocqueville saw in embryo in 1833 has gradually increased ever since.

Moral Sentiments Redirected

Meanwhile, over the century, newspaper stories and church notices told a complex story of community. In the *Times*, we saw declines in the mention of *trust, sympathy,* and *duty*.[21] Church notices reflected a similar trend; in 1900, a parishioner might have listened to a sermon titled "Community of Prayer," "The Escaped Slave: Or Our Duty to Those Who Are Struggling to Be Free," or "The Care of Neglected Children."[22] By the end of the twentieth century, such altruistic themes had begun to fade.[23] The "moral-sentiments arrow" pointed down.

But over the same century, *gratitude* and *sacrifice* dipped and bounced back in the *Times*, and *obligation, commitment,* and *loyalty* continuously rose.[24] As an area of concern, such virtues hung on. Perhaps Americans came to favor some words over others for the "same" moral sentiments or began to think of certain sentiments in new ways. As *duty* appeared less and less over the century, *commitment* rose. This suggested to us a form of *chosen duty*—one that was not imposed by others but chosen by oneself. So in contrast to Nafstad's findings, we suggest that moral sentiments in America have not been forgotten so much as integrated into individualism. To have effect, moral sentiments have become less anchored in the will of the community and more anchored in the will of the individual. As a man who had given up his career to stay home and care for his ill wife told me, "I'm not doing this to be good. I'm doing this because I choose to."

Moral sentiments have also shifted in their aim. Less and less did *sacrifice* and *loyalty* appear in the *Times* together with terms suggesting the civic sphere—*community, nation, neighbor, church, temple,* or *synagogue*. More often, they appeared jointly with words suggesting family—*family, children,* and *kids*. Pooling the articles that mentioned words in all of these spheres—civic, family, or job life—we found movement in terms such as *sympathy, sacrifice, gratitude, duty,* and *loyalty* from civic to family and job life. This finding fits with the thesis of the historian John Gillis, who argues persuasively in *A World of Their Own Making* that a sense of devotion once accorded to church, state, and community has been displaced onto the family—and also, we can add, to the jobs that sustain that family.[25]

The New Market-Self Blur

In individualism, Tocqueville saw an opening of the American cultural door. If we follow these conceptual footprints, what increasingly entered inside was the market. For, since the turn of the twentieth century, readers of the *Times* were increasingly exposed to terms like *profit, buy, sell, market,* and *advertising. Profit* rose by a factor of two, *consume* by a factor of eight.[26]

Over time, even the church and the military developed a market-style "pitch" to their prospective flocks. Tucked into religious announcements were additional notices of offerings beyond the sermon—an organ recital or a talk, for example. These more than doubled between 1900 and 1970; in 2007, their presence in religious announcements was still about 50 percent higher than it had been in 1900. At that point, offerings included such enrichments as wellness shops, meditation workshops, *feng shui* advice, yogic breathing, bereavement groups, exercise classes, adult Bible classes, pastoral counseling, and, in one case, "soul care." Part of this increase over the century was due to the promise of more parishioner-support services—convenient parking, translation services, air conditioning—all of which peaked in the 1970s.[27] Mention also rose of things to buy—books, food, and items from the church gift shop. (Perhaps because of this changed context, one 1970 New York ad reassured parishioners that "All pews are free."[28]) By all indicators on the cultural dial, market culture was on a century-long rise—even in the church and army, which we imagine to be far removed from it.[29]

CORPORATION TO PERSON, PERSON TO CORPORATION

Neither Tocqueville nor Bellah and his coauthors placed the market at the center of their concern. Writing in the 1830s, Tocqueville saw many things for sale and people who wanted to buy them—materialism. Writing in the 1980s, Bellah and his coauthors saw the market as an office-type model for bonds at home: contractualism. But our research reveals something else—a new cultural blur between a personalized market and a marketized self.

Market and personal ties have always been intertwined, of course. The eighteenth-century neighbor was also the village baker from whom one bought a loaf of bread. A friend might devote a week to helping his neighbor build a barn, and the neighbor a while later would give him the gift of a calf. The two were intertwined. But by the early nineteenth century, industrialization had largely split workplace from home, and split a market emotional logic (friendly, efficient, exchange-oriented interactions) from a home emotional logic (devoted, loyal, generosity-oriented interactions). These two emotional logics have now recoalesced in a new way.

This modern blur arises from two directions: the corporate drive to personalize a product's appeal, and the citizen's drive to draw cultural tools from the market. Companies have increased their personal touch in many ways. Over time, they have tagged sacred rituals (Macy's Thanksgiving Day Parade and Santa Coca-Cola ads, for example). They have encouraged communities centered on ownership of goods (Harley-Davidson motorcycle clubs). They have used community practices to sell things (Avon coffee klatches, peer-to-peer buzz advertising, drug-industry representatives attending parent-teacher association meetings, and corporate sponsorship of professional meetings and sports events, to mention a few). But there is another market-style personal touch: branding.

Between 1900 and 2004, the proportion of *Times* articles mentioning *brand* or *brands* rose ninefold. And, over time, the word came to refer to very different things. In the *Times* editions of 1900—and even more, those of the 1860s—the word *brand* almost always referred to markings on animals and slaves, and it was generally spoken of as a neutral or bad thing. Only later did *brand* routinely refer to institutions and people, with the implication that it was something good. Both in newspapers and in everyday life, *brand* came to denote the unique character of a college, museum, politician, or even nation.

The relationship of brand to personal life showed a startling shift as well. When you read the word *loyal* or *loyalty* in the *Times* of 1900, you

Table 1   Loyalty to People and Things
    Articles as % across set[1]

	1899–1901	*1969–1971*	*2003–2005*
Loyalty[2] and[3]			
Loved ones[4]	100% (54)	90% (81)	50% (82)
Brands/products[5]	0% (0)	10% (9)	50% (82)
Total	100% (54)	100% (90)	100% (164)

[1]The number of articles is within parentheses.
[2]This search consists of "loyal" and "loyalty." We did not explicitly exclude "brand" from the searches (e.g., "brand loyalty") because the co-occurrence of "loyal"/"loyalty" and loved one/s, for example, assures it is used in the context we want.
[3]Here we define co-occurrence as the word appearing within five words of the other searched terms.
[4]The "loved ones" search consists of "friend," "friends," "spouse," "wife," "wives," "husband," "husbands," "partner," and "partners."
[5]The "brands/products" search consists of "brand," "brands," "product," and "products."

were likely to see it appear near (within five words of) *friend, wife, husband, spouse,* or *partner*—as in "loyal to my wife" or "loyalty to my friend." In that era, terms suggesting loyalty did not appear near *brand* at all. But turning the pages of the same newspaper in the early 2000s, readers saw the word *loyal* and *loyalty* appearing together with *brand* just as frequently as they did with the terms for loved ones. Loyalty—once reserved for intimate life—had become increasingly associated with brands.

In the world of marketing, brands became personal. Advertisers began to speak of brands as having a birthplace and a creator, and as being the object of a narrative, very like a person. Indeed, as Jeep's vice president of marketing, Jeff Bell, said in 2004, brands are "living, breathing entities that have DNA."[30] Advertisers give brands a "psychographic" profile, imbuing them with personality. As a member of a creative team at a large advertising agency told Arlie in a telephone interview,

When we design a brand, we think of it anthropomorphically. When market researchers do focus groups, the first question they ask is: if the brand were a person, who would it be? So when you design a brand, you're really describing the person. [She is] 35, her name is so and so, she lives in the suburbs, she lives in an apartment, and she is married. If the brand was a person, this is the person it would be. The team is really trying to bring it to life as if it were a *living thing*.

Companies often try to make their branded things befriend a customer they imagine as lonely.[31] As the advertising designer Marc Gobé noted in *Emotional Branding: The New Paradigm for Connecting Brands to People,* customers have a need for a "lasting relationship."[32] So, in a world where a lot of people feel like just a number, he added, "I believe that it is the *emotional* aspect of products and their distribution systems that will be the key difference between a consumer's ultimate choice and the price that they will pay. By emotional, I mean how a brand engages consumers on the level of the senses and emotions; how a brand comes to life for people and forges a deeper, lasting connection."[33]

Behind the corporate drive for the personal touch was the discovery, in the 1980s and 1990s, of the strategic importance of emotion. These insights were introduced by Daniel Goleman's 1995 book *Emotional Intelligence,* which was followed by Kevin Thomson's *Emotional Capital,* Mitch Anthony's *Selling with Emotional Intelligence,* Margot Cairnes's *Approaching the Corporate Heart,* Travis Bradberry and Jean Greaves's coauthored *The Emotional Intelligence Quick Book,* and Martyn Newman's *Emotional Capitalists.*[34] The business world began to see emotion as a kind of capital.

As in the workshop of Geppetto, the wood carver who created the talking puppet Pinocchio, companies try to bring commodities to life. It becomes a problem for them when a commodity remains, in Gobé's words, "a *mere* commodity."[35] For the successful brand now uses appeal to feeling in order to *de-commodify* the shoe, the soft drink, the car, and the service. The market has gone personal.

At the other end of the spectrum, some ordinary citizens have come to think of themselves in more market-like ways—especially in response to increasing insecurity at work. In his article "A Brand Called You," the popular business guru Tom Peters exhorts his readers to accumulate "brand equity" and to increase their "brand energy."[36] Following Peters, Catherine Kaputa notes in her 2010 book *U R a Brand* that when companies fire employees, they do it in three batches: the first batch has negative visibility (they come in late and are cranky); the second has no visibility (they creep in, seldom talk, then creep out); but the third has positive visibility (they succeed and socialize).[37] In winning the race for a decreasing number of jobs, it helps to get in the third category, and one accomplishes this through branding: "A brand is you and you are a brand," Kaputa told Arlie in an interview. "You don't know how *personal* a brand is." To develop one, she advised we aim for a "sweet spot":

> Get a USP—a unique selling proposition or big idea and target a market for it and execute a "self-brand action plan." You'll need a strong visual and verbal identity for it and you can deploy them without seeming promotional or obnoxious. Do a brand "audit"—a detailed study of all your competitors. Smart marketers think in terms of choosing an enemy to position their brands against. Don't think of that as a bad thing to do. Position your strengths against their weakness, and reposition their strengths as not so important. Find the "sweet spot."

To develop a personal brand, we do not need to lie about ourselves, Kaputa explained. "Anyway, people can spot it if you're inauthentic." To brand ourselves is to repackage what is already true about us. It calls on us to reconceptualize our experiences as a collection of assets (such as our ideas and skills) and contacts (our Rolodex), much as we would inventory a company. This way, we position ourselves in the market without lying.

But brands can mislead. "Anything negative in our inventory," Kaputa noted, "is for the *other* guy to find out." Still, she felt that visibility was a moral virtue in itself. Fame was better than obscurity because "even if people don't know what you're known for people think you're better than others they don't know."

Just as some advise us to brand ourselves for work, others advise us to brand ourselves for love.[38] In her bestselling advice book, *Find a*

Husband after 35 Using What I Learned at Harvard Business School Rachel
Greenwald applies branding to the realm of love:

> *Package* [your] assets, develop a *personal brand,* leverage *niche marketing,*
> use *direct mail* and *telemarketing* to get the word out, establish a husband-
> hunting *budget,* and hold quarterly *performance reviews* to assess the
> results. . . . The trick is pulling [these practices] all together into a
> comprehensive and systematic strategic program.[39]

Other authors apply branding to life itself: David McNally and Karl
D. Speak's 2011 book *Be Your Own Brand: Achieve More of What You Want
by Being More of Who You Are* focuses not on getting the perfect job or
marital partner, but simply on being the self you really are—and in
someone else's eyes, getting *credit* for it.[40] It is not enough to be a good
person, he tells us; you have to brand yourself as a good person in order
to receive the benefits of being one.

Companies have pressed American culture to a new edge in other
ways as well, creating a culture of commerce–self blur that makes self-
branding seem slightly less odd. For people are now called on to *help*
companies in their efforts to brand stuff. As Stuart Elliott described the
words of A. G. Lafley, the chief executive at Procter & Gamble, speaking
at the 96th annual convention of the Association of National Advertisers: "'Consumers are beginning in a very real sense to own our brands
and participate in their creation. . . . We need to learn to begin to let go'
and embrace trends like commercials created by consumers and online
communities built around favorite products."[41] For example, Coca-Cola
set up a competition for the best commercial film for its product and
featured the filmmaker in it, thus inviting consumers to become volunteer salespeople. As another conference speaker mused, "Today the customer is in charge and whoever is best at putting the customer in charge
makes all the money."[42]

The California-based company Ruffles sponsored a campaign "to
celebrate the 'rebirth' of the Ruffles brand of potato chips" by offering
$50,000 to a family that would name their baby "Horton" after the cam-
paign's cartoon icon. Sean and Dianna Chesleigh responded to the call,
"won" the competition, and named their son Horton. The *San Diego*

Metropolitan Magazine described the event as a *financial* decision, quoting the "proud father" as saying, "Baby Horton and Mom are happy, healthy and doing well. . . . Although Horton isn't concerned about it, Mommy and Daddy are very excited [that] his college tuition is already paid for."[43]

Of course, some parents name their children after branded commodities quite on their own. According to the U.S. Social Security Administration, out of the 4 million American baby boys born in 2000, there were fifty-five Chevys, six Timberlands, and seven Del Montes about to enter preschool. Among the girls, there were twenty-five Infinitis, five Celicas, 164 Nauticas, 298 Armanis, and twenty-one L'Oreals.[44] Dr. Jui-shan Chang, a sociologist from the University of Melbourne, describes a trend through the 1990s in Australia toward giving children top brand names, often those of cars such as Lexus, Mercedes, Ford, and Bentley.[45]

Some people have thought to auction themselves off as a temporary platform for advertising. As a 2005 notice posted on the eBay Web site, seen by millions worldwide, read:

> Act now and you can rent an entire family of 8 to wear your advertisement (company jackets, hats, shirts) for a month. We have three boys and three girls in addition to a man and woman to hit lots of target markets. Just think of when we are all together and wearing your matching ad! Sure to attract attention. Ads must be family friendly and safe to wear to Church, School and Work. [Starting bid $499.99][46]

The family seated on a couch in the eBay image—arms and legs casually touching, smiling into the camera, wearing identical jerseys—offered itself as a symbol of the cohesive, happy family.

An unidentified mother from Perth, Australia, offered her unborn baby as an advertising platform. She tried to auction off the child's naming rights on eBay for a million dollars. The winning bidder was promised " 'naming, advertising and promotional' rights for five years after the girl, nicknamed Truman baby, [was] born."[47] The mother had no takers, and an eBay spokesperson announced that the listing was removed from the Web site because "it was deemed inappropriate."

Then there is the move to corporate tattoos. A student in marketing at Fox Valley Technical College in Oshkosh, Wisconsin, along with his wife—a psychology and social work major at the University of Wisconsin, Oshkosh—said in their eBay ad:

> "Advertise your Company Or Product On Our Foreheads" [*sic*] . . . Last month we decided to advertise on our foreheads for 90 days. I have to say this form of advertisement has been a great experience for all parties involved. We were on a bunch of radio stations, front page of the newspaper, as well as a special appearance on Fox 11's "Good Day Wisconsin" morning show.

Other people promised to advertise on their arms, backs, and even pregnant bellies.

Citizen-created ads, naming children after brands, auctioning off naming rights, tattooing pregnant bellies—all of this could be dismissed as fringe stuff. And, of course, it is. But that is the point: the fringe has moved—and so has the center.

AN INVITATION TO FEEL

Culture is an invitation to feel.[48] And the modern culture of branding invites us to feel that what is important about us is what is visible to the outside—or, at its extreme, that we only exist in the eyes of others, much as a commodity does. In this way of thinking, it is through our market value that we feel safe and recognized, not through what we and those close to us know about ourselves in private. Branding also invites us to orient ourselves toward rivals: to fear losing out to them, to stay on guard. It does not invite us to relax, or to feel safe or open in communion with others. For how open can we be if, as Kaputa notes, the bad news is what we keep behind the curtain? Branding turns our attention toward the market and away from personal and civic virtues such as duty, trust, and sympathy. The growing practice of "pitching" church and military service as something of personal benefit both reflects and contributes to this trend. Branding keeps us busy, sucking up energy we might otherwise devote to other commitments large and small. In a culture of branding, the self is that which we continually *do* in order to *be*.

There may be very good reasons for this shift. Work and love, the two cornerstones of adult identity, now stand on ever more shaky ground. Especially since the 1970s, many companies have restructured, automated, and moved to cheaper labor pools offshore. Many jobs that were once permanent are now temporary. Benefits and pension plans are more in question. In recent years, government safety nets have eroded while Medicaid, Supplemental Security Income, Medicare, and even Social Security have been attacked as "the nanny state." We have moved from a world of employment and marriage to a world of employability and marriageability.[49] If we lack jobs or become unsure of the ones we have, it makes sense to focus intently on our position and our competition in a wider pool of possibilities—in the market. If we yearn for a partner or feel unsure of the one we have, we do the same thing. In this context, the idea of branding becomes a useful tool, and it is this usefulness that may account for the stealth rise of branding on the American cultural horizon.

At the same time, the post-1970s rising salience of certain moral sentiments—loyalty, gratitude, sacrifice, and commitment—reflects an effort, we believe, to counter a growing uncertainty about job and marriage by affirming the ties that bind.[50] Both the move to branding *and* the rise of moral sentiments may be responses to the same frightening work and family shakeup.[51] So many Americans may be counterbalancing two things: on one hand, preparing themselves for a cold, tough market (getting the right brand); on the other, staking claims to strong bonds with family and friends (affirming loyalty, gratitude, sacrifice, and obligation). Peering through Tocqueville's telescope, it would have been hard to foresee tattooed ads on pregnant bellies, children named for products, smiling families as billboards, or the bewildering struggle to come to terms with it all. To those involved, though, such activities seem like solutions to a problem, not a problem themselves. And in a culture of blur, why not?

But if we are branding ourselves for ever more shaky work and love markets, even as corporate advertisers are breathing life into Pinocchio-like stuff on the shelves, maybe it is time to ask where we are going. Maybe it is time to rehumanize ourselves, and to create the social conditions that make that a safe thing to do.

EIGHT At Home in the Office

WITH BARRIE THORNE

As long-time inhabitants of academic departments, we are familiar—Barrie Thorne and I—with the routines of office hours, hallway chats, committee meetings, and mail pickups in the main office.[1] An academic department is part of an orderly bureaucracy. It houses very smart, well-trained professionals and would seem to invite an attitude of dispassionate concern. So why, we got to wondering one day, do matters of recruitment, course scheduling, and office space occasionally make tempers flare? Why the gossip, occasional intrigue, and sometimes smoldering feuds? Perhaps it is because departments are like families.

Like families, departments are small, face-to-face groups that share space, material resources, and everyday life. Members do not, by and large, choose one another, and, given the tight job market, most anticipate being stuck with one another for the long haul. Periods of adoption

or marriage (faculty hiring) tend to be especially contentious, raising issues of collective identity and fears that the existing balance of power
may shift.

Department members sometimes leave home, having been "courted
away" as happens to eligible young people under the rule of exogamy.
Indeed, departments do not like to hire from among their own graduate
students because it is too "incestuous." Rather, the prospective hire
should come from another village to bring in "fresh blood." Members of a
department may become estranged, or "get a divorce," at which point the
in-laws and children are tacitly required to take sides. Graduate students
may walk into a Ph.D. exam with the hope of "bringing both parents together," just as the children of divorce may try to reunite a broken family
by becoming the symbol of unity at a Christmas party or birthday.

Departments have reputations. They can be known as friendly or
stand-offish ("closed doors"). Departments, like families, are positioned
in systems of social stratification. There is even a national blue-blood
registry: the ranking of "top" departments by the National Academy of
Sciences and the magazine *U.S. News and World Report*. Some departments wage campaigns for upward mobility—requiring six instead of
four peer-reviewed articles for tenure. Others downshift or opt out, affirming missions that break with mainstream criteria for ranking.

Like families, departments have a long tradition of patriarchy. The
vast majority have a male "head" who deploys the labor of other members, and who sits at the end of a long table as he presides over gatherings of the whole. Indeed, department meetings often resemble family
dinners as scenes of ritual solidarity, replete with gestures of subtle defi-
ance and dramatic fights.[2]

Department generations divide into older and younger parents (the
tenured senior faculty and the untenured juniors), and graduate students who, like dependent children, are expected to move on after a period of training and nurture; faculty are pleased if their children "marry
well." The junior faculty are positioned much like adolescents, because
the seniors keep secrets from them and actively control their fates. At
faculty meetings (as at Victorian family dinners), the junior faculty tend
to be seen but not heard, fearful of publicly challenging their more

powerful elders. Behind the scenes, seniors may pressure junior faculty to take sides. The juniors maneuver for position because resources are limited and ascent to the highest, permanent tier (a form of inheritance) is not automatic. When a junior member is up for tenure and fears disinheritance, conflict often erupts.

Tension also surrounds other moments of generational succession, such as the timing of retirements, which will free up departmental offices and tenure lines (the equivalent of land and wealth), or struggles over who will become department chair. A faculty member who becomes chair may find that previously amicable colleagues turn hostile or begin to whine for special favors. The dynamics are like those among siblings when one of their numbers has been singled out and put in charge.

Generational relations often differ for men and women in departments, as they do in families. To advise a student's dissertation is to engage in a professional relationship, but it involves managing dependence, nurture, and often frustration, as the child struggles to become acknowledged as an independent adult. So the dynamics can slide into those between parent and child. As more women become faculty members, mother-daughter and mother-son attachments, resentments, and conflicts have become more widespread.

Gender divisions are marked more subtly in departments than in families, but they persist. Men predominate in positions of authority, and there are relatively few women in the highest ranks.[3] Women have challenged male dominance in departments, as in many families, often focusing on sexual harassment or sex discrimination in pay or promotion, for example. The results, in both cases, have been uneven.

At their core, most departments are also based on a deeply embedded clockwork of male careers.[4] As women have been joining their ranks, many departments have taken on the surface look of equality. But the rules for getting ahead are still premised on the ideal of a full-time worker who has access to full-time help in family care for the rest of life—feeding the baby, taking children to the doctor or dentist, visiting elderly parents or grandparents, sending holiday cards, cooking and cleaning. Women are far less often relieved of these responsibilities than are men.

In departments, as in families, sometimes people complain that a certain faculty member is "never around." Just as children are sometimes left to do homework unattended by hard-working parents, so do graduate students fear the retreat of their "parents" to their studies, leaving them "home alone."

All families manage sexuality, and healthy families manage it well. Although departments do not maintain an incest taboo as well as families do, it is clear that sexual bonds between teachers and students are disturbing to members of the system, and, in a sense, signal trouble in it. There is ambiguity about erotic connections among faculty. They may be seen as mommies and daddies who are free to mate among themselves (for instance, it is seen as fine to have married couples in the same department). Or they may be seen as children of a patriarchal head, and so are less free to mate.

Departments, like families, are sites of a second shift.[5] Just as there are tensions between parents over who should do the less-valued work of making a house a home, so, too, are there tensions over faculty who refuse to "do their share." Some will do the housework (administration) but not take care of the kids (be on dissertation committees). Others do more than their share of both, and still others squirm out of doing either, creating resentment.

Like families, departments have a dominant ethos. Some value the "nurturant" work of the home (tending to student's personal problems). Others only value publishing and politicking). As at home, women sometimes end up spending more time comforting, encouraging, and checking in with students.[6] The tensions—and resolutions—are similar to those in families.

Faculty allocates some of the least desired tasks, such as grading and leading discussion sections, to graduate students. Advanced graduate students are sometimes given their own undergraduate courses to teach, just as older children are sometimes made responsible for younger ones. Like parents, the faculty justify this labor as "training" and "development," but graduate students sometimes question this explanation and resent the work.

Departments, like families, have limited material resources, and professors struggle with one another to get them. The budget is controlled by the department chair, who "brings home the bacon." Staff who have less lofty credentials are responsible for the least valued—clerical and bookkeeping—tasks. Some are seen as "one of the family"—a beloved nanny, a ruler-gripping aunt who is a stickler for procedure, or a sage elder; others are seen as behind-the-scenes service providers.

The chair, like a parent, has discretion in spending the department's income and doles out salary increases (allowances) through an emotionally charged process of "merit review." Sometimes the chair has a few gifts to bestow, such as new computers or extra research stipends. Like children, faculty vie for the extra goodies and sink into states of envy toward siblings who get more. Rumors circulate about parental (chair) favoritism. For in departments as in families, sibling rivalry often rises to the fore.

In both departments and families, space is a scarce and valued resource. Members of equal status are supposed to have equivalent private space, and, like siblings tussling over bedrooms, the faculty scan the size and location of one another's private offices, looking for signs that hint "Daddy loves him best." Sharing an office with a faculty sibling is like sharing a bedroom, a mark of lower status. The head controls the largest and often the most presentable office, which may function as a parlor—a place to receive outsiders and to try to make a favorable impression on behalf of the departmental family as a whole.

Every home has its problems, but in most cases we are so very lucky to be in one. It is the same with departmental "homes." Once we have earned tenure, our department is committed to us. And the vast majority of us commit ourselves wholeheartedly to it. We may be overworked, but we're doing work we love.

But alas, today academia has a rising problem of homelessness. A shocking 68 percent of all faculty appointments in American higher education are non-tenure track.[7] Half are part time—not the "good" part time with health benefits and job security, but the "bad" part time of the contingency labor force, paid only for classroom hours and not for time preparing lectures or talking with students outside of class.[8] To earn enough, many contingency workers commute between two or three colleges, preparing new courses on their own time. In this atmosphere of insecurity, they often avoid anything that might cause complaint—be it civic controversy or tough feedback on student papers—and miss out on meaningful ties with students.

Work homes are wonderful, and we need more of them. The challenge is to make them vital, healing, and thriving places to be. In the meantime, the next time some of us walk into our department's office and feel anxious that we have been displaced by a younger colleague or ignored by a preoccupied elder colleague, we should smile and understand that we are lucky: we have "come home again"—at work.

NINE

Rent-a-Mom

Shortly after her brother and his family paid a week's visit, a working mother told me:

> I wanted to give them a good time—my brother, his wife, their two kids,
> who are 8 and 10. I cooked them nice lasagnas and some great soups.
> I got out games for the kids. But it rained the whole time they stayed
> with us and the kids got bored. My brother and his wife didn't help
> much with the dishes. They didn't say thank you. They just took me for
> granted. And I had my own kids and husband to think about. I had to
> ask myself what *did they think I am—a bed and breakfast*?

Visits can be hard on those visited, but if we compare this woman's complaint to its equivalent in the United States of the 1950s, there seems something new. Envisioning herself at first as a beloved hostess to her kin, the woman discovers herself to be an invisible drone, unappreciated for her troubles. She is in a world of kin that sees itself outside the marketplace, but is *already* inside it.[1] She compares what she *does* feel—unappreciated as a sister—with what she *would* feel—acknowledged as a paid "B-and-B" worker. She is "listening through the wall" between market and non-market life.

LISTENING THROUGH, BORROWING ACROSS, AND JUMPING OVER THE WALL

What if it were true, I would like to ask, that we do not live *outside* the market in private life and are not always *in it* at the workplace and mall? What if there were a larger machine—let us call it capitalism—that has its *own* relationship to our feelings in all these arenas? If this were true, how would we think about personal feelings? In a world of hired daycare workers, eldercare workers, nannies, wedding planners, family photo album assemblers, funeral service workers, "rent-a-Dads," "rent-a-brothers," and "rent-a-Moms," how do we say, "I love you"? How do we consult our feelings to gauge the meaning of gestures filtered through, around, and over the wall between market and non-market life? Does love only feel real if we buy something for another ("I found just what you want."), or does it only feel real if we do not ("I made this myself just for you.")? Or in what proportion each?

Normally, we imagine an impermeable wall between market and non-market life; home is haven from a heartless market world, in the words of Christopher Lasch.[2] But, especially today, this wall is highly permeable, the object of cultural belief and strong emotion. Indeed, people who pay for care services (two-job couples, for example), those who provide services (such as childcare and eldercare workers), and those who are cared for (children, the sick, the elderly) all manage their emotions in accordance with their relationship to "the wall." We assume that the wall between market and non-market life has one fixed and agreed-upon meaning, but, as Viviana Zelizer has beautifully shown, money—one aspect of market life—can have many personal meanings.[3]

We listen through the wall and borrow over it as well. Transplanting rhetoric from work to home, one plant shift supervisor I interviewed (for *The Time Bind,* a study of home and workplace cultures) expressed hope that his family would be a good "production team."[4] Another described his wife as his "best customer." Going the other way, companies often describe themselves as "like a family" (see chapter 5 on this). Advertisements for at-home services often offer homelike qualities. One ad posted on the Internet on Craigslist by someone looking for a home helper said he or she was looking for "another member of the family." In a second Internet ad, a woman searching for a job in eldercare offered to "spend quality time with your grandmother."[5] But for whom does the time have quality?

We also *jump over* the wall. One woman who ran a business called "Rent-A-Mom" was a divorced former homemaker. What began as a complaint against an ungrateful husband ended by giving up any hope of receiving his gratitude, accepting estrangement from him, and making a bitter-happy leap toward paid work. When I asked her how she came to call her business "Rent-a-Mom," she answered, "I was married for twelve years, and I washed, cooked, and raised my children and a garden. But my husband didn't notice much. He thought the only contribution that mattered was his—earning money. So after we divorced, I figured I might as well get paid for all the things I used to do for free." Through the name "Rent-a-Mom," she was stating her *worth* at home as a *price* in the marketplace. She jumped over the wall, even as others, in their quest for meaning, jump back.

Over the last 40 or so years, the United States has witnessed an acceleration of a long-term trend—the commercialization of what has been defined as intimate life. Beginning in the upper classes, this trend has ricocheted down through society as a whole.

FORCES BEHIND THE COMMERCIALIZATION OF INTIMATE LIFE

The market can surge forward or retreat. But over the last fifty years it has mainly inched forward—into intimate life—due to a confluence of trends, some prompting a greater demand for personal services, and other trends propelling the supply. Primary among trends creating a need and demand is the rise of the working mother, the abiding absence of European-style state services, and the loss of community help. Mrs. McGillicuty is not home to watch over the neighbor's kids because she is working 9 to 5 at the 7-Eleven. The majority of American women are now in paid work—making up half the workforce—and, for many, the workday has grown longer.[6]

Part of this is due to a corporate strategy to lure the time and skill of the professional class by engineering a "have fun here" work culture.[7] However, the working class goes daily to jobs—many of them in the "service mall" as maids and childcare and eldercare workers—without such workplace lures. Their low-wage jobs form the basis of another kind of compulsory overtime in which both parents work two, sometimes three or more jobs. As a 2007 survey of Californians showed, those at the lower end of the social class spectrum expect less help from family and friends in meeting their needs and want more market services than do their higher-end counterparts who can far more easily afford them.[8] With what disposable income they have, these weary parents are seeking commercial fixes they can afford for their domestic needs: unlicensed family childcare, Chuck E. Cheese's birthday party setups, McDonald's family dinners.

The growing fragility of the family adds to the need—or at least the yearning—for services. Divorce lowers family income, making services harder to budget. At the same time, it may increase the desire to enjoy services that promise to deliver the "spirit" of home. Indeed, 28 percent of Americans live alone.[9] The culture of "home" may become a prime business selling point for people "going solo."

Other social trends also drive the growing supply for intimate services. As industrial sector jobs move elsewhere around the globe, enterprising workers create new service jobs that peel off tasks along the domestic front. Some services are a modern extension of services familiar to early American history—the maid, the nanny, and daycare and eldercare workers. Others fill newer, more specialized niches—love coaches, friend-finding services, family photo album assemblers, child sleep experts, child namers, and party animators, to name a few. Enveloping all the trends pressing the demand and supply of such services today is a market *zeitgeist*—an unshakable faith that a bigger, freer market is the best solution to just about any problem.

A CULTURE OF OUTSOURCING

In "Beyond Juggling: Outsourcing—Having It All, but Not Doing It All," Kurt Sandholtz and coauthors describe a management consultant named Chris Watson who travels around the world and also volunteers as a youth group leader at her church. She outsources cooking, cleaning, laundry, and even the locating of dating prospects.[10] As she says, "I've found that I can hire someone to do almost anything I don't want to do myself. . . . Mingling at clubs or parties isn't a great use of my very limited social time." Chris Watson applies to herself a principle that business applies to itself: comparative advantage. As the authors write,

> Chris belongs to one of those groups . . . we call "outsourcers"— people who are so clear about their personal priorities that they hire out almost everything else. Outsourcing has worked its way into business lingo as corporations have slashed costs and focused on their core competences—the things they're best at and that make them distinctive. Everything else is turned over to vendors. Individuals have taken the same approach as they try to control their overstuffed lives. They farm out certain tasks and obligations to focus more attention on the activities, relationships and causes they care most about.[11]

In any career we specialize. We try to get very good at what we do and this takes time and mental focus. We want to draw on the knowledge of professional experts. But in clearing the way for that time and focus and desiring expert help, how do we draw a line between the tasks we turn over to others and those we do ourselves? What does outsourcing change? The term *outsourcing* suggests that something inside the home is taken out. And task for task, this is true. But outsourcing also imports cultural images and strips of rhetoric from outside the home into it. Responsibility for the task goes out, and newcomers with their own ideas about "real needs" and "good homes" come in. While outsourcing relieves us of unwanted cares, it can also smuggle in a curiously market-laundered version of hominess. It can bring home *back* home.

Most such ads appeal to clients by offering to do chores they do not have *time* to do or *do not want* to do. As one ad on Craigslist temptingly reads, "Not enough time? Let me help out. . . . Maybe dinner is too much after a hard day's work. I could make you a wonderful coconut curry while you are at work and have it on the table when you arrive." Other ads offer to "organize your home/things/papers, clean house/minor repairs, shop for personal items or gifts." One Internet ad for a personal assistant offers to "do personal shopping, coordinate holiday décor and oversee the design and mailing of holiday cards." Another offers to "organize your closet," to "manage the family calendar," and to "assemble photos in your family photograph album." Other ads offer to assist with e-mail.[12] Ellie and Melissa, "The Baby Planners," run a Studio City, California, concierge service that offers to "organize" and "beautify" the nursery, to hire a muralist, a sleep expert, and a dog walker, to plan a baby shower, and even to organize preschool placement.[13] These services propose the transfer of a certain "executive function" of personal life, and as such call on the client to re-symbolize him- or herself.

Both provider and client "move the wall." The difference between paid and unpaid life remains the same, but the meanings associated with each one shift. What once seemed "too personal" to pay a person to deal with now does not seem that personal after all.

As Jacqueline Salmon, a reporter who wrote a story on such services in the *Washington Post*, described it:

> Brent Lloyd . . . is glad he turned over a hundred years worth of family photos stuffed in shoe boxes and crumbling scrap books to Marilyn Anderson, the owner of Creative Memories in Fairfax Station. Six weeks later, for about $600, Lloyd got back three photo albums with descriptive captions and decorative touches, one for his elderly mother and two to share with his wife and three children.[14]

Brent Lloyd does not want to sort through his family albums; he wants Creative Memories to do it. While others might consider it odd to see a stranger's handwriting under that picture of Uncle Frank and Cousin Martha, or to know that a stranger's judgment had determined which photos to exclude, Brent's focus was on the *result*, not the authorship, of the acts leading to it. Other such services nonetheless raise the question of what feels too meaningful to outsource. One service organizes children's birthday parties, making out invitations ("Sure hope you can come . . .") and providing party favors, entertainment, a decorated cake, and balloons. Virginia-based Precious Places helps parents decorate their children's rooms.

Each party in such transactions develops a new relationship to their feelings. Each checks to see what "feels right" under the new circumstances, and each may live with a strain between what they believe they should feel and what they glancingly know they do feel.

I interviewed a man who ran a maritime funeral service for bereaved clients, which spread the ashes of loved ones on the ocean. The skipper of the boat explained that on a quarter to a third of his trips carrying ashes out to sea, relatives did not accompany him. If they did, he told me, he poured the ashes from a cardboard box into a china urn, and placed it on a table, draped with a brocade cloth. He then dropped nasturtium blossoms into the water before pouring the ashes overboard. He said, "The flowers make it nice. If the relatives are there, I enjoy dropping the flowers as part of the ceremony. If they aren't there, I drop them anyway, just to see what way the tide is flowing, because I don't want the ashes to float to the side of the boat." A certain feeling went with the doing of the task asked of him; he had to consider how to "carry" that feeling, and how to link it to the task. On which side of the wall did the "core" of the symbol lie—in the relatives' participation in the ritual (itself unpaid) or in the fact that the ashes were spread (a task paid for)?

A growing culture of outsourcing deals with such questions of meaning—often through humor. Several *New Yorker* cartoons capture a certain commercial-familial edge. One shows a mother and father wearing faces of impartial wonder at their son who has just pulled the tablecloth off the dining room table, breaking dishes and cups. "Just wait until your nanny gets here," the caption read.[15] In another, a father dressed in a business suit looks expectantly at his son to whom he has given a birthday present. The son says, "Tell your assistant it's perfect."[16] Such humor taps our anxiety or guilt about outsourcing "too much," tacitly establishing a boundary beyond which outsourcing seems funny. It establishes the anxiety/guilt tipping point beyond which it is uncomfortable to go. It reassures us that the wall is "here," so to speak, and not "there"—and that there is a wall at all.

Humor points to serious questions. How do we tell the difference between expressions of emotional bonds that feel real, deep, and whole, and those that feel sloughed off, partial, or fake? Is the boy really more grateful to his father's assistant than to his father? Or is he getting back at his father for passing the buck? If so, what does the father feel or think he should feel? And how about the assistant? The shifting wall between paid and unpaid life continually challenges our distinction between what is personal and what is not, and where we should look to recognize and display feeling.[17]

THINKING ABOUT COMMERCIALIZATION

Three schools of thought offer different approaches to this interface of family and market life. One would see it as part of an evolutionary march of history. Such thinkers as Talcott Parsons focus not on the market, or profit motive, or medium of money per se, but on the overall trend toward modernization—a societal move from simple to complex, from less division of labor to more.[18] In this perspective, the artisanal family progresses to a postmodern one, specializing in adult intimacy and the raising of children and, when possible, gradually outsourcing everything else.[19] Because domestic outsourcing fits modernization and because modernization is not, in this view, a problem, outsourcing seems natural. It arouses little curiosity. This march-of-history perspective tells us little about what goes on when we de-commodify services—as, for example, in the movement to abolish slavery. We can see smaller examples of de-commodification as well. In Renaissance Europe, for example, upper-class women used to send their babies to village wet nurses to be breast-fed for a fee.[20] Today, we condemn slavery and wonder at wet-nursing—facts the march-of-history story does not explain.

A second line of thinking focuses not on the grand march of history but on the wondrous cultural pageant resulting from various collages of market and non-market culture. In *The Social Meaning of Money,* for example, Viviana Zelizer beautifully illustrates the many ways that we achieve personal ends through what would seem like impersonal means—such as paying money for adoption, allowances, alimony, inheritance, and gifts. As with the march-of-history thinkers, Zelizer does not posit a market "encroachment." From the dawn of history, the idea is, we have had markets, so there is little here that is new or a problem. Zelizer's notion of market is closely linked to the use of money, and she brilliantly analyses aspects of social life inside capitalist economies. But she does not link it to the principle that runs the system—the pursuit of profit—or to the powerful companies based on it, or to the quiet cultural colonization that their presence can cause to unfold.[21]

A third line of thinking focuses on the profit motive but neglects the importance of symbols of personal connection. Many such theorists admire the market's capacity to produce and distribute goods and services.[22] But mindful of the limits of the profit motive in achieving the good of all, such scholars keep a nervous eye on market expansion into various arenas—including that of intimacy. They focus on the new inequities caused by the privatization of public functions, the erosion of the commons, and the destruction of natural resources.[23] In *The Great Transformation,* Karl Polanyi argues that during the nineteenth-century Europe changed from being a society with marketplaces to a marketplace with small islands of society.[24] The market ripped free from "society," he argued, and from its customs for helping the needy—a system for which the modern state would have to substitute. Following Polanyi, the economist Robert Kuttner argues that when companies beholden to stockholders take over services that everyone needs—schools, hospitals, transport—those most in need lose.[25] For-profit hospitals often drop the sickest patients; for-profit schools do not admit the worst-off students; for-profit nursing homes refuse the neediest elderly. The aim of business is to make money, not to help the needy; but, as he rightly notes, those in need still need help.

Not just the student, the poor, or the ill, but all of us, David Bollier argues in his book *Silent Theft*, are part of the encroachment of the market on the commons. We swim in the ocean and enjoy a natural commons. We sit in a public park and enjoy a social commons. We consult Wikipedia and enjoy an informational commons. Bollier makes a special case against for-profit companies reducing the free exchange of information on the Internet, and against for-profit companies engaging in genetic research so as to sell human genes.[26] In *The Age of Access: The New Culture of Hypercapitalism, Where All of Life Is a Paid-For Experience*, Jeremy Rifkin also offers a broad-brush critique of the fake culture of malls and planned communities now replacing historically rooted communities and neighborhoods.[27] In a similar vein, the economist Juliet Schor critiques the growth of consumerism for its overuse of the world's resources. We all benefit from our natural commons—that is, the earth itself—she observes, but the twin headless horsemen of profit-seeking companies and commodity-hungry customers pose a threat to this environment.[28]

By focusing on the most powerful institutions of our time (for-profit companies), I think the encroachment theorists—Polyani, Kuttner, Schor, Bollier, Rowe, and Rifkin—help us see the big picture. They lift capitalism as a specific system out of a more general concept of modernization and they hold it there. This is an important starting point. But they do not explain why so many of us yearn for what commodification offers to personal life—from rent-a-friend to party animator.[29] What is the story behind our need?

In addition, none of these schools of thought ask how we know when something *feels* saleable or not. How do we cast a halo around certain events and not around others? Seeing a baby breathe her first breath, a child take his first step, a casket lowered into a grave, or ashes thrown on the sea—at what points do we locate our notion of the sacred? And how is our idea of the sacred related to our ideas about what is unthinkable to sell or buy? Where do we discover our anxiety tipping points?[30]

SAYING I LOVE YOU

The market has become a third party in many of our intimate relationships. Like the woman who compared herself to a worker at a bed-and-breakfast inn, we often put our ear against a wall to overhear news about life on the other side of it. ("How much would I be paid over there for what I do unpaid here?") We borrow across the wall. ("I would be worth a lot for what I can do.") We jump over it and back. Starting from this premise—and drawing from the march-of-history, cultural-pageant, and market-encroachment thinkers—we can finally ask: How is it we say "I love you" in a market society? And how do we use our feelings to tell us we "know"?

Before we were a market society, misery and disappointment and missed connections occurred in old-fashioned ways, such as when a person failed to visit, or a pie was not thought of or not baked, or was baked badly. The would-be recipient thereby got—or was given—a message of disconnection or disparagement. In a context where gifts should be made, such meaning resided in the failure to make them. The same held true for activities: a child would not invite an elderly parent to live with him or her, or to visit, or a father would neglect his child. These were premarket ways of saying "I don't care."

In much of America today, the market—in its most recent rationalized, bureaucratized incarnation—has changed this. Today, more people say "I love you" by proxy. The one who thinks of giving and the one who does the giving are often different people.[31] The mind, heart, and pocketbook of a gift are less often the hands who accomplish it. So I wish to grow flowers to give to a friend, but then I do not have the time or place to grow flowers. So I buy them to give to my friend, but then I do not have time to pick them up. So I order the flowers online, but then I do not have time to search for an appropriate arrangement. So I e-mail a Bangalore-based concierge service, and an employee there makes a note to send birthday flowers to my friend every year and to automatically bill me. Similarly, I wish to make a cake for my child, but then I do not have the time, and the store cakes are more beautiful and taste better. So I wish to buy a cake, but then I do not have the time to shop. So I order the cake for the birthday along with—if I can afford it—a birthday planner. I share authorship of these acts; they are no longer a "just-me-to-just-you" thing. The expression of a gift, a service, or an object is often standardized. The birthday planner may offer her customer the Winnie-the-Pooh birthday or the Harry Potter birthday, but the menu from which one makes an "individual" choice is standardized. (See chapter 5 for more on this.)

Finally, services such as these are also based on fees. Paying and being paid money—a transaction—offers those on both sides of the deal an out. The deal is as permanent or as temporary as the money is. On the one hand, this flexibility is the great appeal of the market; the customer gets what he needs and does not have to pay for what he does not need. The corporation, too, can withdraw from bad customers and move on to good ones. On the other hand, when we commodify personal services, we draw them into a framework of present-time tit-for-tat deals, and we withdraw them from the ebb and flow of abiding relationships. As Georg Simmel long ago noted, the market introduces the potential for freedom *and* estrangement.[32] But what ratio of freedom to estrangement do the prevailing circumstances—cultural, psychological, economic—make us come to want or need? We do not really know.

In short, the use of proxies, standardized procedures, fees for services, and personal services as a way of saying "I love you" raises key questions. What is personal? What is *too* personal? What is not personal *enough*? Looking at the impact of industrialization on nineteenth-century England, Marx observed how workers could become alienated from both the products they made and from those they bought. In the "fetishism of commodities," we focus, Marx observed, on the commodity itself, and forget who made the things we buy and under what conditions.[33] Today, customers of personal services are also invited to focus on the service *itself*, divorced from the context in which it is produced.

FEELING RULES AND EMOTION WORK

In everyday life, we are often called on to evoke or suppress—in a word, to *manage*—our feelings according to our sense of what we ought to feel.[34] The commercialization of intimate life places a new kind of call on us to manage our emotions. We may feel the wall to be in one location but want it to be in another. For example, we may not want, or feel that it is "right," to place an elderly parent in a nursing home and pay for the service of a proxy caregiver. Our feeling rules put us on the non-market side of the wall, but circumstances force us onto the market side. Maybe we do not like it, but Grandma has to go. Or maybe the elderly parent and child both clearly want a good nursing home but cannot afford it. In either case, how we imagine acts to symbolize love may not accord with what we are able to do or honestly feel like doing. We may be living on one side of the commercial wall, while our feelings put us on the other.

Increasingly, it seems the case that the spending of time has become less the language of love, and the spending of money more so. This transition has allowed us to desymbolize one line of action as a sign of love and resymbolize another. But we know so very little about the emotional intricacies of this moving of symbols. A client who has placed a parent in a nursing home may come to symbolize his love as "managing the caregiver." So this middle-aged child may shift his symbol of love from "taking daily care of Mother, myself," to managing the hired caregiver. This can create problems for the caregiver, of course, who may now resent the man's repeated complaints about her care of his mother. She may see him as ungrateful or distrustful. For her part, the elderly patient may go willingly to the nursing home, not wanting to be a burden living together with a busy, overcrowded family, or live alone. Or she may feel "warehoused," in which case only living back home would symbolize love. Whether as givers, proxies, or receivers, people sense some contradiction between a desire to give a personal gift and the increasingly impersonal means by which it is given.

From each vantage point, we try to put the personal element back in—but in a new place. We repersonalize. The mother who, in a previous decade, symbolized her love by making a birthday cake with her child now symbolizes her love by co-enjoying the purchased cake. A mother may have once devised party games, but now she hires a party planner; her symbol of love is now to co-consume—and co-enjoy—those games and the whole purchased experience. Or she may photograph the child and in this way symbolize her love.[35]

So for the modern market person the meaning or fun is often not in growing a vegetable garden but in eating from it. The fun is not in building the house but in living in it. The fun is not in training the dog but in having a trained dog. The advertisements in toy catalogs today often describe precisely these desired results of their products. Among the ads Allison Pugh studied was one for a Winnie-the-Pooh that turns the pages of a book, its audio reading a story. The result? A child is happily read to by a mechanical bear.[36] It is not only that we cannot grow vegetables, build houses, train dogs, or read to our children, but that we seem to be in the process of ceasing to look for primary meaning in doing so. We are moving our personal symbols from the production side of life to the consumption side of it. As we do, we are left to wonder which symbols to leave attached to the production side and which symbols to remove from it.

In all of this, the cared-about must look for expressions of care in different places than they might have a generation ago. Does a child feel hurt or disappointed that mother is not in the kitchen making cookies? Or that she did not spend the time to think up fun games for them to play together? Does an elderly person feel like a burden when others are paid to talk to her? Or does she feel that the thought to hire someone or the money to pay them was *itself* the gift?

As for a service provider such as Rent-a-Mom, how personal or impersonal is the task of organizing an underwear drawer? Does the maritime funeral service worker feel, as he drops the nasturtium petals and then the remains of the deceased onto the water, "There go the ashes of a person who once lived, like I do"? Or does he simply think, "Another order fulfilled"? All parties live with this series of questions because one set of ground rules for daily life has been removed and another not quite yet set down, leaving many of us to arrange our affairs in an atmosphere of slight uncertainty.

In the end, the walls between market and non-market life are permeable: what we are doing on one side of it we are comparing to what we *could be* doing on the other. In addition, our feelings about the wall have themselves shifted with time. In America over the last forty years, various trends have jointly pushed us in the direction of commodifying intimate life. What happens, we may quietly wonder, when we lose our personal holds in a capitalist system—our job, our pay, our ability to buy goods and services—and, with all of these, our passport to the symbols of love? Even when we have firm hold of our passports, we may ask ourselves how much our love depends on money. We take the measure of a commercial age within the magnified moments of our dearest relationships, and we discover what would stand firm if we did not have—or spend—a dime on Rent-a-Mom.

Women on the Global Backstage

TEN Two-Way Global Traffic in Care

An ever-widening two-lane global highway connects poor nations in the southern hemisphere to rich nations in the North, and poorer countries in Eastern Europe to richer ones in the West. A Filipina nanny heads north to care for an American child. A Sri Lankan cares for an elderly man in Singapore. A Ukrainian nurse's aide carries lunch trays in a Swedish hospital. Going in the other direction, an elderly Canadian migrates to a retirement home in Mexico. A British infertile couple travels to India to receive fertility treatment and to hire a surrogate mother. In all these cases, Marx's iconic male, stationary industrial worker has been replaced by a new icon: the mobile as well as stationary female service worker.

If we step behind the front stage of the global free market—the jet-setting, briefcase-carrying businessmen forging deals in fancy hotels—to a lonelier backstage, we find, along one such global pathway, the female migrant worker.[1] She is not doing the physical labor of paving roads, constructing buildings, or mowing lawns, but the emotional labor of caring for people. One part of that emotional labor is to address her relationships with those she cares for and who hire her, and another part addresses the wrenching ruptures with those she leaves behind. This hidden part of her work reflects the great potential costs of life in a grossly unequal world.

At the moment, such women are moving in five main migratory streams—from Eastern Europe to Western Europe, from Mexico and Central and South America to the United States, from North Africa to southern Europe, from South Asia to the oil-rich Persian Gulf, and from the Philippines to much of the world—including Hong Kong, the United States, Europe, and Israel.[2] Sometimes both parents leave. In western Ukraine in 2003, the *Christian Science Monitor* reported that "most of the adults in the mountain villages have made the crossing in order to work illegally in Central and Western Europe. But the price is high; a generation of children left behind with grandparents, and a region increasingly drained of its working population."[3] Many factors force people to migrate—stagnation or collapse of Second and Third World economies, political unrest, or the chance to fulfill economic ambitions.

Over the last century, migration studies have been dominated by the paradigm of the male migrant worker. This for good reason: half the world's 214 million migrants (3.1 percent of the world population) are men, and historically, most of those who have migrated in search of paid work have been men.[4] Meanwhile, most of those who have migrated in order to reunify their families have been women. Today, however, we are witnessing the "feminization" of migration, in which a growing proportion of female migrants move in search of jobs.

Until recently, First World scholars have focused on female migratory flows as matters of money and labor whereas scholars of work-family balance have focused on First World families. But emotional life for migrant workers is as real as it is for anyone else—and more anguishing than for most. The same is true for the many Third World women to whom clients travel for service.

Women migrate to earn money that they transfer back to their home country in the form of remittances, which pay for different things. The Sri Lankan maids studied by Michele Gamburd and Grete Brochmann were funding desperately needed basic food and shelter.[5] The wages of the Filipina nannies studied by Rhacel Parreñas mainly covered children's school fees, housing upgrades, and money to hire a home-based nanny.[6] Many in the sending countries benefit from the nanny's income—her children, spouse, parents, other relatives, her local church and community. Third World governments also greatly gain from the inflow of hard currency. Indeed, the Philippine government has long recruited, trained, and supported female migrant workers, counting the revenue they bring in as an important part of the nation's gross domestic product (GDP). At the receiving end, First World employers welcome the badly needed services migrants offer. All these parties agree on the benefits of female migration and talk of these women's decision to migrate as the expression of a well-thought-out family strategy, a wise government policy, and, over the last thirty years, a developing national cultural norm.

But there is an emotional cost that is often lost to view in all the talk of money and tasks. I focus on that here in order to highlight the ways in which talk of globalization, with its focus on "free choice" in a "free market," speaks more to the life of those on the front stage of globalization than to those on its backstage, for whom the phrase "free choice" exacts a higher emotional price.

Much of the research on male migrants has focused on their role as economic providers, not on the emotional costs of their work. We can imagine a male Turkish migrant sweeping the streets of Amsterdam or a male Mexican gardener trimming the hedge in the backyard of a California suburban home, harvesting Florida oranges, or slaughtering chickens in a Chicago factory. But the emotional sides of their lives have often gone unnoticed. In the South African migrant labor system under apartheid, for example, many African men migrated to jobs in coal, gold, and diamond mines for eleven months at a time, far from the barren "homelands" to which their families were confined and to which they returned one month a year. As one wise miner told the South African economist Frances Wilson, he missed the chance to be with his children every day and to raise them. But even more, he told Wilson, "I miss having my children raise me."[7]

Over the last forty years, women have become a growing proportion of migrant wage-earners. And compared to most male migrant workers, female migrant workers have based more of their identities on the nurture of children, the sick, and elderly. Many such women migrate in their late twenties, thirties, or forties—key childrearing years. Research suggests that, compared with migrant fathers, mothers leave behind children who are more strongly attached to them, a painful situation for both mother and child.[8]

To be sure, not all female migrant workers do care-based work, and care workers have not always come from abroad.[9] African American slave mothers and poor American women of many races often left their own children behind to spend long hours caring for those of others, and we are tempted to believe their stories have faded into history. But in truth, they have continued and gone global. While many American black women have left domestic and personal care work for better paying jobs, many migrant women are filling their shoes. Earlier in the century migrant women seldom left children behind in their natal land. Robles and Watkins estimate that in 1919 only 7 percent of women immigrating into the United States left their children behind in their home country—a figure that is vastly higher today.[10]

VICKY: MIGRANT NANNY

Vicky Diaz, a 34-year-old mother of five, is a migrant nanny. She had been a college-educated schoolteacher and travel agent in the Philippines before she migrated to the United States to work as a housekeeper for a wealthy Beverly Hills family and a nanny for their 2-year-old son. Vicky explained her situation to the ethnographer Rhacel Parreñas:

> [My children] were saddened by my departure. Even until now my children are trying to convince me to go home. . . . The children were

not angry when I left because they were still very young when I left them. My husband could not get angry either because he knew that was the only way I could seriously help him raise our children, so that our children could be sent to school.[11]

Vicky left for the sake of the family but without their active consent. As she saw it, she made a free choice. But from a wider perspective her free choice was her way of compensating for the absence of good schools or well paying jobs.

Vicki's free choice and that of many others help to redistribute the wealth of the world in the absence of national and global mechanisms for doing so. But it also adds to a global *emotional inequality.* She subtracts daily maternal care from her own five children back in the Philippines and adds a second layer of loving care to the child she's hired to tend in America. The American child enjoys one more caring adult while Vicky's children grow up with one less. Like others, Vicky participates in this emotional redistribution:

> Even though it's paid well, you are sinking in the amount of your work. Even while you are ironing the clothes, they can still call you to the kitchen to wash the plates. It . . . [is] also very depressing. The only thing you can do is give all your love to [the 2-year-old American child]. In my absence from my children, the most I could do with my situation is give all my love to that [American] child.[12]

The children left behind have their own point of view, of course. One mother told Parreñas that she had returned to the Philippines after a long period only to discover her grown daughter asking to be carried, as if time had stopped at the point her mother left.[13] (See chapter 11 for more on the experiences of the children of migrant parents.)

We often imagine such anguish as a temporary sacrifice that will bring about economic growth in the poor countries. And it is true that a lot of money changes hands. According to the World Bank, the officially recorded remittances in 2010 exceeded $440 billion—nearly three-quarters of which went to residents in developing countries.[14] Additionally, the unrecorded transfers have been estimated at about half again the value of the recorded ones.[15] These funds make up 10 percent of the

GDP of the Philippines, 21 percent of Haiti's, 22 percent of Nepal's, and 47 percent of Tajikistan's.[16] Even ten years ago, these monies were reaching about a tenth of the world's population—the leading beneficiaries being India ($27 billion), China ($26 billion), and Mexico ($25 billion).[17] Such remittances often pay for food, housing, dowries, wedding expenses, and school fees for the migrants' families. But, as Elizabeth Gibbons of UNICEF notes, "Behind every remittance, there's a separated family."[18]

Remittances do reduce poverty, but they do not foster economic development.[19] That is, remittances do not lead to investments in enterprises that would offer enough places for the well-educated children of migrant workers at home. If they did, Dilip Ratha and his coauthors at the World Bank argue, by now the Philippines would be a thriving South Korea and Sri Lanka a booming Singapore. Such structural changes have to begin with new international trade agreements, with "fair trade" pricing, and national government support for birth control, health care, and free quality education.

Instead of revitalizing local economies, female migration has paid vital family expenses but also contributed to a culture of remittance dependence. In many countries, it has led to a self-perpetuating system: the children of migrant mothers grow up, face the same dearth of good local jobs that their mothers earlier faced, and migrate to better-paying jobs abroad. They too have children they leave behind, many of whom will one day migrate themselves.

GEETA AND SAROJ: COMMERCIAL SURROGATES

Parallel to the movement of migrant women inbound from the Third to First World is an outbound flow of First World clients to care workers who remain in the Third World. Some retirees from the North, for example, make long-term moves to take advantage of the cheaper care and sunnier climates of the South. After cuts in pensions, a 65-year-old American whose middle-aged children work long hours and live far away might find it more affordable to retire and live—at a third of the cost, according to recent MetLife data—in an assisted living facility in Mexico.[20] Indeed, 1.2 million American and Canadian retirees now live in Mexico. Similarly, a divorced or childless Japanese man might retire to northern Thailand. A French elderly person of modest means might retire to Tunisia or a Norwegian to Spain to be cared for by women who—in contrast to Vicky—stay in their country of birth.

Northern clients also make short-term trips to the global South as so-called "medical tourists." A middle-class American may fly to Mexico to get a tooth capped at lower cost. A Canadian woman might travel to Brazil for half-price cosmetic surgery or to Mexico for a tummy tuck. A western European might turn for less expensive treatment to Thailand or India.

In 2012, medical tourism to India was worth about $2 billion and had become second only to Internet technology as a source of national revenue.[21] Advertisements describe India as the global doctor offering First World skill at Third World prices with shorter waits, privacy, and—especially important when hiring surrogate mothers—an absence of legal red tape. At various Indian offices and hospitals, a bone can be reset, a knee replaced, or a heart valve repaired. In addition to medical or dental treatments, many facilities offer "pre-care" and "after-care" that can last some time.

Westerners have grown used to the idea of a migrant worker caring for a First World child and even to the idea of hopping an overseas flight for surgery, but a growing part of medical tourism now centers on reproduction, in particular on the sale of eggs and sperm and the rental of wombs. In India, commercial surrogacy is legal and, as of early 2013, still unregulated; nowadays a Westerner of moderate means can go to an Indian clinic to legally hire a surrogate mother to carry a baby to term. Normally the surrogate is implanted with a fertilized egg from the client couple, but if the wife cannot produce an egg, one can be bought and fertilized with the husband's sperm. Egg, sperm, and womb can all be bought or rented in India or (as the documentary film *Google Baby* shows) from elsewhere around the world.[22]

The Akanksha Infertility Clinic in Anand, Gujarat, houses the world's largest collection of gestational surrogates—women who rent their wombs to incubate the fertilized eggs from clients in India and from around the globe. Since 2004, when Akanksha began offering surrogate services, it has supervised the births of over 500 babies. Sixty surrogates are gestating babies at any one time.[23] Since 2002, when surrogacy was declared legal in India, well over 350 other assisted reproductive technology (ART) clinics have opened their doors around the country.

As the clinic's charismatic director Dr. Nayna Patel views the matter, the client and the provider enact a mutually beneficial transaction.[24] A childless couple gains a child, and a poor woman earns money. "What could be the problem?" she asks. If one looked only at the front stage of the global free market, Dr. Patel has a very good point. But more goes on backstage. Like nannies, surrogates do a great deal of emotional labor to suppress feelings that might interfere with the performance of their job—including feelings about the babies they bear.[25]

In January 2009, I followed a kindly embryologist, Harsha Bhadarka, to an upstairs office of the Akanksha Infertility Clinic in Anand, India, to talk with two surrogates whom I will call Geeta and Saroj.[26] They entered the small room, nodding shyly. Both lived on the second floor of the clinic, although most of its residents live in one of two hostels for the duration of their pregnancy. The women are brought nutritious food on tin trays, are injected with iron supplements (a common deficiency), and are kept away from prying in-laws, curious older children, and lonely husbands, with whom they are, for nine months, allowed no visits home or sex. (For more on surrogates, see chapter 12.)

Typical of the other surrogates I spoke with, Geeta had only a brief encounter with the parents who paid her to carry their genetic baby. "They're from far away. I don't know where," she said. "They're Caucasian, so the baby will come out white."

Seated next to Geeta was Saroj, a heavy-set, dark woman with intense, curious eyes, and a slow-dawning smile. Like the other Hindu surrogates at Akanksha, she wore *sindoor* (a red powder applied to the part in her hair) and *mangalsutra* (a necklace with a gold pendant), both symbols of marriage. She was, she told me, the mother of three children and the wife of a street vendor who sold vegetables. She had given birth to a surrogate child a year and three months ago, and she was waiting to see if a second implantation had taken. The genetic parents were from Bangalore, India. (It is estimated that half the clients seeking surrogacy from Indian ART clinics are Indian, and the other half are foreign. Of the foreign clients, roughly half are American.)[27] Saroj, too, knew almost nothing about her clients. "They came, saw me, and left," she said.

Saroj's husband's wages were 1,260 rupees (or $25) a month, so she turned to surrogacy so that they could move out of a shed with an earthen floor to a rain-proof house and she could feed her family well. Yet she faced the dilemma of all rural surrogates: being suspected by neighbors or distant relatives of adultery, a cause for shunning or worse. I asked the women whether the money they earned had not also improved their social standing. For the first time, the two women laughed out loud, and talked to each other excitedly. "My father-in-law is dead, and my mother-in-law lives separately from us, and at first I hid it from her," Saroj said. "But when she found out, she said she felt blessed to have a daughter-in-law like me because I've given more money to the family than her son could. But some friends ask me why I am putting myself through all this. I tell them, 'It's my own choice.'"

Geeta and Saroj freely chose to become surrogates, but what were their options? Their villages reflected appalling government neglect—rundown schools, decrepit hospitals, and few well-paying jobs. Given these circumstances, surrogacy was the most lucrative job in town for uneducated women.

The director at Akanksha organized surrogacy much as she would have organized the manufacture of shoes. She proudly sought to increase inventory, exercise quality control, and improve efficiency. In the case of surrogacy, that translated into the goals of producing more babies, monitoring the surrogates' diet and sexual contact, and ensuring a smooth, emotion-free exchange of baby for money. (For every rupee that goes to the surrogates, observers estimate, three go to the clinic.) In Akanksha's hostel, the women slept on cots, nine to a room, for nine months. Their young children slept with them; the older children were not allowed to stay in the hostel, though they could visit. The women also exercised inside the hostel, rarely leaving it and then only with permission.

Dr. Patel also advised surrogates to limit contact with the clients. Half-hour meetings to sign a contract, perform the implantation, and pick up the baby were typical. Staying detached from the genetic parents, she said, helps the surrogate mothers give up their babies and get on with their lives and on with the next surrogacy. It increased efficiency.

What happens when a surrogate dies in labor? Or when the commissioning genetic parents reject a disabled newborn? Or the money does not come through? The laws regulating commercial surrogacy have been under consideration since 2004; but as of March 2013, no laws have been passed.[28] Even if the laws were to pass, they would do little to improve the life of women such as Geeta and Saroj. The law currently under consideration specifies that the doctor, not the surrogate, has the right to decide on "fetal reduction" (abortion). Under no circumstances can the surrogate decide because, legally speaking, she is not carrying *her* baby.[29] Moreover, federal laws in India are merely advisory to powerful state governments which are free to disregard federal law.

Most Indian courts are woefully backlogged, causing years, even decades, of delay, and even if the laws were enforced, what surrogates can read the contracts they sign? Most have a seventh-grade education in Gujarati (some illiterate surrogates sign by thumbprint), but their contracts are written in English. Even if she could read her contract, what aggrieved surrogate could *afford* to hire a lawyer?

Should the law pass in the Indian parliament, it would do nothing to address the crushing poverty that presses women into surrogacy in the first place.[30] The Indian government itself considers surrogacy a form of "economic development." It gives tax breaks to the private hospitals that treat overseas patients and lowers import duties on medical supplies. As a $455 million a year business in India, surrogacy improves the national bottom line.[31] But, as in the case of migrant remittances, revenue helps individual surrogates alleviate their poverty without doing much to revitalize the overall economy.

Moreover, the surrogates are also exposed to the global free market's "race to the bottom." Indian surrogates charge less than American surrogates by a factor of one to ten.[32] But Thailand could undersell India,

Cambodia could undersell Thailand, Laos could undersell Cambodia, and Sri Lanka could undersell Laos. Each country could undercut the next cheapest, cutting fees and reducing the legal protections for surrogates along the way. If the race to the bottom, as William Greider calls it in *One World, Ready or Not,* can apply to the global competition to sell cheaper cars, computers, and shoes, it could tragically apply to the global competition for inexpensive surrogacy.[33]

Like immigrant nannies, surrogates do a hidden form of emotional labor. If nannies suffer separation from their biological children who grow up half a world away, surrogates suffer detachment from the babies they carry but must give away. Both struggle with the issue of self-estrangement (see chapter 12).

ON YOUR OWN IN THE FREE MARKET

Vicky says she freely chose to leave her children behind, and Geeta and Saroj freely chose to give up the babies to whom they gave birth. Given their extraordinary circumstances, their choices made sense to them, as they would to many in their shoes. By their own accounts, in no sense were those choices easy. Yet our free market culture invites us—and them—to look past the painful circumstances to their "free" choices in an imagined world of "win-win" market transactions.

In the free-market imagination of those on the front stage of global life, the object of fear and dread is Big Brother government. Such novels as George Orwell's *Nineteen Eighty-Four,* with its "Ministry of Truth," or Ray Bradbury's *Fahrenheit 451,* with its image of Nazi-type book burning—offer an image of coercion, intrusion, and utter control over what we think and do.[34] Aldous Huxley's 1932 *Brave New World* offers the image of the London Hatchery in which babies are designed by white-uniformed eugenic scientists.[35] Margaret Atwood's disturbing 1985 novel *The Handmaid's Tale* describes a right-wing Christian state that divides women into Handmaids who procreate, Marthas who tend house, and Wives who are wives.[36] In all these nightmares, our fear is directed toward an all-powerful government that undermines and replaces the family and community.

But the stories of Vicki, Geeta, and Saroj point toward another nightmare. In this one, there is no menacing policeman, no harsh jailer, no Big Brother. Indeed, the free-market exchanges go on with almost no government regulation—or help—at all. Instead of a paramilitary trooper breaking into one's home at night, there is the opposite sense of no one coming to one's aid in an hour of need. Indeed, in this nightmare, the government provides no fine schools, no well-equipped hospitals, no reliable police service, no beautiful parks, no safety-checked water or food, and no effective safety net. We face a world starved of public services, where helpless people make "free choices" between harrowing options. Many of us are poised to look for a Mack truck coming from the left where Big Bad Government is found, but the other big truck of unregulated capitalism is already approaching from the right, though the purr of its engine is hard to hear. The so-called free market—composed of international treaties governing the flow of goods, services, and people, and the flow of things and people itself—can be shaped by the policies of do-nothing governments in the Third, Second, and First Worlds. In this dystopia, a "structural tragedy," as the German sociologist Kai-Olaf Maiwald calls it, takes place.[37]

Most migrant care workers want a government that neither oppresses nor abandons them and a world more equal than the one they have. But in the absence of a more positive alternative, Vicky, Geeta, and Saroj may say they are freely choosing to take part in the two-way global traffic, but what they really need is the freedom to choose between the world we have and a world that tends to the happiness of those on the backstage—a world that brings the backstage to the front.

ELEVEN Children Left Behind

WITH S. UMA DEVI AND LISE ISAKSEN

An increasing proportion of the earth's population—3.1 percent, or 214 million people—are migrants.[1] Nearly half of these migrants are women.[2] Of such women, an increasing number migrate not to reunite with their families but to seek jobs far from them.[3] For many, these jobs are to care for the young, the elderly, the sick, or the disabled of the First World. Thus, many maids, nannies, eldercare workers, nurse's aides, nurses, and doctors leave their families and communities in the weak economies of the South to provide care to families and communities in the strong economies of the North. In such countries as the Philippines and Sri Lanka, female migrants outnumber male migrants, and many are young mothers. Once in the North, female migrants tend to stay longer than male migrants do. Just as poor countries suffer a brain drain as trained personnel move from the South to the North, so too they suffer a care drain.[4]

This drain occurs through a series of substitutions of one caregiver for another across the globe.[5] Scholars who study women migrant workers often focus on the poor pay, long hours, and sexual exploitation they face in the North.[6] Missing, until recently, has been much inquiry into their relationships with their children or other family and friends left behind. Without falling into maternalism (the idea that only biological mothers can care for children), without imposing northern middle-class cultural ideals on families of the South (presuming a nuclear family), and without being mistaken as an opponent of migration, we can inquire into the emotional costs of female migration.

Usually migrants' children are cared for by female relatives, husbands, other nannies, or boarding schools. Sometimes they are left in orphanages, as shown in Nilita Vachani's heartbreaking documentary *When Mother Comes Home for Christmas* about a divorced Sri Lankan mother of three who worked as a nanny in Greece.[7] One out of four children in the Philippines has one or both parents working overseas, so this is no small matter.[8]

A 2006 UNICEF-UNDP (United Nations Development Project) field office survey of three states in Mexico—Zacatecas, Jalisco, and Michoacan—reported that a third of households with children in each state were without both father and mother.[9] A 2003 study of domestic workers from Mexico and Central America working in California estimated that 40 to 50 percent left children behind, usually in the care of grandparents or aunts.[10] Yet partly because mother-child bonds in particular are taken for granted, and partly because family problems are seen as private, these separations have remained until recently a hidden aspect of the backstage story.

In her pioneering work, Rhacel Parreñas focuses on both the Filipina migrating mother and the children she leaves behind.[11] Over half of Filipino migrants are women; their median age is 29 years, and they have on average 2.74 children who stay back in the Philippines. Building on Parreñas' work, I have suggested the term "global care chains"—the series of personal links, paid and unpaid, between people around the world.[12] A Sri Lankan nanny leaves her children in the care of her sister and a nanny in Colombo so that she can take up the paid care of twin sons of an upper-middle-class couple in Los Angeles, the wife of whom gives, as a personnel officer, her own "care" to the human resources division of a multinational company. Meanwhile, the Sri Lankan's nanny has left her own youngest children in the care of a 15-year-old daughter, and her sickly mother in the care of a neighbor.[13]

Global care chains have long spanned great distances across regions, states, and even countries. Between 1850 and 1970, for example, thousands of women from rural Slovenia migrated to Egypt to take up work as domestic servants and wet nurses, leaving their own children behind. As one Catholic nun in the Saint Francis Asylum in Cairo, Egypt, observed:

> We witnessed the sufferings of these young mothers on those Sunday afternoons, as they were giving their own body and milk to the child that was not their own, for the sake of their family. In spite of their suffering, they returned to Egypt as wet nurses after each baby, for they were well paid, and the family property was enlarged—but their suffering was too high. Let not this situation happen again, never more.[14]

So how can we understand such transfers of care? In "Global Care Chains: Critical Reflections and Lines of Inquiry," Nicola Yeates systematizes the idea of care chains, broadens the scope of its applicability, and adds to it a clearer picture of global labor networks.[15] Here we extend Yeates' work by describing what *anchors* the care chains: the socioemotional *commons*—a community of give and take of which any one person is a small part.

The term "commons" originally referred to the land on which eighteenth-century English villagers could freely graze their sheep and cattle, collect firewood, and hunt game. The land was shared—either because it was owned in common or was owned by a person who offered others the right to hunt, graze, and forage. Through a series of Enclosure Acts, the British Parliament privatized this land, preventing the commoners from using it.[16] But the term "commons" has remained and has come to refer to other physical resources to which a wide community has free access—Internet data, the ocean, or nature preserves, for example. It is not just physical resources that can be held in common: community itself is a form of emotional commons. Based on the principle of "generalized reciprocity," community means that each individual is poised to give to others, and each can expect to receive something from others—small favors in normal times or large favors in times of emergency. Just as public spaces can be placed off-limits to commoners, so too can access to social ties. In showing how care chains are anchored in such commons, and drawing upon S. Uma Devi's extensive research, Devi, Lise Isaksen, and I hope in this chapter to open a conversation about how to think about what is gained and lost.[17]

THE TABOO ON TALK ABOUT MIGRANT MOTHERS' CHILDREN

The hush and tension that accompany talk about migrants' children are themselves a clue that one has encroached upon a painful topic. One reason for the anxiety about this topic is surely the fact that the Third World state, the First World employer, and often the migrant herself clearly want this global arrangement to work. Given the huge financial incentives, workers badly want the jobs. At home in the Philippines, the domestic workers who migrated to the United States and Italy, interviewed by Rhacel Parreñas in the 1990s, had averaged $176 a month as teachers, nurses, administrators, and clerical workers.[18] By doing less skilled though no less difficult work as nannies, maids, and care-service workers, they earned $200 a month in Singapore, $410 a month in Hong Kong, $700 a month in Italy, or $1,400 a month in Los Angeles. The Sri Lankan Muslim maids studied by Michele Gamburd and Grete Brochmann migrated to pay for basic food and shelter.[19] Most of the lower- to middle-class Filipina migrants studied by Parreñas, and the Kerala-born, Persian Gulf–based medical workers studied by Devi had migrated to pay for school fees, better housing, larger dowries, and more lavish weddings.[20]

For their part, the spouse, the parents, and even the mason who builds her family's new house and the priest at the village temple who receives her larger donations want migration to work because they benefit from it. Of course, the Third World governments also greatly gain from the influx of taxable hard-currency remittances (see chapter 10 for more on this). Indeed, many parties—the worker, her kin, her overseas employer, the businesses that arise to train, transport, and house her, and her local government—have a powerful vested interest in female migration.[21]

But as S. Uma Devi's research shows, there *is* a cost. Most of the migrant mothers she interviewed in Kerala, India, were proud to work overseas, but at the same time they felt sad to leave their children behind.[22] Relatives, teachers, and child advocates also expressed concern about such children. Sometimes the government itself issues an alarm. As a 2004 report of the National Statistics Office of the Philippine government concluded, "The country faces huge social costs to migrant families as a result of prolonged separation, the breakdown of families and the deterioration and underdevelopment of the psycho-social growth of their children."[23]

Devi's first discovery in her interviews with the kin of Kerala female migrant mothers was the taboo among the kin about discussing "how the children were doing." Mothers especially felt their departures to be a sensitive, private matter, not an expression of a larger public issue.[24] Many migrant mothers face accusations by neighbors back home of being a "bad mother" or a "materialistic person," and they themselves feel anguished at the long separations from their children.

One final obstacle faces those who write about the children left behind: fear of the misuse of their findings. Scholars who champion, as we do, the rights of migrants may also fear that any research illuminating the family problems of migrant workers could be used against them by nativists of the North. Although such fears are well founded, far more important is expanding our understanding of the hidden costs of female migration, both to advance our thinking and to influence global policy regarding the development of poor countries.

Given these obstacles, the small but important line of research now filling this gap is especially welcome. Early studies focused on the effect on children of departing fathers; recent studies point to the effect on children when both parents leave.[25] Kandel and Kao, for example, find that the children of Mexican migrants earn better grades in high school and can, courtesy of their parents' remittances, better afford to attend college than the children of non-migrants. But, poignantly, they were less likely to want to.[26]

Other studies focus on children's emotional well-being. In their survey of 709 Filipino elementary school children, average age 11 years, Battistella and Conaco compared the children who lived with both parents to those in "father absent," "mother absent," or "both absent" families.[27] Most children "show an understanding" for why their parents are sojourning abroad—to earn money for private education or a better house, for example.[28] But the children also viewed their parents' departure with "a sense of loneliness and sadness."[29] Compared with the children who had absent fathers, the children with absent mothers were also more likely to say they felt sad, angry, confused, and apathetic.

In one of the few in-depth studies of what she calls "parenting from afar," Leah Schmalzbauer studied 157 Hondurans, among whom were 34 transmigrant workers living in Chelsea, Massachusetts, twelve of their family members back in Honduras, and six others whose family ties had been severed. Both the migrant fathers and mothers, Schmalzbauer discovered, worried whether their children truly understood why they had left. In addition, she noted, "Dissension within transnational families is common. Some migrants completely cut themselves off from families back home."[30] In yet another study of the children of migrant workers, Rhacel Parreñas compared the children of Filipino male migrants and female migrants.[31] When the husbands migrate, she discovered, the wives usually assume the role of both father and mother. However, when the *wives* migrate, most husbands stand aside from childrearing, leaving it to female relatives (grandmothers, aunts, or others). Some even take their wives' departure as a divorce and move to another village to find a different woman with whom to raise children. Parreñas sensibly calls for such husbands to take on the task of raising their children, just as the stay-in-the-Philippines wives do when the fathers of their children migrate.

In her book *Divided by Borders: Mexican Migrants and their Children*, Joanna Dreby documents the strong emotional strain that coexists with an equally strong sense of family responsibility in migrant families. Young children often flouted the authority of their absent parents, turning for guidance to grandparents and other on-the-scene caregivers, even as they sometimes complained to their overseas parents that their caregivers were misspending the remittance money. The children told Dreby that they even missed being disciplined by their parents.[32]

LEFT BEHIND CHILDREN IN KERALA

In 2003, Devi and her assistant Ramji interviewed 120 people, twenty-two of whom were working mothers from Kerala, a state in the southwest of India, who delivered health care in the United Arab Emirates.[33] Among these women were six doctors, ten nurses, five laboratory technicians, and one hospital cleaner. For each such migrant, Devi and Ramji averaged interviews with five family members back in Kerala, including children, spouses, parents-in-law, siblings, and other caretakers. Of the thirteen children under the age of 5 years, seven lived with both parents in the United Arab Emirates; one lived with the father and paternal grandmother back in Kerala; two lived with maternal grandparents and two with paternal grandparents; and one lived with another relative back in Kerala (not with the parents or grandparents). Of the nine adolescents, four attended boarding school in Kerala, and five lived with their fathers. Despite years of living apart with only occasional meetings, in no cases did migration sever relations between spouses.[34]

Migration out of Kerala has become an accepted way of dealing with the discrepancy between its excellent schools and its struggling economy, which is unable to absorb its graduates. As one "solution" to this disparity, Kerala exports its educated workers. One out of every five working adults in Kerala is or has been a migrant worker.[35] Of such migrants, one out of every ten is a woman, and many of these are mothers. In the Devi study, migrant mothers averaged two children each, and they visited their children, on average, once each year for a month.

Mothers who migrated from Kerala often experienced a conflict, Devi found, between wanting to be a good mother and wanting to be a

financial heroine. By migrating, these mothers were defying the prevailing ideal of motherhood. To be sure, the idea of an "ideal mother" varies
from one ethnic or religious group to another within Kerala. (Sixty percent of Keralans are Hindu, 20 percent Muslim, and 20 percent Christian.) Yet migrants from all these groups shared roughly the same vision
of the ideal mother as a woman who lives with her children. She might
work away from them during the day, but she returns to them in the
evening.[36]

Most Keralans favored the idea of a joint household, in which elderly parents live together with their sons, daughters-in-law, and
grandchildren. A mother within the ideal joint family household is one
who is physically present and the object of a child's primary attachment, but who gladly shares the emotional limelight with loving grandparents, aunts, uncles, and cousins. Both ideals—that of mother and
family—persist in the popular imagination, but exist less and less in
reality.

So Keralan mothers find themselves in a cultural cross-current of
criticism and praise, disapproval (as being "heartless" and "materialistic") and approval (as being "heroically sacrificing" and "generously
providing"). Though few mothers said they had been criticized to their
face, all were highly aware of criticisms "going around." At the same
time, given the high unemployment in Kerala, many well-trained, able-
bodied Keralans from both the middle and working class yearned for
the golden opportunity to migrate. Migrant mothers also felt that some
negative gossip rose out of envy for the larger homes, more lavish wed-
dings, larger dowries, and better schooling that their migration afforded
them.

Despite their inner conflict of ideal mother versus financial success,
the migrant mothers claimed that they did not feel alone because usually they were following a family plan. Still, when they spoke of their
children in the interviews, Devi observed that most mothers teared up
or openly wept. Even mothers who had long been reunited with their
children recalled past separations with anguish. A number of nurses
worked for hospitals in the Persian Gulf that had stringent pregnancy
policies allowing only forty-five days' postpartum leave for the birth of

a worker's child. Thus, mothers would fly from the Persian Gulf back to Kerala, give birth to their babies, stay for forty days, then return to their full-time jobs back in the Gulf. Many would then work for a full year, or in a few cases, longer, before seeing their babies again.

Infants left by their mothers at the age of one month can develop a wide variety of alternative attachments to which this study cannot begin to do justice. But Devi was struck by some of the open statements by older children of migrant workers. For example, Priya, a Keralan college student and the daughter of a nurse practicing in the United Arab Emirates, said:

> I want you to write about the human cost for people like us, to be apart for year after year. I'm living here in this hostel, and my classes are fine, but I can't talk to my mother. I can't tell her things. I can't see her face. I can't hug her. I can't help her. My mother misses me, too. My mother will retire at some point, but how old will I be then?[37]

Leela, another daughter of a nurse working in the United Arab Emirates, lives with her father and brother in Kerala:

> I cannot go home even for weekends because my father is alone at home and in a traditional setting I would not go and live with him, when he is alone. . . . You know you cannot discuss everything with your father. I wait for my mother's call every Friday, from the hostel phone. Also, I cannot talk freely with her, because the matron [a nun] is always hovering around. . . . My father is very strict, he has become more strict now and is very conservative . . . if I do anything non-conventional he tends to blame my mother for bringing me up the way she has, so I try to be very careful to see that my mother is not blamed. This is a big burden, which I would not have if she was here.[38]

Many children spoke of envying friends who enjoyed the luxury of living with their mothers. When her mother left for a nursing job in the Gulf, Vijaya, now 20, took her mother's place in the household with her father and brother:

> When I see my classmates accompanying their mothers to church or shopping, I miss my mother badly. . . . Actually I need my mother now

at this age. Anyway, later they would marry me off and I would miss the opportunity of living with my mother. I miss her.[39]

When Vijaya's mother was interviewed in the United Arab Emirates, she asked, "How is my daughter? I know she misses me. [The family] call[s] me every day in the evening from the STD booth [an outdoor phone store, with a private booth]. She sometimes cries. I do too."[40]

Even in their absence, migrant mothers became an emotional presence to their children. Mina, the 2-year-old daughter of a nurse in the United Arab Emirates, for example, daily looked at a blue dolphin toy hung in the center of the living room. Her paternal grandparents encouraged Mina to play with it, reminding her "your mommy sent the dolphin for your birthday." When it was decided to take a photo of Mina, her grandmother immediately dressed her in a frilly dress and brought her beaming into the living room. "Tell them who sent you this frock," the grandmother coaxed Mina. Mina, shyly looking down, held her grandmother by one hand and put her hand over her face as she replied in a whisper, "Amma-chi" ("my mother" in Malayalam, the language of Kerala).[41]

The memory of the missing parent was not suppressed for these children, as can happen in the case of a bitter family rupture, a divorce, or a suicide. Nor was the mother's absence completely normalized, as in the case of the absent seafarer or soldier. Nor, again, was the role of mother fully absorbed by the grandmother or sister-in-law or father. Rather, a place was reserved in the child's heart for a mother who was not there.

At the same time, to varying degrees, children managed their private doubts about the arrangement. Why, the older children recalled asking themselves, did my mother leave me when the mothers of my school friends did not leave them? Did my mother have to leave, or did she want to? Or did she leave me because I was naughty? Answers to these questions seemed to differ depending on how a child imagined a parent's role as well as that of fathers, grandparents, friends, and others. But the more the child was exposed to friends whose mothers had not left, the more these questions arose. As one grown child of a migrant worker put it, "I wondered why she couldn't have stayed back or I couldn't have gone with her. I still wonder."[42] She was managing doubt.

A few children, Devi found, had moved from doubt to distrust. They felt they had been promised a trustworthy bond with their mother that they did not have; they felt betrayed. This may correspond to what psychologists call "empathic rupture"—the breaking of an empathic connection. As a headmaster of a boarding school for children of migrant workers in Kerala said, "Most of the children we have in this school have parents working in the Middle East. The children we have here range in age from 5 to 16. Many of them have lost trust in adults. They are very independent, but not always in a healthy way. They distrust adults."[43] Each relationship between child and migrant mother, like that between any child and parent, is surely unique. Not all children of migrant workers are sent to boarding school, nor do most end up losing trust in adults, but the headmaster's comment points to an issue we know far too little about: the hidden price tag of global inequality.

The children left back in Kerala find themselves in an "emotional commons" in which there is a busy adult-to-adult exchange of favors, large and small, between kin, friends, neighbors, and teachers. This is governed by a complex web of understandings: grandparents care for a 4-year-old child, the migrant mother pays a builder to construct a house for a brother, and the brother and his wife stand ready to care for the grandparents in old age. The mother later finds a job in the United Arab Emirates for the brother's wife, so the favor exchange goes on.

So children ask themselves, "How do I fit in? Is the care I receive from my grandparents or aunts freely given as a gesture of love, or is it paying Mother a favor? Is this care offered out of commitment or desire, and in what measure each?" When the migrant mothers send gifts to "the household," are these gifts "payment" for the care? Or to what measure are they "purely" gifts?

Some children reported feeling "like a guest" in their caregiver's house. They tried to behave like little adults vis-à-vis their grandparents or aunts and uncles in the household so that they could "earn their keep," especially the older girls who tended to make themselves useful as little mothers to younger siblings.[44] In taking on the care of children—especially the very young—the migrant mothers' relatives often felt they were offering the migrant a gift far greater than any material return. So,

Devi discovered, both the migrant workers and their children felt beholden to the caregivers.

Removed from the day-to-day lives of their children, the migrant mother was forced to "materialize" love—to express through money and material gifts what she could not express through hugs. For the child, the arrival of a package of toys or electronic gadgets could mean "Mother is thinking of me" or "Mother knows what I like."[45] On the school playground in Kerala, a new toy often made a migrant's child at once a prince and object of pity, for it meant both that one's mother was absent but that one's family was relatively rich. The meaning that migrant parents meant to convey to their children through gifts was "I'm thinking about you, and I am devoted to you." But some children, Devi reports, interpreted such gifts as ways of saying "I'm sorry" or "Here is this gift instead of me."

Some children of absent parents continued to feel ambivalent about such gifts years after they had received them. For example, Divya, 26 years old, had grown up separated from both her parents who worked in the Gulf in order to accumulate a large dowry for her in the form of a "Gulf house." (The name given to large, upscale houses built with remittances.) Now well-married and raising her newborn son in this house, Divya has still never opened the small gifts that her parents sent her during their long absence. As she told Devi during the interview, "My parents sent me many glamorous pens and pencil boxes from the Middle East. But I never used them, even now, 20 years later."[46]

Overall, the children of Kerala migrant workers faced many issues related to the departure of their mothers: the management of sadness at the lost company of one whose emotional centrality remained despite their absence, the envy of children with resident mothers, doubt about why a mother "had to" leave, an aversion to "being a burden" to relatives, and the task of figuring out the meaning of a material gift.

The migration of these mothers also led to shifts in the family system and the community beyond it. Although other research has uncovered stories of ruptured relations between wives and husbands, and even between parents and children, Devi came across no such stories in her Kerala interviews.[47] Nor did migration in Kerala divide the community between the migrating rich and the non-migrating poor as it did in some places because most families at each occupational level had one migrant contributor to the family coffers. However, it did create cross-currents of envy (of the migrants' money) and criticism (of the migrants' motherliness) through communities of kin and family. It also unsettled the standing of children throughout the migratory system; for if the mothers of *some* children could leave, then *other* mothers might also leave as opportunities opened up. More importantly, migration stripped away the patterns of care that *would have taken place* between a woman and her child, her husband, her parents, her neighbors, her friends, and her temple had she not had to migrate: it raids the commons. S. Uma Devi's fieldwork opens a door into a world of hugely important and still largely unanswered questions.[48]

TRANSFERRING CARE CAPITAL OR ERODING A CO-LIVING COMMONS?

The nurse who leaves her children in the care of relatives in Trivandrum, Kerala, while she cares for patients in Dubai on the Persian Gulf is part of a care chain. But how do we think about this? Should we understand a care chain as the transfer of "care capital"—simply the caring capacity—from one family and nation to another? Or is it best understood as an erosion of an emotional "commons"—or of a "life-world," to quote Jurgen Habermas—that is, a care *drain*?[49] Or is it a monification of bonds that nevertheless remain strong?

We can speak of migration as leading to a transfer of a migrant's care skills—her care capital—from South to North. But how is care like capital? Alejandro Portes sees social capital as "social chits," a series of favors that are owed or owing.[50] They differ from money in two ways. In a pure economic exchange, we borrow money, and we repay money—the *currency remains the same*. In the exchange of social chits, we give in one currency but repay in many others. In a pure economic exchange, if we borrow money, we pay it back at *a specified time*, but in the exchange of social chits, we leave open the time for repayment.

Between a migrant mother and her caregiving kin there is indeed an exchange of social chits. A favor is given (a relative cares for a child) and is eventually repaid (the mother pays various expenses and gives gifts). For example, the migrant health-worker Sujatha had asked her sister and her sister's stepdaughter Prithi to care for her 6-year-old daughter, Anitha, Devi reports.[51] Sujatha sends money for Anitha's upkeep and education, and she pays for her sister's medical treatment and for Prithi's education; she also sends Prithi gold jewelry as gifts and sends checks to be put toward a *sari* or a computer, not "just money," to make the transfer more personal. Although Prithi is hoping that one day Sujatha will be able to find her a job in the United Arab Emirates, as Sujatha told Devi, "I know Prithi expects me to bring her over to Dubai, but if she comes, who would look after my daughter? So I don't want to help bring Prithi here now." In this case, receiving one chit prevented Sujatha from giving another.

Money was not in every instance depersonalizing, but in the exchange of favors, the simple keeping of company—dinners, birthday celebrations, daily conversation, and visual or physical contact—was lifted away from relations between family members. Children and caregivers alike tended to experience money as a substitute for shared experiences and love. Paradoxically, money for these cross-national caregivers came to loom large as a *symbol* of love, even as it also *commodified* love.

The accumulation of chits between Sujatha, her sister, and her sister's daughter Prithi implied a hidden inequity between Sujatha and the other player in the game: the employer in the North. Sujatha appeared to her employer as unencumbered by children: Prithi and Sujatha's daughter, half a world away, were invisible. But Prithi's caregiving is utterly necessary to liberate Sujatha for her fifty- or sixty-hour-a-week job. Were Sujatha to formally "hire" her sister's stepdaughter, it would be seen as necessary to add the cost of that childcare to the wages Sujatha is paid in Dubai. That cost might, in turn, lead to higher costs of services in the Middle East. But, given her child-free presentation of self, Sujatha cannot be compensated for the remote care of her daughter. The employer in Dubai never sees the care chain, the sacrifices, or the need to pay, so Sujatha is absorbing a cost that the Dubai employer ignores. The idea of "care capital" illuminates this inequity.

At the same time, thinking of these things as any kind of capital inhibits us from appreciating the *communal* world in which children and their chit-exchanging mothers live. And it hides a basic inequality in physical *access* to the integral *collectivity* that gives a social chit meaning in the first place. The idea of social capital leads us to imagine that social chits are individually owned and are independent of life in a community. It is as though a person could put a stack of bills (capital) in their private suitcase, get on a plane, and go. We are led to forget all the favors—the chits—that *would have been exchanged directly* and would have enriched the community had the person stayed.

As the social linguist George Lakoff argues in his book *Metaphors We Live By,* every metaphor implies a cognitive frame, itself based on a view of reality.[52] Social capital is drawn from the same cognitive frame as material capital—money. It describes what a migrant mother or child *has,* not who she *is,* by participating in a social whole. If family and community are absent from the picture—that is, from the cognitive frame—we cannot see what is distorted, strained, or eroded by this Third World care drain. To put it another way, we cannot really see the effects of pollution on the ecology of the lake if we do not understand the concept of ecology, and think of each fish as an "on-your-own" fish. Similarly, we cannot fully understand the gift exchange if the only thing we can think to compare it to is a financial transaction. If we think of care as a form of capital, and we miss the idea of a rich, social ecology—an emotional commons—it is harder to see what migration subtracts from it.[53]

As the economic anthropologist George Dalton notes, to apply market terms to the "non-market sectors of primitive and peasant economies is as distorting as it would be to use the concept of Christianity to analyze primitive religion."[54] As a belief system, animism may be just as complex as Christianity, but it rests on very different premises. In parallel fashion, we are fitting the wrong idea to the anguish of a migrating mother and the doubt, sadness, and envy of the child she leaves behind. Migration can "dis-embed" the informal exchange of favors and *turn them into* capital. But we cannot see how it does this if we start off by assuming that such favors are—and only are—expressions of capital.

Thinking about anything as "capital," we are led away from the idea of inalienability.[55]

We often speak of the yawning monetary gap between haves and have-nots, but a person can have or not have far more things than money. What seems missing from the capital/market view is the opportunity *to live as part of an integral whole* family and community. One thing that helps create such a whole is being together, seeing one another, talking face to face, and physical touch.[56] Today we can talk by telephone or Skype, of course. But we envision this technology as tiding us over until we can see, touch, or hug one another.

Most ideas of community are anchored in reality, but some are based in fantasy. Many migrants forced off their land into the city, or out of their country into another country, look back with longing at a community of their dreams "back home." Indeed, many migrants wax lyrical about their hometowns back in Estonia, Tunisia, Uruguay, or the Ukraine. As whole villages have been emptied out by migration, the idea of an "imaginary" commons emerges to absorb a yearning for community. In Cinzia Solari's extensive research on Ukrainian "grandma nannies" who care for elderly people in a graying Italy, she discovered a number of nannies who remitted funds to construct grand houses; one jokingly called hers a "monument."[57]

But no one lived in those houses. These vacant homes instead housed the nanny's fantasy of a three-generation family, in which the family all lives together—the grandparents, their children, and their grandchildren—a family she had dreamed of but never lived in as a young mother, given the cramped apartments available during the Soviet era. They dreamed of caring for their beloved grandchildren in this large house, while their daughters left in the morning to pursue professional careers like those they themselves had once pursued before they migrated. But alas, the young daughters of these grandma-caregivers led very different lives. Discouraged by the Ukrainian government from working, many were stay-at-home moms who were asking their migrant working mothers for money to buy apartments to accommodate their own nuclear families in the Ukraine.[58] Meanwhile, the spacious, empty, remittance-secured homes, the symbol of the older migrant mothers' dreams, occupied the photos they would flip out of their wallets in Italy to show their employers, to say, "This is who I am."

Just as the market eroded the commons in eighteenth-century Europe, so too the market of the rich North is eroding the commons of the southern and eastern Europe today.[59] Looking at the growth of market capitalism in Europe, observers have noted that the market relied on and then, in a sense, used up the pre-existing non-market social ties based on trust and mutual commitment.[60] As Durkheim wrote, the idea of the contract was first based on a precontractual solidarity, confirmed by a gentleman's handshake or over the clink of two mugs of beer.[61] To lend money, tools, or labor to a neighbor, a man relied on a culture of trust and the watchful eye of a stable community. From this original basis, contracts, courts, and jails were derived. Once more impersonal mechanisms were established, they tended to undercut the trust, rendering it irrelevant.[62] Speaking of the effects of the market on nineteenth-century European society, Karl Polanyi noted,

A principle quite unfavorable to individual and general happiness was wreaking havoc with his [the worker's] social environment, his neighborhood, his standing in the community, his craft; in a word, with those relationships to nature and man in which his economic existence was formerly embedded. The Industrial Revolution was causing a social dislocation of stupendous proportions, and the problem of poverty was merely the economic aspect of this event.[63]

For Durkheim and Polanyi, both society and market existed in the same place: Europe. But the relationship between them had changed over time—roughly from the 1800s to the 1900s. In the global migration of women today, the same process is taking place; only now the places are different, but the time period—the twenty-first century—is the same. Now the market of the North is indirectly eroding the social solidarities of the South and East, causing a care drain. Mothers are still mothers, but their children are forgetting what they look like. Mothers are making great sacrifices for their children, but the trust required to make those great sacrifices is sometimes undermined. Absent mothers leave for their children's sake, but the children are left with private doubts about why their mothers left. Just as man's relationship to man and nature was "disembedded," in Polanyi's general term, so too, we suggest, migration can "disembed" relationships between parents and children. This effect occurs within the family, but by introducing the idea of a commons we can see the price paid in southern and eastern Europe for the services enjoyed by the North.

To be sure, migrants are choosing to migrate, but this is only true in the limited sense that eighteenth-century European peasants "chose" to seek jobs on the margins of the expanding cities of their day. The vast majority of the migrant mothers of Kerala, Thailand, and Latvia would far rather work at good jobs near home. Moreover, most migrants see themselves as using their remittances (drawn from the market) to better the lives of their families (part of the social commons). But over their heads, the powerful global market in service work—of which they form the core—is distorting and eroding that Third World commons. Indeed, as whole "sending" villages are emptied of their mothers, aunts, grandmothers, and daughters, it may not be too much to speak of a desertification of Second and Third World caregivers and the emotional commons they might have sustained.

In the end, the global care crisis raises concerns for both social theory and policy. For social theory, it highlights vital issues that market-derived concepts prevent us from grasping. For social policy, it raises the issue of what we can do to reduce the hidden injuries of the global gap between rich and poor. At the very least, we can call for arrangements by which children and perhaps other caregivers can follow mothers to their new places of work. We could also call for measures to be taken by the World Bank, the International Monetary Fund, and the North American Free Trade Agreement to reduce the economic gap that motivates much migration to begin with. But to solve a problem we first need to see it, and to see it we need the guidance of an idea.

TWELVE

The Surrogate's Womb

At dusk one evening in January 2009, a Muslim call to prayer in the air, I walked around mud puddles along the ill-lit path through a village on the edge of Anand in the northwest state of Gujarat, India. Sari-clad women carrying pots on their heads, gaggles of skinny teenage boys, scurrying children, and elderly men shuffled along the jagged path past brick and tin-roofed shacks and mildew-stained concrete homes. Aditya Ghosh, a Mumbai-based journalist, was with me. We were here to visit the home of a commercial surrogate, 27-year-old Anjali, seven months along with a baby grown from the egg of a Canadian woman, fertilized by the sperm of her Canadian husband, and implanted in Anjali's womb at the Akanksha Infertility Clinic.[1] In several dormitories, the clinic houses the world's largest known gathering of commercial surrogates— women who carry to term the genetic babies of infertile couples living anywhere around the globe. I was to learn from Anjali and others how it feels to finally afford a house secure against the monsoon rains; to rent one's womb to a couple who would remain strangers to her; to manage a detachment from her womb, her baby, and her clients; and to feel she was acting out of "free choice."

I had come to Anand because it seemed to me the ultimate expression—in the words of Robert Kuttner—of "everything for sale."[2] Over the past three decades, in the United States, India, and many other parts of the globe, influential thinkers have pressed for a free market and the policies that would strengthen it—deregulation, privatization, and cuts in public services. The late Nobel Prize–winning University of Chicago conservative economist Milton Friedman, for example, linked these policies to the idea of progress and to the welcomed movement of a market frontier into nearly every sphere of life.[3] On one side of this frontier lies the idea of personal, unpaid favors, gatherings of family, friends, and neighbors. On the other side lies the idea of these activities as available for rent or sale. Some services, such as life coaches, offer expertise that help us do personal, unpaid tasks ourselves—like bring up a baby. Other services take the activity off our hands. Some services have become modern-day essentials (childcare and eldercare, for example), while others seem optional (Internet dating services, life coaches, wedding planners).

What is the human story behind a world of everything for sale? In the *Economic and Philosophic Manuscripts*, Marx noted that a person could become estranged from—as a stranger to—the object he makes (say, a shoe), from the making of it (the cutting and hammering), and from himself.[4] The more capitalism and commodification, he argued, the more estrangement or alienation; he used the terms interchangeably. Not only did the worker become estranged from himself, his tools, and his product, Marx thought, but the customer, too, felt separated from what he bought. Through a "fetishism of commodities," the customer comes to focus on the shoe itself and forgets his relationship to the maker of the shoe, and to the circumstances in which the worker lives and works. For Marx, the growth of factories, the division of labor, and capitalism estrange us from our work and from our being, regardless of culture or human agency.

But what if we flip his statement into a question? Instead of declaring "The worker and client are estranged," we *ask* "Is the worker estranged?" or "Is the client estranged?" What if cultural ideas about what makes for intimate life or a market—and about what makes for a "good" mix between the two—play a part in a loss of connection or meaning? When does a person become so detached from what she makes or buys as to be estranged from it? To draw a mundane example from modern middle-class life, in my interviews for *The Outsourced Self,* I heard many busy workers say, "I never have time to cook." And yet, many became oddly attached to their newly purchased oven. *It* seemed to become personal, as it was associated with the fantasy of cooking, which itself remained a warm, homey thing to do. In everyday life, we often become separated from symbols representing our core identity. But when and how? And in what ways do we relocate symbols of self in order to keep personal life feeling personal?

How, we can ask further, do we distinguish estrangement from the many good, necessary, and normal forms of detachment in everyday market life? A checkout clerk cannot sustain friendly feelings toward all 300 customers whose groceries he daily scans at the checkout counter. Nor, again, can a train conductor personally like the holder of each ticket he punches. What feeling rules guide our sense of just how emotionally involved or uninvolved we should be in any given circumstance?[5] In addition to sensing *what* we feel—joyful or sad, for example—there is the question of *how much* we should care at all (see chapter 1 for more on this).

This is a strange line of questioning. Normally, we imagine we know what personal life is and assume there is nothing we are doing to "keep" it personal. And we are not "doing" anything to keep relationships impersonal, either. We detach—render impersonal—the inconvenient, uninvited, dropped, or culturally ignored bonds. To understand how and when we attach or detach, we are led to wonder about that which is attached or detached—feelings. When we become estranged from a person, we don't *feel* anything for that person. Acts symbolically linked to that person—searching for a photo, visiting—cease to matter. Knowledge symbolically linked to that person—their favorite songs, their sense of humor—cease to matter. When we become estranged from something, we stop having feelings about it.[6]

The realms in which we often think we should feel the most deeply involved—family, community, church—are governed by an overarching ethic, what Lewis Hyde, drawing from Marcel Mauss, has described as "the spirit of the gift."[7] If the world of the market centers on the efficient monetary exchange of goods and services and a capacity for finely measured degrees of emotional detachment, the world of the gift moves through a continual affirmation of bonds, based on responsibility, trust, and gratitude and premised on our capacity for wholehearted attachment. To be sure, these realms can be fraught with difficulty. Families can be confining, churches can promote harsh ideas, and communities can exclude. But as an *ideal*, the spirit of the gift governing all of these defines what we think should go on within these realms. When we affirm symbols of the spirit of the gift, we reaffirm our attachment to—our nonestrangement from—others, even those we meet in the market and those living across the globe.

ANJALI: FREE CHOICE ESTRANGEMENT

As I sat on a cot in her new concrete house, Anjali, now in her second surrogate pregnancy and contemplating a third, explained how she had become one of hundreds of surrogates to give birth at Akanksha since it opened in 2004. Anjali told me how she tried to detach herself from her baby, her womb, and her clients. So I wondered how she reordered the parts of herself that she claimed and disclaimed, and what emotional labor that might require her to do.[8] I wondered if Anjali's story could shed light on lives far closer to our own.

Her husband, a house painter, had gotten lime in his eye from a bucket of paint. A doctor would not attend him unless he was paid an amount of money the family did not have. After fruitless appeals to family and friends, Anjali turned to a money lender who charged an exorbitant fee. The couple used the money to hire the doctor who helped the painter recover his eyesight. Afterward, the money lender hounded them mercilessly for repayment, and the family took to paying twice-daily visits, heads hung low, to the Hindu temple for daily meals. It was under these desperate circumstances that Anjali approached the Akanksha clinic and offered her services as a surrogate. At the same time, mindful of the scorn neighbors felt for surrogates, whom they confused with adulterers and prostitutes, Anjali moved her family to another village.

As her relations with extended kin and neighbors atrophied, those with her fellow surrogates grew closer. For her first pregnancy, Anjali stayed nine months in Akanksha's hostel with other surrogates, nine cots to a room. (Women were only selected for surrogacy if they were married mothers, so all of them had husbands and children at home.) Their young children were permitted to sleep with them; older children and husbands could pay daytime visits. During their confinement, the women rarely left these premises.

Meanwhile, the clinic's director told Anjali to maintain a business-like detachment from her clients, the genetic parents of the baby she carried. Partly, as other gynecologists explained, this protected their Western clients from the possibility that poverty-stricken surrogates would later approach them to ask for more money. Partly such detachment also reduced the chance that, for the next baby, the client and surrogate would not cut out the middle-man—the director, who took a large cut of the fee.

Anjali met the genetic parents on three occasions, and then only briefly. The first time she spoke to them through an interpreter for a half-hour and signed a contract. (Her fee could range from $2,000 to $8,000.) The second time, Anjali met them when eggs were harvested from the wife, fertilized in a Petri dish with the husband's sperm, and implanted in her womb. The final time she met them was when she gave over her—and their—newborn baby. When I asked about her clients, she could not recall their names but told me that they "came from Canada." Other surrogates were similarly vague: "They come from far away."

Surrogates should think of their wombs as "carriers" and themselves as prenatal babysitters, the clinic director told them. So, as a matter of professional attitude, they were to detach themselves from their womb, a task that might be especially hard in a strongly pronatalist culture such as India's.[9]

When I asked Anjali how she managed not to become too attached to the baby, she repeated what the director said: "I think of my womb as a carrier." Then she added, "When I think of the baby too much, I remind myself of my own children." Instead of attaching her idea of herself as a loving mother to the child she carried, she prompted herself to mentally substitute the idea of the child she already had, whose school fees her surrogacy would pay for.

Another surrogate, a mother of a 3-year-old daughter who could not afford to have the second child she greatly wished for, told me, "If you put a jewel in my hand, I don't covet it. I give it back to its owner." And others said simply, "I try not to think about it." In another case, a surrogate said, "I have three children, I don't need one more." Or "When children grow up, many become disloyal to their parents. They don't help you." Surrogates living together in the clinic and dormitories helped each other detach, and they were guided by the practices and philosophy of the clinic itself. For their nine months under the clinic's direction (as briefly described in chapter 10), Anjali and her fellow surrogates became part of a small industry run according to three goals: *to increase inventory* by recruiting surrogates and producing more babies (it now produces a baby a week); *to safeguard quality* by monitoring surrogates' diets and sexual contact; and *to achieve efficiency* by ensuring a smooth, emotion-free exchange of babies for money. By applying this business model, the clinic hoped to beat the competition in the skyrocketing field of reproductive tourism, which has been legal in India since 2002 and remains unregulated today.[10]

Anjali's story raises a host of issues: the life of desperate poverty, the appalling absence of the most basic government services, the lack of legal rights for surrogates or clients, the question of cultures that assign greatest honor to biological parenthood, and the absence of nonprofit or community answers to infertility. But the issue that so strongly drew me to Anjali's home was the very idea of applying to the most personal act of surrogacy a business-like model of relationships, one that called for a high degree of emotional detachment on all sides.

Others I interviewed for *The Outsourced Self,* a book on the meanings we attach to outsourcing, responded to Anjali's story by drawing different moral lines:

Why do we need genetic offspring? There are so many orphans in the world, why don't infertile couples adopt babies already born who need parents?

Or

I can understand couples wanting their own genetic offspring, but why not inquire whether a friend or acquaintance could help you out?

Or

I can understand preferring to deal with a stranger rather than a friend or acquaintance, but it should be under the auspices of a nonprofit agency, not a for-profit one.

Or

It's fine if a couple finds a surrogate through a for-profit agency, so long as parents and surrogate have a warm relationship with one another and the surrogate isn't doing it strictly for money.

Or

It's fine if a surrogate carries a baby strictly for money, if she needs the money . . . Up to two births; after that she becomes a baby-making machine.

The sociologist Amrita Pande, who spent nine months at the Akanksha clinic talking in Gujarati to the surrogates, described the conversations the surrogates had among themselves about Anjali, whom they felt had become too driven, too strategic, and too materialistic with her fancy new house and stereo surround-sound system. She had crossed their moral line.[11] A photographer for the *Hindustan Times* told me that he had earlier photographed Anjali weeping just after she had a miscarriage. He asked her what she was thinking, and she answered, "We were going to redo the first floor of the house. Now we can't." That seemed to cross his quietly held line.

In their dormitory life together, some surrogates blamed Anjali for carrying a baby "only for money," which made her therefore "like a whore." But it was a dishonor they themselves feared: sadly, all the Akanksha surrogates were renting their wombs because they desperately needed money. There was little talk in the dormitory of altruism, Pande reports, and many enjoyed their nine months for all "the coconut water and ice cream we want." Yet most also took pride in not giving in "too much" to materialism and not imagining their wombs as "only" money-making machines. They were motherly. They were givers. They did not want to be or to seem too detached from their bodies or babies. So they ate for the baby, and they felt the baby kick. They felt their ankles swell and their breasts grow larger and more tender. So it was no small matter to say about the baby "this is not mine." As one surrogate told another interviewer, "We will remember these babies for as long as we live." But they had to prepare to let their babies go and to do the emotional labor of dealing with the potential sadness or grief that evoked.

Like Anjali, many surrogates seemed to take certain actions in order to walk their path along the market frontier. First of all, they avoided shame by avoiding visibility: they moved out of their villages, they kept their pregnancy a secret from in-laws, and they lied about where they were. If photographers came to the clinic, they wore surgical masks. As their doctor instructed, they developed a sense of "me" that was distinct from "not me." For "me," they embraced the pride-saving idea of giving a gift to the clients and giving money to their families. Some felt they were babysitting the baby before it was born. In the "not me" or "not mine"—much of the time—were the womb and the baby. Beyond this, they did the emotional labor needed to avoid a sense of loss and grief, working on their feelings to protect their sense of self as a caring mother in a world of everything for sale. Each woman drew for herself a line beyond which she would be "too" estranged from the baby she carried, up to which she might not be estranged enough. She guarded that line through work on her feelings.

Anjali had reached her own line in a very unexpected way. A deeply devoted Hindu, Anjali and her family had become deeply suspicious of Muslims, for she lived a hundred miles from the site of the 2002 Godhra train burning, in which dozens of Hindu pilgrims were killed by Muslims in revenge for the destruction of a mosque, a series of events which led to further widespread violence throughout Gujarat. After giving birth to the child of the commissioning Canadian couple, Anjali was horrified to learn that the baby and the receiving family were Muslim. "I have sinned," she told the journalist Aditya on the phone. "Still you got the money didn't you?" he replied. "Yes, but I should have waited for another [non-Muslim] client." Anjali had imagined she would be detached from the baby, but on learning of its parents' religion, she was struck by her *attachment* to the baby as a being who reflected on her own identity. She had crossed her own line.

ECHOES ON THE AMERICAN MARKET FRONTIER

Anjali's circumstances were drastically more desperate, her options far fewer, and her clientele more specialized than those of the other service providers I interviewed. But her calibrations regarding "how much to care" echoed a theme I heard among upscale First World consumers, starting with one American couple who were clients at the Akanksha Clinic.

Sitting in the living room of their home in Jackson, Louisiana, the genetic father-to-be, a mild-mannered musician named Tim Mason, recalled meeting the Akanksha surrogate who would carry their baby:

> The surrogate was *very, very short* and *very very, very skinny* and she didn't speak any English at all. She sat down and she smiled, then kept her head down, looking towards the floor. She was bashful. The husband was the same way. You could tell they were very nervous. We would ask a question and the translator would answer, just to try and make conversation. They would give a one or two word response. We asked what the husband did for a living and how many kids they had. I don't remember their answers. I don't remember her name.

Tim's 40-year-old wife, Lili Mason, an Indian-American who described a difficult childhood, a fear of motherhood, and an abiding sense that she was not "ready" to be a mother, gave her own impressions:

> I was nervous to meet the surrogate just because of this Indian-to-Indian dynamic. Other client couples—American, Canadian—all react *more emotionally*. They would hold hands with her [their surrogate]. I was thinking, "That's weird." We don't do that touchy-feely *goo-goo gaa-gaa* thing—especially for a service. "I am so glad you are doing this for me, let me hold your hand." She is doing a service because of the money, and the poor girl is from a poor family. I am a little bit rough around the edges anyway, and this meeting isn't going to put me in a touchy-feely mood.

Lili did not feel she should try to attach herself to the surrogate, nor did she want to. For her, motherhood was a core identity, but she disconnected the idea of a close relationship with her surrogate from it. Although they did not say so, perhaps the couple also wished to avoid the shame of admitting to friends and acquaintances that they needed a surrogate to have their baby. If they remained detached during the pregnancy, they could feel freer to leave the surrogacy a secret. The clinic's ethic encouraged this detachment. Finally, there was the gaping chasm between First World and Third, the moneyed and non-moneyed, those with more power and those with less, all factors that discouraged the forming of a bond.

It is hard to know how typical Anjali is of Indian surrogates or how typical the Masons are of her clients. Still, their experiences lay bare the deeper questions about how we detach ourselves from symbols of self on the production side of intimate life, and attach ourselves to symbols of self on the consumption side of it.

"THE EXPERTS KNOW WHAT MAKES 5-YEAR-OLDS LAUGH"

It would be easy to assume that Anjali's estrangement from her womb and Anjali's life itself have no bearing on life among the affluent of the global North. Anjali is desperately poor, and she lives in a poor nation.

To compare any part of her life to that of privileged people in privileged nations might seem to trivialize Anjali's serious plight. But it need not. Comparing moments of estrangement across worlds can help us pry open questions we seldom ask and extend our compassion.

In an upscale neighborhood in the San Francisco Bay area, friends of the nearly 5-year-old daughter of Michael Haber all had birthday parties organized by hired planners. Still, Michael, a professional who worked long hours but was eager to declare himself a hands-on dad, told his wife one day, "It's stupid to hire a party planner. *I'll* do everything for her birthday." As his wife recalled,

> All of Raquelle's friends' parents hired a party planner named Sophie. All the kids loved Sophie's parties. Kids would write her thank you notes, "Dear Sophie, Thank you very much for the fun birthday. Love from your friend, Harrison." Or even, "Dear Sophie, I was wondering how you are today. Love, Maya." Kids around here come into birthday parties these days and immediately ask, "Where's the coordinator? Where's the itinerary?" It's what they *expect.*

Sophie might be wonderful, Michael granted, but Sophie had moved in where dads and moms had moved out, as he saw it—he, for one, was going to buck the trend.

So Michael sent out invitations to Raquelle's friends. He ordered a cake. He blew up the balloons. He taped up pink and blue streamers. He planned games. Even though he was rebelling against paying a party planner, he borrowed the idea from party planners that a party needed an entertainer. His wife described the event:

> Michael dressed up as a cowboy from the Australian outback—like Crocodile Dundee [an alligator wrangler portrayed in a film of that name]. He put on a broad-brimmed hat, khaki shirt and shorts, and tall leather boots. He stalked about on a pretend stage in front of the girls, describing this and that wild animal in a flat Aussie accent. And he went on for three or four minutes. Then he ran out of things to say. Michael hadn't thought out more to say. Worse yet, the children didn't think his jokes were funny. They began to examine his knobby knees. Then they began to fidget. Then the whole thing fell apart.

When Michael recalled the same event, he put it differently:

> Do you *know* how *long* two hours is? I didn't know it would be so
> *hard!* . . . It's a skill running groups of twenty or thirty 5-year-olds. . . .
> It's like being a continual standup comic. It nearly killed me.

Meanwhile, a neighbor standing at the kitchen door, watching the entire event, told him, "Michael, leave it to the experts. *They* know what 5-year-olds think is funny. *They* know games 5-year-olds like. We don't. Don't embarrass yourself. Leave it to them."

Michael concluded that his neighbor was right. Sophie could do it better. Like Lili, he moved his symbol of himself as a "hands-on dad" from the production side of personal life to the consumption side of it. Michael decided he "couldn't have the baby himself."

Michael was not, like Anjali, forced by desperate need into estrangement from a womb. His was an apparently trivial matter woven into ordinary upscale American life: he was detaching himself from the idea that "I should know what makes my child laugh." But by juxtaposing extreme examples of estrangement—Angali from her womb, and Michael from knowledge about what makes his daughter laugh—we can better recognize the many moments of life between these extremes.

THE MOMMY MALL

A working mother named April was looking over an array of ads for parenting services available to middle-class Americans in her city. These services included offers for coaching parents on what to buy for one's baby (baby planners), installing safety gates and cord-free windows (safety proofers), choosing a baby's name (nameologists), potty training a child (potty trainers), teaching a child to sleep through the night (sleep specialists), teaching a child to ride a bike (sports coaches), picking a summer camp (camp consultants), and creating a fun ambiance at a teen party (party animators).

At 35 years old, April was a marketing specialist and mother of two small boys. For her, the important encounter was not between "me" and "my body" (Anjali), or between "me" and "what I should know" (Michael). Rather, April was struggling with the relationship between her sense of "me" and an idea of parent and child that she felt was implied by this entire tempting "mommy mall." In her time as a mother, April had gladly employed a wonderful babysitter, paid a neighbor to drive her children various places (the babysitter did not drive), hired a hair delouser (when the kids had gotten lice), and was the client of a much revered psychiatrist. But she also suspected that the mall was inviting her to worry about meeting the standards it invented and was preying on her anxiety about being a good mom.

In the realm of work, she believed a person should get very good at one special thing—for her, it was corporate public relations. In that arena, she was a great believer in the principle of specialization: outsource what you can to experts and become a specialist in something yourself. But how far should she take that idea, especially when this principle impinged on her identity as a mother? "I'm not the earth-mother type," she said. But, on the other hand, "If you outsource all these tasks to different specialists, your kid is going to feel like the car you take in for the tune-up, oil change, wheel rotation, lube job. How would he remember his childhood? Appointment, appointment, appointment . . ."

She felt the need to distinguish between the "me" who was a good mother and the "me" who might be tempted to anxiously over-rely on expert help. She gave a recent example:

All the second- and third-graders in our school district are supposed to do a special report on the California missions [built by eighteenth- and nineteenth-century Spanish missionaries]. They are supposed to build little replicas. A few years back, parents hunted up the materials themselves. Then Jimmy's Art Supply began to provide the tile material for the roof, the yarn for your trees, the green paint for your garden. Now the store has a special section that has even the precut foam board, trees, railroad, grass. There's one kit for Mission Dolores, another for San Juan Bautista. You pull it off the hook at Jimmy's, take it home, glue four walls together, put on the roof, glue the trees, and take it to school. What are the kids learning? That the store-bought mission is better than the mission they could build on their own.

This meant that a child who didn't make it to Jimmy's would bring to school a ridiculous-seeming mission. "You may be a parent who says to their kid, 'build the mission out of things you scrounge around the house,'" April explained, "but then your kid is embarrassed to walk to school with his home-made mission. I *know*."

Like Michael's neighbors, April felt that experts knew more than parents. The baseball-coached child threw a better ball. The cyclist-trained child rode a steadier bike. But she also saw that parents eager to help their kids become good at a wide range of things could feel surrounded on all sides by raised standards against which to measure their perfectible child. She felt the easy trip to Jimmy's was wiping away something parents and children should know—how to work on something together. Reflecting on party animators paid to get the party going at bar and bat mitzvahs, she commented, "I want my kids to learn, *themselves*, what to do when the party gets dull." Like others I talked to, April was trying to do invisible repair work—a work of reattachment—in a system of outsourcing that, like new technologies, had divided her from her symbols of connection.

Anjali, Michael, and April all benefited from one aspect of modern capitalism: its giant web of buyers and sellers had attached them to a wondrous array of goods and services they wanted. For Anjali, that was money; for Michael, it was an entertaining birthday; for April, it was time for work. Seen from this perspective, the free market has brought them and others like them much good.[12] Through this market, we cooperate to produce, sell, and buy many useful goods and services of our own choosing, and so improve prosperity for the many. This is the market triumph story, the story we celebrate and know by heart.

But a vast chasm has opened up between the world of Anjali on the one hand, and that of Michael and April on the other. As a system, the free market has no governing purpose other than to perpetuate itself. And the current terms of global trade have acted to increase the gap between the world's rich and poor. Now more than ever, the Anjalis of the global South want to escape to the North.[13] While they were waiting to give birth, the surrogates of the Akanksha Clinic stitched together a large patchwork quilt, made of individual embroidered squares, and on many squares they have sewn images of airplanes pointing up toward the sky. Each plane carries a dream of escape to the North. Maybe the fantasy is to fly to the country of the genetic parents of their babies to care for them, or to care for other children or the elderly to make money and become part of the global care chain (as described in chapter 10).

If we can so easily detach ourselves from the small details of personal life in the global North, how vastly more easy it is for those of us in the rich North to detach ourselves from the concerns of the Anjalis of the poor South. Next to our detachment from the crying needs of this green earth itself, it is the detachment of the world's rich from the poor that looms as our biggest challenge. But re-charting our "under-developed" empathy maps, we can find ways to meet it. So when we ask "how's the family?" there will be a whole world to answer.

Notes

1. U.S. Department of State 1963, "The Personal Call," 4. According to protocol, everyone rises whenever the ambassador or his wife enters a room, even when many people are present. Chiefs of mission and their wives precede others in entering or leaving rooms, and no one should leave a function before the Ambassador and his wife leave. This means that, out of courtesy to restless subordinates, the chief of mission and his wife usually leave fairly early in order to allow their subordinates to go home.

2. One very important key for me was the entire body of works by Erving Goffman, starting with *Presentation of Self in Everyday Life* (1959).

3. Major nineteenth-century thinkers who took on the big questions of their age—Karl Marx, Émile Durkheim, Max Weber, and Sigmund Freud—all touched on emotion. In the *Economic and Philosophic Manuscripts of 1844* (1844/1986), Marx spoke of the nineteenth-century factory worker's alienation from the things he made and the work he did to make them. He saw in the worker a lost pride and joy that comes with the idea "I made that." In *The Elementary*

Forms of Religious Life (1912/1995), Émile Durkheim studied the religious rituals of Australian aborigines in search of conditions inspiring self-transcendent rapture. In *The Protestant Ethic and the Spirit of Capitalism* (1930/2001), Max Weber singled out fear and desire for loving approval—feelings the early Protestant believer directed toward a forbidding God—as the motivational source of the Protestant work ethic. To Freud (1960), emotion, and especially anxiety, was fundamental to understanding the self, although for him emotion was hard to distinguish from instinct and underwent many transformations, as detailed in his theory of the ego and superego. To all of these nineteenth-century thinkers, the sociologist of emotion owes a great debt. Indeed, something like a "sociology of emotion" might be said to have existed for a long time without the name. But during the nineteenth and first part of the twentieth centuries, it was a confusing warren of conceptual tunnels and fascinating empirical observations without a sustained focus on emotion as something in and of itself. I first used the term "sociology of emotion" in a 1975 essay entitled "The Sociology of Feeling and Emotion: Selected Possibilities."

4. Curiously, those lacking power and authority have been most vulnerable to being labeled "emotional" or "overemotional," and have been considered to have something a bit "wrong" with them as a result. In nineteenth-century America, blacks were characterized as childlike, instinct-driven, expressive, and emotional. In early modern Europe and America, women were linked to witchcraft, to the myth of the "wandering womb," and later to hysteria and an overall childlike absence of emotional control (Hacker 1993). Emotion had a bad name.

However, we need to focus on emotion. In my interviews, I have often focused on the experience of women, partly because their lives have been less valued and understood, and partly because I believe their lives often give us better access to the emotional codes that men feel obliged to hide or repress, but by which they, too, live. So it is not that women are *not* emotional, it is that *men are too*. If either one appears "unemotional" in stressful situations, it is likely they are managing their emotions—doing "emotion work," as I called it in *The Managed Heart* (1983). It is not because they are not feeling emotions.

5. See Mueller and Thomas 2001; Spector et al. 2001; and Cherry 2006, among others.

6. For a comparison between students in the United States, Croatia, Slovenia, Canada, Ireland, Belgium, Germany, Singapore, and China, see Mueller and Thomas (2001). For a comparison of Mexican and American male business students, see Mahler (1974). See Spector et al. (2001) for cross-cultural comparisons of the belief in one's control over the environment as control via interpersonal relationships. When researchers expanded their concept of control to include control "via interpersonal relationships," the Americans showed a lower sense of control than respondents from Hong Kong and the Peoples Republic of China.

7. Borges 1998, 6.

8. Elias 1978.

9. Elias 1978, 157–58. The exposure of flesh—in modern beachwear and sports—presupposes more sexual control than was, during the more modest eighteenth century, presupposed.

10. Kundera 1992.

11. Hochschild 1983.

12. Personal communication, Haruo Sakiyama, College of Social Sciences, Ritsumeikan University, Kyoto, Japan, 2008.

13. Grandey, Diefendorff, and Rupp 2013.

14. Ehrenreich and Hochschild 2003.

15. Mills 1963, 1967.

16. Roosevelt quoted in Kelly 2001, 7.

17. In 2009, forty-four out of the one hundred largest economic entities worldwide were corporations (Keys and Malnight 2012).

18. Kuttner 1997.

19. The self that is best suited to the market is focused on the individual's own separate, highly differentiated wants and tastes—or what economists call "revealed preferences." As one person put it, consumers have wants, but citizens have values—including commitments to the public good. The market self bargains for himself, not for others. Often, he comes to conceive of himself as a free agent, uninfluenced by his surrounding context—social class, race, nationality, geographic locale, society. To him, his society is itself never more than the sum of its separate parts. A town meeting, a congregation, a nation, or any emergent community is, to the market self, but an aggregation of individuals, each with separate wants. The market self is oriented to commercial time (when payments are due), not to generational or religious or national or historical time (when commemorations are marked or commitments reaffirmed).

To someone who extends market culture to every realm of life, everything from marriage vows to the Ten Commandments makes sense only as a barter of individual interests. The metaphors the market self brings to bear on such relationships—"profitable investment in the relationship," "brands," "He divested himself of his wife," "He's rebranded himself"—support a *norm of emotional detachment*. People may be obliged to do emotion work to detach themselves enough to live up to the norm.

20. "SocialJane.com" offers to help clients find a friend, just as dating services help one find a romantic partner. For a person new in town, it is easy to see the appeal. Walking along the street, sitting in a park or cafe, it is often hard to make eye contact with strangers—a first social gesture—because many are talking on their cell phones or reading e-mail on their iPads. As the SocialJane.com

Web site's blog explains, finding friends online can be "Convenient, Efficient, with a High ROI":

> In financial terms, ROI stands for return on investment, and is a measurement of the investment or risk that you make, and the result or return derived from that investment. So let's say you bought a painting at a yard sale for $10, and then sold it on eBay for $20. Your ROI would be 100% return in this case—you doubled the value of that initial investment.
>
> In terms of a friendship, the ROI is not as easily calculated since the amount of investment or effort you put into finding and forming a new friendship varies greatly, and is completely depends [sic] on circumstances. For example, one day you are out getting the mail and a new neighbor happens by. The two of you start chatting, then laughing, and the next thing you know you are planning dinner out and a new friendship has begun. The investment here was pretty small, relatively speaking—after all, you were just checking the mail.

The ad appeals to what a client gets, not what she could give—an act we usually associate with friendship. Ironically, SocialJane.com's sales pitch impoverishes the very thing it offers to help one find: friendship. SocialJane.com even suggests that a client who has goods or a service she wishes to sell can use her membership to market them.

21. "What Is the Cost?" GirlFriendCircles.com, 2012, www.GirlFriendCircles.com/staticWhatIsCost.aspx.

22. SocialJane.com and GirlFriendCircles.com are the "mom and pop" stores of the Internet. As industrial jobs disappear from the American workplace, more such services are likely to appear. And through them, a market way of speaking and thinking is inadvertently applied to personal life. In truth, we do not need to buy anything at all in order to talk, think, and feel in a buy-and-sell sort of way. Market culture has "escaped the iron cage" of the market, to paraphrase Weber, and now stalks about our civic and personal lives. We are left to draw lines between a world governed by an ethic of emotional detachment and that governed by an ethic of attachment.

CHAPTER ONE

This essay is based on a paper given at a meeting of the International Society for Research on Emotion, July 29, 2011, in Kyoto, Japan, and takes off from one interview reported in chapter 1 of Hochschild 2012.

1. See Hochschild 2012, chapter 1.

2. One can become a member of Match.com for free. However, to communicate with other members and participate in its core services, a paid subscription is required. In 2009, Match.com was charging its 1,438,000 subscribers

$34.99 for one month or $17.99 a month for a six-month contract. As of July 2012, the rates were $35.99 and $19.99, respectively.

   3. Habermas 1985. Like Herbert Marcuse (1955), Habermas speaks of a wider social complex of which the market is one part.

   4. See chapter 7 of this book.

   5. Cacioppo and Patrick 2009.

   6. Cacioppo and Patrick 2009; Cacioppo 2011.

   7. In a three-volume work, *Attachment and Loss* (1969–80), the psychologist John Bowlby describes various patterns of attachment between small children and their caregivers. Mary Ainsworth (1978) set up a laboratory experiment (the Strange Situation Protocol) through which to observe and analyze different styles of attachment in children. Later, Cindy Hazan and Phillip Shaver (1987) and Kim Bartholomew and Leonard Horowitz (1991) adapted Bowlby's and Ainsworth's theory of attachment to adult love attachments. People develop a fairly steady working model of attachment, they argued, that is derived from childhood experience. Bartholomew and Horowitz identified four adult attachment styles. Securely attached adults are comfortable depending on others and having others depend on them and balance intimacy with independence. Others are insecurely attached, including the "anxious-preoccupied," who seek great responsiveness from partners and become highly anxious without it. Those who are "dismissive-avoidant" avoid dependence on others and having others depend on them, and they avoid rejection by avoiding rejecters. The "fearful-avoidant" have difficulty trusting the intentions of others, and tend to deny and suppress their need for attachment.

   8. These strategies can be conscious, semi-conscious, or forms of unconscious mechanisms of defense. In *The Outsourced Self* (2012), I detail some of these—compensation, take-backs, back-channeling, empathic reach, and flight.

CHAPTER TWO

This essay is based on a talk given at a panel entitled "The Future of Emotional Labor," held on April 17, 2009, at Pace University, New York, published in 2010 as "Invited Commentary: Can Emotional Labour Be Fun?" *International Journal of Work Organization and Emotion* 3, no. 2: 112–19.

   1. See Hochschild 1983 (rev. ed. 2012).

   2. To feel emotion while on the job is not the same as doing emotional labor. A truck driver may, for example, feel anxious about the slick roads and rising price of gas. He may be friendly toward fellow drivers and hear out his boss's bad family news. But this is not central to the truck driver's job, which is to drive a truck. Plumbers, telephone repair people, and other service workers relate to

customers and coworkers, of course, and they need minimal relational skills to do so. But usually relating to others is not the centerpiece of their job description. As Max Scheler (1912/1961) has also pointed out, we can attune ourselves to the needs of another without empathizing with him or her.

3. Hochschild 2012, 189.

4. Here I add to an insightful, lively, corrective literature on these questions. See Lopez 2006; Paules 1991; Tolich 1993; Bolton and Boyd 2003; Taylor, Mallinson, and Bloch 2008; Baugher 2012.

5. Solari 2006a.

6. The older and highly educated caregivers of the elderly in Rome, interviewed by Cinzia Solari, were displaced *babushki* who were no longer needed to care for the children of their stay-at-home daughters back in Ukraine. Most saw themselves as wage earners for—and enjoyed the gratitude of—their families back home (Solari 2006a, 2011).

7. Baugher 2012. Mihaly Csikszentmihalyi (1996, 1997), a University of Chicago psychologist, explored the concept of "flow": the experience of total engrossment, of release from a consciousness of time, and of feeling at one with the activity in which one is engaged. See also Stets 2010.

8. Winnicott 1965.

9. In *The Managed Heart* (1983), I distinguish between "emotion work"—the purposeful evocation or suppression of feeling we do in everyday life—and "emotional labor"—the same kind of emotion management we do for pay as part of a job.

10. Hiestand 2001. Also see Harrington 2010; Harrington, Carrillo, and Blank 2009.

11. Dizon 2000. To save on cost, many American insurance companies are also removing patients from hospital acute care wards and placing them in nursing homes with surgical wounds and intravenous lines still in their arms (Hiestand 2001). Also see Harrington 2010; Pear 2008.

12. Hiestand 2001.

13. Foner and Dreby 2011, 551.

14. Parreñas 2005.

15. Tragically, World Bank economists find that the remittances sent by workers in the global North back to families in the global South do not result in more developed economies back home (Ratha and Xu 2008). See chapter 10 of this book, and Hochschild 2012.

16. In general, while many aspects of global migration are beneficial, the migration of parents away from children has uncounted high costs and points to the need for other means of equalizing the wealth of the world.

17. Even when her clients are very visible, a caregiver may find herself taking the invisible and devalued part of her client's work off his shoulders. For

example, as one California-based personal assistant said, "A lot of my clients have been thirty-something dot-com executives and they talk very fast. *Rata-tat-rata-tat-rata-tat.* 'Call Jim at the office . . . tell him we need the order by eight a.m. tomorrow. . . .' [She snaps her fingers—snap, snap, snap.] So I call Jim's office. I'm friendly with his receptionist. I talk to Jim himself, answer questions, and make sure he's got the message straight and is in a good mood about it. I respond to any hesitancy or resentment I sense in his voice. I'm patient. My clients outsource patience to me" (Hochschild 2012, 169).

18. Interview with childcare worker, conducted as part of my research for *The Outsourced Self* (Hochschild 2012).

CHAPTER THREE

1. In *The Empathic Civilization: The Race to Global Consciousness in a World in Crisis,* Jeremy Rifkin (2009) argues that through the broad swath of human history we have increased—indeed, have begun to globalize—our empathy for other people. Some evidence for this comes from the Harvard psychologist Steven Pinker (2011), who argues in his book *The Better Angels of Our Nature* that over the centuries violence has decreased, including tribal warfare, homicide, cruel punishments, child abuse, animal cruelty, domestic violence, lynching, pogroms, and international and civil wars. Pinker attributes this to a growing exercise of self-control, reason, and empathy. Still, in 2011, we should note there were no fewer than thirty-seven armed conflicts in the world; in each one, twenty-five or more people died as a cause of battle during the year (Themnér and Wallensteen 2012). In 2011, thousands died, but eons ago, the *proportion* of people killed in the armed conflicts of tribal societies was ten times greater, Pinker argues. War-related deaths as a proportion of modern populations are about a tenth as high as they once were when the world's people lived in tribes. For the definition of armed conflict, see Uppsala Conflict Data Program 2012. Also see Azar Gat 2012.

2. As Adam Smith (1776/1875) observed in *The Wealth of Nations,* "Little else is requisite to carry a state to the highest degree of opulence from the lowest barbarism, but peace, easy taxes, and a tolerable administration of justice" (13). Smith famously argued that self-interest was a glue strong enough to bind buyer to seller, but some small measure of trust and empathy is surely also required.

3. See chapter 2, "From Consumer Boom to Ecological Bust," in Juliet Schor's *Plenitude: the New Economics of True Wealth* (2010).

4. In addition, the expansion of the market has greatly widened the gap between rich and poor in the world, creating envy and hardship. Adam Smith (1776/1875) also speculated that "an industrious and upon that account a wealthy nation, is of all nations the most likely to be attacked" (551).

5. Kessler and McLeod 1984; Weissman and Klerman 1977; Nolen-Hoeksema 1987; Piccinelli and Wilkinson 2000.

6. Kessler and McLeod 1984, 621.

7. Kessler and McLeod 1984, 620; Gove 1972; Barnett, Biener, and Baruch 1987. Married women also reported higher rates of depression than single or divorced women, and the question was, again, why? Do married women cope less well with life than unmarried ones? Others have speculated that women have been dealt a more depressing role in marriage than men have been, or even that depression-prone women are more drawn to marriage.

8. Kessler and McLeod 1984, 628.

9. Kessler and McLeod 1984, 629.

10. Kessler and McLeod 1984, 629; Fischer 1982; Gove, Hughes, and Galle 1983.

11. In her forthcoming book on rich and poor families living in Silicon Valley, Marianne Cooper (2013) compares the way rich and poor define and handle economic insecurities. In the working class, women in poor families become the family's "designated worriers"—the ones who wake at night with nightmares about paying the bills—while, in the upper class, it is mainly men who take on this kind of worry.

12. The National Altruism Study, based on data collected from 1,366 people in the 2002 General Social Survey, is one of the few nationally representative studies we have of empathy (Smith 2003). The report found empathy, altruistic values, and helping behaviors all fairly common among Americans. According to the study, three-quarters of Americans said they were "often touched by things that happen" and are "pretty soft-hearted" (3). Forty-three percent "feel selfless caring for others on most days or more often," and 33 percent feel it "once in a while or less often" (3). The study distinguished between altruistic values (agreeing, for example, that it is personally important to assist those in trouble) and altruistic behavior (giving directions, letting someone cut in line, talking to a depressed person, loaning items). Women tended to hold more altruistic values but did not perform more altruistic acts than men (12). Also see Bernard 1981.

13. Eagly 2009, quoting Burleson and Kunkel (2006), 647.

14. Eagly 2009, 648.

15. Eagly 2009, 648.

16. Eagly 2009, 649. Also see Taylor 2003; Leyens et al. 2007.

17. Eagly 2009, 649.

18. Eagly 2009, 646–47.

19. Eagly 2009, 647.

20. See, for example, the work of Claude Fischer (1982, 2011) and Barry Wellman (Wellman and Berkowitz 1988; Wellman and Wortley 1990) on networks of friendship.

21. Stack 1974.

22. Do sadists empathize with their victims in the sense of trying to understand what would hurt most so as to better inflict pain? They can exercise something *like* empathy, but I would have to believe such a thought process is more mechanical and somehow bypasses the feeling of standing in a victim's shoes.

23. Tronto (1993) defines "care" broadly as a "species activity that includes everything that we do to maintain, continue and repair our 'world' so that we can live in it as well as possible" (103). Also see Halpern and Weinstein 2004.

24. The omnipresence of cell phones has led to a culture of interruption, which may thin and loosen empathic bonds. I interviewed a San Francisco–based psychotherapist whose specialties included helping clients to limit the use of iPhones, BlackBerries, and computers during in-person communications with loved ones. As he recounted, "This is a real problem with about 10 percent of my clients, but a bit of a problem with nearly all of them." A number of his iPhone-glued clients complained that their own listeners seemed to be tuning an ear for their next call, and so serving a thinner slice of empathy.

25. Thanks to Neil Smelser in helping me articulate the meaning of empathy. In *The Social Edges of Psychoanalysis* (2002), Neil Smelser argues that structural and social psychological forces are mutually embedded and that patterns of empathy may be an instance of this.

26. Empathy is also related to, but not the same as, sympathy. *Sympathy* is a sentiment of feeling sad on behalf of another person but without necessarily fully empathizing with all of their experience. If I sympathize, I feel sorry for a person even if I cannot imagine being in the same predicament myself. As a term, *compassion* blends empathy with sympathy: "I can imagine myself in those shoes" and "I'm sorry that person is in them." *Altruism* refers to a disposition to act generously and not to what specifically motivates those acts. *Selflessness*, in turn, is altruism extended to the act of casting aside one's own needs.

27. Thanks to Gertraud Koch for the connection between moral ideas and feeling rules.

28. In the early 2000s, with the help of Allison Pugh, I also conducted a set of exploratory interviews with some fifty individuals on informal cultures of care, and I am drawing on those. In the interviews, we asked who individuals turned to in their hour of need, and who turned to them. This particular example draws on an interview I conducted for *The Outsourced Self* (2012).

29. Twain 1885/1992.

30. Twain 1885/1992, 330.

31. Twain 1885/1992, 234, 237.

32. Twain 1885/1992, 330.

33. Lomax 1995.

34. Lomax 1995, 132.

35. Lomax 1995, 143.
36. Lomax 1995, 255.
37. Lomax 1995, 266, 268, 274.
38. Lomax 1995, 275.
39. Thomas 2005. The camp was started by the U.S.-based Kabbalah Center and the Palestinian Abu Assukar Center for Peace and Dialogue.
40. Roots of Empathy, "About Roots of Empathy," www.rootsofempathy.org /en/who-we-are/about-roots-of-empathy.html, accessed January 15, 2012. Roots of Empathy gave rise in 2000 to another school-based program called Seeds of Empathy, focused on 3- to 5-year-olds.
41. Warner 2010.
42. Warner 2010; Piff et al. 2010.
43. When those who make more than $200,000 a year account for more than 40 percent of taxpayers in a given zip code, the wealthy residents give away 2.8 percent of their discretionary income to charity. This compares with an average 4.2 percent for all those earning $200,000 or more (Gipple and Gose 2012).
44. Finding from a 2007 report from Indiana University's Center on Philanthropy, as cited in Warner 2010.
45. Warner 2010; Piff et al. 2010.
46. Konrath, O'Brien, and Hsing 2011. This study was based on a meta-analysis of seventy-two studies of American college students. In a parallel study, another team of researchers found that 44 percent of students in college between 1966 and 1978 ("Boomers") gave priority to "being very well off financially," while 71 percent of those in college between 1979 and 1999 (Gen Xers), and 74 percent of those in college between 2000 and 2009 (Millennials) reported the same (Twenge, Campbell, and Freeman 2012, 1049). This growing preoccupation may reflect a growing fear of economic hardship, a turning inward, and a vulnerability to an "empathy squeeze." See "The Chauffeur's Dilemma" (Hochschild 2005).
47. Konrath, O'Brien, and Hsing 2011, 183.

CHAPTER FOUR

This essay is based on a talk entitled "Five Conversations to Re-Balance Work-Family Balance" that I gave at an international conference sponsored by the Center for Research and Studies in Sociology and Instituto Superior de Ciencias do Trabalho e da Emresa (ISCTE), Lisbon, Portugal, April 12, 2007.

1. To many political conservatives, the term "family" refers to one chosen kind of family: the middle-class, heterosexual, two-parent family. "Family

values" refers to both an embrace of that kind of family and an exclusion of gay and lesbian families, cohabiting couples, and women who have exercised their right to abortion or affirmed the right of others to do so. I use the term "family" here and throughout this book to refer to people—heterosexual, lesbian, and gay—who commit themselves to the feeling rules of family—to love, to help, and to nurture—and who, in the words of a Boston judge, "hold themselves out" to the community as family.

2. Elder and Schmidt 2004.

3. OECD 2011.

4. In some countries, women's move into paid work proceeded slowly—as in Italy, from 28 percent in 1960 to 46 percent in 2010. In Norway, it took a flying leap from 26 percent in 1960 to 73 percent in 2000 (OECD 2011). The data refer to the population of women aged 15 to 64 who are employed. Source for rates in the 1960s: Pissarides et al. 2003, drawing on OECD data.

5. Schwab's text (from Schwab and Zahidi 2010) is excerpted from Hausmann, Tyson, and Zahidi 2012, v. In the preface to the 2010 report (Hausmann, Tyson, and Zahidi 2010), Schwab also writes:

We are at a unique turning point in history. Never before has there been such momentum around the issue of gender parity on the global stage. Numerous multinational companies have aligned core elements of their businesses and products to support and provide opportunities for women in the communities in which they are active. The United Nations has created a new entity for gender equality and the empowerment of women. There is a strong movement around greater investment in girls' education in the developing world. Businesses around the world are starting to take into account the increasing power of women consumers. As women begin to make up more than half of all university graduates in much of the developed world, there is an increased consciousness that this talent must be given the opportunity to lead. Several countries have introduced legislation that mandates minimum requirements for women's participation, in both business and politics.

6. Hausmann, Tyson, and Zahidi 2010, see figures 7 and 8 (28–29). Interestingly, the gender gap does not measure absolute levels of economic, educational, medical, or political attainment but rather the relative gap between women and men along these dimensions.

7. Hausmann, Tyson, and Zahidi 2010, 29.

8. Hausmann, Tyson, and Zahidi 2010, 31.

9. According to Ursula von der Leyen, the family minister for Germany's chancellor Angela Merkel and a mother of seven, given its current births-to-deaths ratio, the German population stands to shrink by 100,000 each year. If Germans do not produce more babies, she grimly concludes, "We will have to turn out the light" (Shorto 2008).

10.   Clark 2011; Minder 2011; Saltmarsh 2010; Social Security Administration 2009. The worry about "too many old people" has led a number of European governments—Italy, Spain, and France—to try to raise their birthrates by setting incentives for women to have more children. Those pressing for a higher birthrate sometimes run counter, rhetorically, to those pressing narrowly for "female empowerment" and economic development. Florence Jaumotte (2005), an OECD economist, noted in one study that "any increase in paid parental leave beyond 20 weeks has a negative effect on women's labour force participation."

11.   Fertility rates, which represent 2012 estimates of the children born per woman in each country, are from the Central Intelligence Agency's *World Factbook* (2012).

12.   Comparison of the difference in nonwork time between full-time-working mothers and fathers with young children, as found in Hochschild and Machung (1989), and Milkie, Raley, and Bianchi (2009).

13.   Fey 2011.

14.   Glass 2013.

15.   Why the rise in "free market" talk? Perhaps, as Robert Kuttner (1997) has argued, globalization—and the ability of rich countries to seek cheap labor and new consumers—has raised the power of large corporations and reduced the power of governments and labor unions to act as counterweights. In "As Corporate Profits Rise, Workers' Income Declines" (2011), Floyd Norris reported that corporate profits have reached the highest level in American history while at the same time workers' real wages have stagnated. Meanwhile, as a share of federal tax revenue, corporate taxes have dropped from a high of 30 percent in the mid-1950s to less than 10 percent in 2008. Not only have corporate tax rates declined, so have taxes on individual millionaires—which were 66 percent in 1945 and 32 percent in 2010 (see Gilson and Perot 2011).

16.   See Good Jobs First's "Corporate Subsidy Watch" profiles at www.good jobsfirst.org/corporate-subsidy-watch. According to B. John Bisio, the Community Affairs Manager of Wal-Mart Stores in Bentonville, Arkansas, a third of Wal-Mart's 3,500 or so U.S. retail stories have requested public assistance from state and local governments (Mattera and Purinton 2004, 14n5). In their study of Wal-Mart distribution centers, Good Jobs First documented public subsidies to 84 out of 91 centers, averaging $7 million each ("Corporate Subsidy Watch"). What government has done for Wal-Mart it has also done for dozens of others— biotechnology companies, private prisons, foreign auto plants, semiconductor plants, and agribusiness—through a wide variety of means. Such payments are usually described as "incentives" rather than as "tax-payer subsidies to companies" or "companies on the public dole."

17.   UNICEF 2007. The report covered—in order of overall ranking in child well-being—the Netherlands, Sweden, Denmark, Finland, Spain, Switzerland,

Norway, Italy, Ireland, Belgium, Germany, Canada, Greece, Poland, Czech Republic, France, Portugal, Austria, Hungary, the United States, and the United Kingdom. The OECD countries excluded for insufficient data were Australia, Iceland, Japan, Luxemburg, Mexico, New Zealand, the Slovak Republic, South Korea, and Turkey. Sometimes the report also offered information on non-OECD nations such as Israel, Slovenia, Estonia, Malta, Croatia, Lithuania, Latvia, and the Russian Federation. The report could not get sufficient information to report on children's exposure to violence or mental health, and it excluded data on very young children. A more recent report (UNICEF 2010) finds that among rich countries the United States has one of the largest gaps between the well-being of rich and poor children.

18. All capitalist economies—including Sweden, Norway, and Denmark—operate on the principle of a free market, of course. But, as the political scientist Gosta Esping-Andersen (1990) has noted, capitalist economies greatly differ among themselves: the Nordic countries have built a "social democratic" welfare regime, the central Europeans—Germany, Austria, and Italy—a "conservative" one, and the United States, the United Kingdom, and Australia a liberal one.

19. UNICEF 2007.

20. UNICEF 2007.

21. UNICEF 2010.

22. UNICEF 2007, 2. Labor force participation rates are drawn from 2010 rates and 2012 estimates as reported in International Labour Office (2011). The rates refer to the population aged 15 years and older in each country. The UNICEF report did not compare the children of working and nonworking mothers within each country. What we observe here are findings that strongly suggest that children do well in family-friendly working-mom states.

23. Others focus on the high number of single-parent homes in the United States as compared with the countries of Europe. Yes, compared with the United States, Sweden has a similar proportion of single-parent homes, but they—importantly—receive government subsidies and so are much less likely to face the financial hardships that befall most single mothers in the United States.

24. He assumed that such children would not be going to good schools, studying in nice libraries, or otherwise enjoying public help.

25. The percentage made up by immigrants in each country's population ranges from 10.7 percent (France), to 13.1 percent (Germany), to 13.5 percent (United States) (United Nations, Department of Economic and Social Affairs 2009). Minority populations are harder to compare across nations. The CIA *World Factbook* does not distinguish between Hispanic and non-Hispanic, for example. Immigrants and non-white minorities in France overlap but are not the same, and France banned the census that distinguishes between people of different ethnic origins.

26. Wilkinson and Pickett 2009. Some scholars have criticized the authors for confusing class and status. Their empirical evidence concerns income gaps, but, critics suggest, their reasoning concerns gaps of status. See Goldthorpe 2010; Fischer 2010.

27. Wilkinson and Pickett 2009. In the most unequal societies such as Singapore, the United States, Portugal, and the United Kingdom, the richest 20 percent are eight to ten times as rich as the poorest 20 percent. In the most equal societies—Japan and the Scandinavian states—the richest 20 percent are about four times as rich as the poorest.

28. Wilkinson and Pickett 2009, 186.

29. Wilkinson and Pickett 2009, 179.

30. Wilkinson and Pickett 2009, 107, 123, 136, 149.

31. Fischer 2010, 30.

32. Snowdon 2010. See also World Health Organization 2012.

33. Murray 2012.

34. Murray 2012, 159.

35. Murray 2012, 268.

36. Murray 2012, 248.

37. Murray 2012, 282.

38. Walkerdine and Jimenez 2012.

39. The growing income gap has other causes beyond free-market policies. These include the OPEC oil crisis of the 1970s, the continuing automation of the workplace, globalization, and the weakening of labor unions, among other things.

40. I am grateful to Deirdre English for a helpful conversation on this.

41. Schor 2004. A survey of youth in seventy cities in more than fifteen countries found, Schor notes, that American children are more "bonded to brands," as they say in advertising, than are children elsewhere in the world. More American children believe, for instance, their clothes and brands describe who they are.

42. Schor 2004, 19.

43. Schor 2004.

44. Children are also sought as an indirect route to their parents and their pocketbooks, a so-called influence market. "That persuasive power is why Nickelodeon, the number one television channel for kids, has had Ford Motor Company, Target, Embassy Suites and the Bahamas Ministry of Tourism as its advertisers" (Schor 2004, 25).

45. Schor and Ford 2007.

46. Borzekowski and Robinson 2001; Zimmerman and Bell 2010; Linn forthcoming.

47. Ogden and Dietz 2010. In 2010, 17 percent of children were diagnosed as obese and at risk for diabetes and heart disease.

48. Schor and Ford 2007, 12.

49. Schor and Ford 2007, 18.

50. Hood 2011; Campaign for a Commercial-Free Childhood 2012.

51. Molnar, Boninger, and Fogarty 2011; Lewin 2011.

52. Molnar, Boninger, and Fogarty 2011.

53. Cohen 2011.

54. Consumers International 1996. In general, nations in which neo-liberal policies prevail (the United States, United Kingdom, and Australia) averaged 11 minutes of advertising per hour; the more social-welfare capitalist states (Netherlands, Belgium, Germany, Austria, Denmark, Sweden, Finland, France, and Norway) averaged 3.3 minutes of ads. Also see Kasser 2002, 2011.

55. Hawkes, Lobstein, and the Consortium for the Polmark 2011.

56. Hawkes, Lobstein, and the Consortium for the Polmark 2011.

57. Hawkes, Lobstein, and the Consortium for the Polmark 2011. In the 1970s the U.S. Federal Trade Commission tried to end television commercials for sugared products aimed at young children, but this effort failed. Commercials for candy and other products aimed at very young children have expanded exponentially since then. Behind this, Schor suggests, is the political power of the so-called child industry (2004, 29).

58. Kasser 2011.

59. On the question of who uses such services, see More and Stevens 2000; Ostergren, Solop, and Hagen 2005; Dougherty 2011; Dearen 2011. The for-profit library company, Library Systems and Services, is now the fifth largest library system in the United States. It has replaced the pensions that long characterized positions in the public library system with retirement funds (Streitfeld 2010).

60. Coalition for Evidence-Based Policy 2012b.

61. Bornstein 2012.

62. Coalition for Evidence-Based Policy 2012c.

63. Coalition for Evidence-Based Policy 2012a.

64. Child Trends 2007.

65. Decision Information Resources, Inc. 2007.

66. In a study of national attitudes, Leslie McCall (2005) found that Americans had become decreasingly tolerant of inequality except after the late 1990s economic boom when they became more tolerant of it. See also Kenworthy and McCall 2008.

67. Faced with the dark side of the market, Americans often do not feel entitled to indignation. If we are let down by a family member, we feel upset or angry. If a government official steals money, we can "kick the bums out." But in the realm of the market, on what grounds can we appeal? If jobs disappear, an American company can politely remind us that its promises are to its

stockholders, not to workers or citizens. Free-market policies uphold stockholder values, not necessarily worker or family values.

68. Kantor 2011.

69. In 1958, when the National Election Study of the Pew Research Center first asked Americans about their trust in the government "to do what is right," 73 percent answered either "just about always" or "most of the time." In 2010, only 22 percent answered this way (Pew Research Center for the People and the Press 2010).

CHAPTER FIVE

1. Christensen and Porter 2004; Family360/LeaderWorks 2012, www .family360.net.

2. Tough 2002. See also Hochschild 2012, chapter 8.

3. Tough 2002, 80.

4. Family360 is part of a larger two-way cultural exchange. The language, ideas, and sense of time of the workplace have traveled home, even as the idea of home has gone to work. Larry Page, CEO of Google, boasts of his company's "family environment." McDonalds promises to keep the information that its customers offer online within the "McDonald's family"—which includes the McDonald's Corporation and its franchises, subsidiaries, and affiliates. IBM refers to certain kinds of computer software as part of the "IBM family."

5. Tough 2002, 80.

6. See chapter 8 of Hochschild 2012.

7. Gilbreth and Gilbreth Carey 1950/2005, 2; *Cheaper by the Dozen* 1950. The film was even culturally resonant enough to inspire a 2003 remake and 2005 sequel.

8. So the goal of Family360 affirms the idea of family, but it coaches dads in the means to affirm the cultural importance of the office. As John Dewey wisely noted, any idea is only as good as the means for achieving it (Dewey 1976, 1981).

9. Time is a problem for many working parents, who put in far longer hours at work now than their counterparts did 30 years ago (Schor 1992; Fischer and Hout 2006, figure 5.13). So Family360 is a response to a real problem that many men and women at every class level face, regardless of whether they can pay a $1,000 fee. But as a time strategy, Family360 resets the scene, leading us to wonder at what point a solution becomes a problem.

10. Hochschild 1997. These strategies were not present in my first analysis of the material gathered for the book, but are based on further reflections.

11. Endurers develop a work-entrenched self, but the deferrer develops what I call in *The Time Bind* a "potential self." This father resolved the contradiction between the demands of work and fatherhood by claiming to be an attuned

dad now, while doing what might earn him that identity later. Thus, he deferred. Hochschild 1997, 192–93, 235–37.

12. Heidmarsdottir 2002.

13. Each strategy has its light side. In a charming but telling story about his three-year-old daughter's life as a New York child, Adam Gopnik (2002) describes, in the *New Yorker*, overhearing Olivia talk to an imaginary friend she names Charlie Ravioli. Charlie is "too busy" to play with her because he is working. In fact, Charlie hires an imaginary personal assistant to answer Charlie's calls because Charlie is too busy to say he is too busy.

14. Every time strategy is linked to an orientation toward symbols, but we realize what is a symbol in our own eyes or those of others only in retrospect. We say "that act meant so much to me" only when we later discover how much it meant. Although people often intend to communicate meanings that they wish to last ("here we are, all together at Christmas"), what actually turn out to be lasting symbols are those well ensconced in the psyche of others. For example, many working families hold to sharing "a home-made meal" as a symbol of family unity, but many also have ceased to cook. So a new oven comes to resymbolize family unity: the oven becomes like a fireplace, seldom used but sentimentally important.

CHAPTER SIX

1. Correspondence from an ambassador's wife. This research is based on participant observation and upon a 1965 survey sent out to 100 wives of chiefs of American diplomatic missions, of whom thirty filled them out and returned them.

2. Stolberg 2012.

3. Stolberg 2012.

4. Bloch 2004.

5. De Callières 1716/2000, 23.

6. Although I had lived for ten years as the child of a diplomat, in larger and smaller embassies than this one, I made no systematic records of my observations in those posts.

7. When the questionnaires were mailed in 1965, there were 116 embassies, two of which were headed by women, some by bachelors, and six were vacant. Two-thirds were held by career diplomats and a third by political appointees. Interestingly, the responses from wives of political appointees did not differ significantly on any question from those of the wives of career men.

8. Fourteen percent did not specify the country to which the husband was assigned.

9. Bloch 2010; Association for Diplomatic Studies and Training 2012. The first female ambassador was appointed in 1949.

10. Reputations can bring honor or shame on the person so bestowed, and these can result in admiration or envy on the part of a bystanding community. We can perhaps speak of soft reputations (easy to carry) and hard ones (difficult to carry). As a "carrier" of another's reputation, we can also respond in many ways—hide under another's reputation, feel stifled by it, compete with it, or bust out from under it. Each of these responses calls for a certain amount of what I have called "emotion work" (see Hochschild 1983).

11. Papanek 1973.

12. As de Callières, the eighteenth-century expert in diplomacy, pointed out, "The diplomatist must . . . bear constantly in mind both at work and at play the aims which he is supposed to be serving in the foreign country, and should subordinate his personal pleasure and all his occupations to their pursuit" (de Callières 1716/2000, 127).

13. In this respect the wife's role, compared with that of her eighteenth- or nineteenth-century counterpart, has become more important (see Thompson and Padover 1963; Foster 1906; Roetter 1963). Judging from de Callières, the role of women in eighteenth-century diplomacy was more a source of influence upon powerful men than a source of information humbly gathered and loyally relayed to a spouse.

14. Post 1960; Satow 1917; U.S. Department of State 1963.

15. Hoover 1962.

16. Morgan 1965a, 1965b. Although her main task is to represent the "American people" (as distinct from the American government) to the local country, the diplomat's wife actually represents a small segment of American people to local officials. There are no Southern hominy grits or tamale pies every tenth night or spaghetti every twelfth, for example. For the most part, she represents the lifestyle of the upper-class Protestant East Coast. The servants, the mansion, the chauffeured car, the six-course meals represent a small elite. This is, of course, equally true for the diplomats from most other countries.

17. Peterson 1965, 20.

18. Peterson 1965. But as the *State Department Newsletter* further advises, a wife has to mean what she says: "To announce an attitude and then not seem to live up to it is to many people in the host country a form of dishonesty that reflects against the United States. For example, to say that you like the local food and then refuse to touch it does not win friends."

19. However, she went on to explain that she felt that being an ambassador's wife is a profession. "I'm still practicing my profession [she was a cultural officer in the Foreign Service before marriage] but in an unpaid and unacknowledged

capacity." Of the wives sampled, slightly over half had been trained for and had practiced an occupation. This group included journalists, teachers, executive secretaries, a cultural officer, a hospital dietitian, a public relations officer for an investment firm, a musicologist, an artist, and an editor. Others, while not professionally trained, took a strong interest in their hobbies of music and teaching dance. Of the occupationally trained, half said that, in a way, they were still practicing their professions. For example, one former hospital dietitian said that she practices her profession "every day in the home" and "outside the house in under-developed countries by talking over nutritional problems. . . . My college and internship training and my two years of work before marriage are very valuable for my life in the foreign service and as the mother of six children." Another, formerly an investments public relations officer, reported, "I have a chance to practice my profession as an ambassador's wife, and must try to be all things to many types of people."

On the other hand, a former journalist said about keeping up her profession, "It's okay back in the United States, but never while abroad." A trained nurse said she was not continuing her profession: "I think being an ambassador's wife is a full-time job and should not be delegated to wives of subordinate officers. I retain my interest by encouraging wives to participate in volunteer work at hospitals and arranging benefits for hospitals." Most agreed with one wife who warned, "If an ambassador's wife wishes to practice her profession, she can't be too careful."

20. Bohlen 1962.

21. Some wives did not feel hampered by this in their choice of friends. When asked, "What do you feel about the chances to make close friends in your present position?" one wife stationed in east Africa replied, "Excellent among those in the community who have my interests in museology and art."

22. Bohlen 1962 (italics mine).

23. Veblen 1899/1912.

24. The official car, for example, is actually the property of the American government, not the ambassador.

25. Nicolson 1952, chapter 10, 219.

26. De Callières 1716/2000. "It is not enough to think aright, the diplomatist must be able to translate his thoughts into the right language, and conversely he must be able to pierce behind the language of others to their true thoughts" (62).

27. There is also a message system between hostess and servant. At diplomatic dinners, the wife communicates by hand and eye or under-the-table electric buzzer, which sounds in the kitchen and which the hostess steps on when the last guest has finished each course.

28. To avoid an interpretation that is not intended in the covertly political language but that might be interpreted in that language, the ambassador's wife and her husband may devise certain formulas.

29. See Salcedo 1959; U.S. Department of State 1963. Also see U.S. Department of State, "Protocol, Precedence and Formalities," last updated in 2009.

30. Bohlen 1962.

31. Often the problems of seating determined who was omitted from the guest list, because protocol might seat people next to each other who were known to dislike each other or whose countries were in major disagreement on an important issue at the time.

32. U.S. Department of State 1963, "The Personal Call," 4. According to protocol, everyone rises whenever the ambassador or his wife enters a room, even when many people are present. Chiefs of mission and their wives precede others in entering or leaving rooms. And no one should leave a function before the Ambassador and his wife leave. This means that, out of courtesy to restless subordinates, the chief of mission and his wife usually leave fairly early.

33. Hall 1959.

34. Norms of dress, for example, can communicate political messages. The modest way in which early American and post-1917 Russian diplomats' wives dressed was "an expression of scorn for the pomp and flummery of bourgeois manners and dress of diplomats from other countries" (Roetter 1963, 167).

35. Bohlen 1962.

36. Hall 1959.

37. Thirty-eight percent spent most of their time with local officials and/or their wives, 23 percent with American embassy wives, 8 percent with other Americans (mostly businessmen), 3 percent with their families, 10 percent with foreign envoys, 5 percent with other local women, 3 percent with servants (who are usually local), 3 percent with Peace Corps volunteers, 2 percent with local artists and intellectuals, 2 percent with foreign visitors, 2 percent with local students, and 2 percent with local wives married to American officers. Three percent said it was "hard to tell." Altogether, 36 percent spent most of their time with other Americans of some sort or another, 12 percent with foreigners not from the assigned country, and 52 percent with locals.

38. In the 1960s, the average age of the career chief of mission was 53 years old. For the political appointee it was slightly younger, 51.9 years. In 1963, the youngest ambassador was 38 years old (U.S. Department of State 1964). The average age of a Foreign Service officer was 41.

39. U.S. Department of State 1963, 8.

40. See U.S. Department of State 1967, 9. Also see Fisher 1966.

41. If she did not actively participate, she kept herself informed about their activities, which included preparing booklets, directories, and shopping guides,

setting up thrift shops, holding bazaars to raise charity money, holding flower shows, teaching (usually English), or doing social work.

42. The relation between the ambassador's wife and her female subordinates depended on the size of the embassy. One ambassador's wife distinguished the way relations with wives should be handled between small and large embassies:

> I have always assumed that the morale and efficiency of the distaff side of the Embassy is largely the responsibility of the ambassador's wife. . . . In small embassies one can bring the senior wives in for a monthly coffee or lunch and discuss the general problems of the local scene. Informal talks about how the different wives are getting on, whether there are any problem children and what can be done about them, enable the ambassador's wife to keep her finger on the pulse of things without becoming unnecessarily involved in individual problems. In a large Embassy, of course, this is more difficult, but it is usually possible for even the busiest ambassador's wife to set aside one morning every four or six weeks to talk with the senior wives, who should be prepared to talk briefly and knowledgeably about the junior wives in their sections of the Embassy and whether the general morale is good or bad.

43. As Robert Merton (1965) points out, the formal secondary group does not allow for primary relations that are disdainfully labeled as "apple polishing," nepotism, or favoritism.

44. "The higher one's rank, the harder it is to make friends," one wife explained. "Any chief officer's wife—be she that of a consul, consul-general, minister, or ambassador—probably has this experience. Among your own wives you have to take care to treat all carefully to avoid jealousies and rivalries." Another noted, "Within the Embassy family it's a delicate matter. I feel my relationships with all the other Embassy wives should be on an equally friendly but not intimate footing. My best friend is the wife of another ambassador at the Post."

45. Emphasis mine.

46. The barriers that inhibit close friendship also applied to American wives whose husbands worked for parallel hierarchies of wives in the U.S. Information Service (USIS) and the Agency for International Development (AID), which are under the general supervision of the ambassador. "Jealousy and rivalry among the services and missions is a problem," one wife noted, "if one devotes too much time and attention to any one [agency]." Talking, telephoning, and visiting time were all distributed equitably among the wives of subordinate officers in the organizations under her husband's authority.

47. Penfield 1963. She continued, "Naturally this file is given to one's successor," suggesting the passing on of the social requirements to the next occupant of the role.

48. Bohlen 1962. She suggests to young wives that "in the junior ranks you will not have to invite senior officials; keep your entertaining simple and

confine the guest list to those whom your husband should know and with whom he works."

49. Even the embassy-furnished car and chauffeur are associated with a sense of territoriality. In London in 1661, "the attendant of the Spanish Ambassador in London fell upon the French Ambassador's coach, killed the postillion, beat up the coachman and hamstrung two horses in order to make certain that the Spanish Ambassador's coach went first" (Roetter 1963, 162). While this is no longer such a symbolic object, there are still some rules of protocol attached to car seating. The official guide, *Social Usage*, suggests, "In order to have the ranking person sit there [at the place of honor on the right] it may be necessary for the junior person to enter the car first, or to go behind the car and enter from the other side" (U.S. Department of State 1963, 23). *Social Usage* also suggests that in many countries, the right side of the sofa is "considered the seat of honor" and "should not be occupied by the junior wife or husband unless specifically invited to do so" (23).

50. Although most of the furnishings are supplied by the State Department and are not of her choosing, the house often reflects an American standard of living and customs. It has air conditioning or heating, the windows usually have screening so that rooms are free of flies and other insects, and there are carpets on the floor. Even the smells (from the furniture and the cooking) are American and make Americans feel at home and foreigners feel to some extent not at home.

51. Bohlen 1962.

52. De Callières 1716/2000, 127.

53. De Callières 1716/2000, 118. He elaborates, "Indeed it is the nature of things that good cheer is a great conciliator, that is, fosters familiarity, and promotes a freedom of exchange between the guests, while the warmth of wine will often lead to the discovery of important secrets" (119).

54. See Wolff 1951, 51. There are also certain rules of thumb concerning with whom one talks. "Talk to foreign guests and not with Embassy friends, introduce yourself to people you have not met. At dinner parties be sure to talk to your neighbor—even when language barriers exist you can usually manage something with your hands . . . or just be friendly. But above all try—a hostess cannot bear pools of silence halfway down her table" (Bohlen 1962).

55. De Callières 1716/2000, 132.

56. If it is a fairly large embassy, there may be a staff of up to five or six, one being the head steward. The diplomat's wife may take them with her from post to post or train each staff as she meets them at a new post. In some cases, they may provide her with deep insight into the indigenous culture. One of the biggest problems with her staff is petty stealing or "borrowing." As one ambassador's wife reported, "Your staff is your biggest problem. Without their loyalty

and respect you cannot entertain. In spite of this you must constantly safeguard against stealing—thus insulting them. Thievery is common. We've just caught our cook at it. The guardienne and the other steward reported it. If I fire him, two years of training in a hot kitchen goes down the drain as well as a good cook. If I keep him, the morale of the others goes down and they think it's acceptable to steal. I've learned to accept cheating up to a certain point. Cooks are hard to find [here]."

57. Winfield 1962. Her communication with embassy wives is similar to the advice given to junior wives: "Keep your eye on the hostess, she may need an errand done or want some information."

58. According to one ambassador's wife, "Old friends may become more precious also." Said one wife, "Maintaining friendships with old friends in the Service in previous posts, by correspondence, is one of my pleasures. Old friends have almost become my roots in this nomadic life of ours, and becoming a principal officer's wife does not change one's contact with them."

59. Winfield (1962) noted, "Another thing which frequently is revealed is that in a new and strange situation family members are pulled closer together and there is a closing of the ranks" (96).

60. Merton 1965.

CHAPTER SEVEN

1. Viviana Zelizer (2005) distinguishes between three approaches to the intersection of market and personal life. These she calls the a) "hostile worlds," b) "nothing but," and c) "connected lives" approaches—the latter being her own. Tocqueville, Bellah, Kuttner, Sandel and others—including us—focus on *points of tension* between market and personal life, and studies with this focus constitute, we feel, a missing fourth category.

2. Tocqueville 1840/1945, 98.

3. Tocqueville 1840/1945, 99, 104.

4. Tocqueville 1840/1945, 99. To be sure, Tocqueville counterbalanced his fear of this inward-facing individualism with an admiration for American voluntary associations—based on a faith in collective action. Latter-day commentators—from Bellah to Amatai Etzioni and Robert Putnam—have rued the loss of this communal aspect of American life. A number of social scientists, including Margaret Levi, Karen Cook, and Claude Fischer (1982, 2011), have studied the question of whether we have lost, retained, or redirected our sense of community. See Cook, Harden, and Levi 2007.

5. Smith 1759/1976.

6. Tocqueville 1840/1945, 22.

7. Bellah et al. 1996, 147.

8. Bellah et al. 1996, 17.

9. Bellah et al. 1996, 108.

10. Certainly changes in our basic context—the rise in suburban, urban, and airport mega-malls, for example—deeply affect us, as does the climate of public opinion. See Cohen 2003.

11. Nafstad et al. 2009. See also Nafstad et al. 2007.

12. Searches from before the turn of the century proved to be less reliable, possibly because of inconsistent encoding of the newspaper scans. The number of articles published in the *New York Times* varied over our search periods: 155,827 in the 1900 period; 272,817 in the 1970 period; and 183,921 in the 2004 period. To be able to assess historical trends in the representation of particular concepts in the newspaper, we standardized all findings relative to the number of articles published in each period. When we discuss increases in a given term, for example, this trend is thus independent of the different sizes of the newspaper in each era. For more information about the data and analyses presented in this chapter, please contact the authors.

13. See Inglehart and Norris 2007; Kohut and Stokes 2006 (chapter 5); Morin 1998.

14. Andrew Cherlin argues this in *The Marriage-Go-Round* (2009).

15. We could not, for technical reasons, replicate Nafstad's searches for *I* and *me*, but we were able to trace other words—singly and in pairs— suggesting both relationships typical of close community and those typical of the market.

16. DeWall et al. 2011.

17. From the *Chicago Times* (February 14, 1970) and the *New York Times* (February 17, 2007, two articles), respectively.

18. From the *New York Times* (February 17, 2007) and the *Los Angeles Times* (February 3, 2007, and February 10, 2007), respectively.

19. From the *New York Times* (February 10, 2007) and the *Los Angeles Times* (February 3, 2007), respectively.

20. In our sample of military recruitment materials, the ratio of ads appealing to individual gain to those appealing to national duty, pride, or need was approximately 1 to 2.53 during World War I, 1 to 3.21 during World War II, and 1 to 2.15 today. These figures reflect coding that allowed for recruitment ads to represent *both* individual gain and national duty/pride/need. Analyses of the subset of posters that represented only *one* of the themes reveals a decline in national duty/pride/need (26 percent to 20 percent) and an increase in appeals to self-interest (14 percent to 26 percent).

21. The unit of analysis here is the article; that is, these findings are all based on the proportion of articles in each three-year period found with a

particular search term or set of search terms (for example, *trust*, or the set of terms denoting family). We look at these counts in terms of their raw number, but also with regard to the same counts in other years, counts of articles containing other terms, and the changing size of the paper. In these and all other searches in the *New York Times*, we searched for the word reported as well as variations of it. For example, we searched for *trust* as well as *trusting*. As initial searches revealed that *trust* was frequently used in a financial instead of a relational sense, we employed search strategies designed to exclude from our analyses the articles in which *trust* was used within five words of *fund* or *financial*. Over the course of the century, the proportion of articles in which *trust* and related words appeared declined by about half; *sympathy* and *duty* each declined by about 60 percent.

22.   From the *Chicago Times* (February 4, 1900), the *New York Times* (February 3, 1900), and the *Chicago Times* (February 11, 1900), respectively.

23.   The proportion of sermon titles that evoked giving, selflessness, community, and/or communal roles declined from 13 and 12 percent in 1900 and 1970, respectively, to 4 percent in 2007. There was also a decline in the proportion of sermons that focused on selfless, compassionate leaders. Among the 278 sermons announced in early February 1900, about 10 percent focused on figures such as Abraham Lincoln and Jane Adams. That proportion had sunk by half by the 1970s, and (though the small number of sermons published in 2007 make the data less certain) it seems to have continued at this low level into the new century.

24.   See note 21 for a description of our *New York Times* analyses.

25.   Gillis 1996.

26.   That is to say, the proportion of articles including the term *profit* and its variations doubled over the 100-year period, while the presence of *consume* and *consumer* together increased almost eightfold.

27.   Although services available through large mega-churches have increased over time (for example, childcare for different age groups), the proportion of Americans who describe themselves as unaffiliated rose from 7 percent in 1970 to 20 percent today. A third of those under age 30 say they are unaffiliated. See Hout and Fischer 2002; Pew Research Center 2012.

28.   *New York Times* (February 7, 1970).

29.   Indeed, the military has invested significant funding in honing their market message. In 2006, Ira Teinowitz reported that the U.S. army spent "more than $200 million annually on marketing—the biggest ad contract in the federal government."

30.   Piccalo 2004.

31.   And objects can seem to offer lasting connections. Indeed, as James Burroughs and Aric Rindfleisch (1997) write, for children of divorce, the purchase of

things may support a useful "coping mechanism . . . helping to restore a sense of stability, permanence, and identity in their lives" (91).

32. Gobé 2001.

33. Gobé 2001, xviii (emphasis in original).

34. Goleman 1995; Thomson 1998; Anthony 2003; Cairnes 2003; Bradberry and Greaves 2005; Newman 2008.

35. Gobé 2001, xvi.

36. Peters 1997.

37. Kaputa 2005.

38. See also chapter 1 in this volume.

39. Greenwald 2003, back cover and p. 4.

40. McNally and Speak 2011.

41. Elliott 2006.

42. Elliott 2006.

43. Cruz 2003. See also Reyes 2004, and Frito-Lay's announcement of the competition: "Would You Name Your Baby Horton?—If So, Ruffles Wants to Pay for College" (May 12, 2003), www.fritolay.com/about-us/press-release-20030512 .html.

44. Deam 2003.

45. Smith 2005.

46. Posted on eBay on February 25, 2005.

47. Smith 2005.

48. Thanks for this insight to Neil Smelser, Sociology Department, University of California–Berkeley.

49. Wallulis 1998.

50. Our finding that rhetoric reflecting the values upholding communal ties has persisted through the century fits with other research on friendship. See Fischer 2011.

51. See Pugh forthcoming.

CHAPTER EIGHT

1. Barrie Thorne, my friend and colleague in Sociology at U.C. Berkeley, was the lead author on the original article, and I made later revisions. Also see Hochschild, *The Time Bind: When Work Becomes Home and Home Becomes Work* (1997).

2. In the early 1990s, approximately 10 percent of chairs in "doctorate-granting I and II institutions" were women (Carroll 1991). More recent data suggest that the proportion is increasing, "especially at non-research oriented institutions" (Carroll and Wolverton 2004; Niemeier and González 2004). In 2000, women made up about 20 percent of chairs, with variation across departments (Niemeier and González 2004; Roos and Gatta 2009).

3. Niemeier and González 2004; Roos and Gatta 2009.

4. See "Inside the Clockwork of Male Careers" in Hochschild 2003, 227–54.

5. Hochschild and Machung 1989.

6. Mokros, Erkut, Spichiger, and the Spencer Foundation (1981), for example, found female advisors engaged more with the personal concerns of their students than did their male counterparts.

7. American Association of University Professors 2012.

8. American Association of University Professors 2012.

CHAPTER NINE

1. This point is carefully made by Zelizer 1994, 2005; Hyde 1983; Mauss 1954/2000.

2. Lasch 1977.

3. Zelizer 1994.

4. Hochschild 1997, 114.

5. The quotes are from classified advertisements found on the Internet, most from Craigslist.

6. See chapter 4 for more discussion.

7. Fowler 2011; Guynn 2012; Useem 2000. What are now called "new company towns" also offer many paid services that a homemaker or the man of the house used to do at home: laundry and dry cleaning services, car washing and maintenance, bicycle repair, and chef-cooked dinners. Even civic life has come to work. Lands' End, a mail-order clothing company, and Amgen, a biotech firm, developed employee clubs for "chess, genealogy, gardening, model airplanes, public speaking, tennis, karate, scuba diving and charity" (Useem 2000). Another corporation has a singles group called Mingle. According to Useem, in the early 2000s, a thousand companies nationwide offered onsite Bible study groups. With the mall and civic life brought in the door of the workplace, the professional and managerial worker tends, of course, to work long days and have less time to live the nonwork side of life.

8. This survey was administered by the University of California–Berkeley's Survey Research Center as part of their Golden Bear Omnibus program. Using random digit telephone sampling and computer-assisted telephone interviewing, investigators surveyed Spanish- and English-speaking adults 18 years of age or older, residing in households with telephones, within the state of California, between April 30, 2007, and September 2, 2007. During the study, 1,186 phone interviews were completed, with an overall response rate of 15.9 percent. Our module about engaging personal services was completed by 978 respondents.

9. Klinenberg 2012. Also see Livingston 2011; Martin et al. 2011.

10. See Sandholtz et al. 2004, which grew out of their book (Sandholtz et al. 2002).

11. Sandholtz et al. 2004.

12. These classified ads were accessed on the Internet, mainly from Craigslist, between 2000 and 2010.

13. "Ellie & Melissa TheBabyPlanners," http://web.archive.org/web/20120615170036/http://www.thebabyplanners.com/contact.html.

14. Salmon 1996.

15. Barbara Smaller, *New Yorker,* May 31, 2004.

16. C. Covert Darbyshire, *New Yorker,* July 22, 2002.

17. Nippert-Eng (1996) focuses on ways we draw boundaries between symbolic realms of home and work—by putting up family photos at work, placing keys for home and work on the same key-chain, using the same or separate calendars for home and work events, keeping one or two telephone books for colleagues and friends. Some people, she notes, use integrating whereas others use segmenting strategies.

18. With modernization, Parsons and Bales (1955) argued, the family has moved from an institution that performed many functions (education, entertainment, economic activity, socialization, and procreation) to one that performed few. The factory system took over economic activities, schools and summer camps, education, and so on.

19. Parsons and Bales (1955). The market itself is welded into a notion of modernity. Meanwhile, families are a matter of roles—the differentiation between male and female roles, in Parsonian theory, and matters of role-overload or role-spillover in later formulations (Barnett and Marshall 1992; Barnett, Marshall, and Sayer 1992; Burley 1991). The hostess who compared herself to a worker at the bed and breakfast inn might be said to be suffering from "role overload."

20. Fildes 1988.

21. Zelizer 1994. As Ralph Fevre (2003) has argued, economic sociologists who once launched a major critique of Weber's "iron cage" have quietly climbed inside it to study and comment on it "from within." To look at the market with greater perspective, we need to focus on the overall balance between the market "realm of worth," as Boltanski and Thévenot (2006) call it, and those of the state, civic life, and family. We should also look to the "take-away give-back" syndrome embedded within capitalism itself. See Hochschild 2012.

22. Marx both admired and faulted capitalism. His major concern, of course, was with the owners' exploitation of workers, the growing class divide between rich and poor, and the individual's alienation both from what she makes and from what she buys (for instance, see Marx and Engels 1887/1967).

23.   For natural resources, see Schor 2004; Schor and Holt 2000. For human resources, see Ehrenreich 2001. For inequalities, see Kuttner 1997. For erosion of the commons, see Bollier 2003; Rowe 2002.

24.   Polanyi 1944.

25.   Kuttner 1997.

26.   Bollier 2003. This is because a system based on the profit motive simply is not designed to protect the public good.

27.   Rifkin 2000. See also Fevre 2003; Hochschild 1997.

28.   Schor 2004.

29.   Many services are advertised in such a way as to invite us to question the adequacy of who we are or what we have. Just as the ads for skin products feature young women with impeccable complexions, so do ads for personal services raise the bar on personal fulfillment almost out of reach. (Thanks to Mark Kramer for the comparison to such an ad.) In pursuing this line of questioning, we can draw on the distinction Christina Nippert-Eng (1996) makes in her book *Home and Work* between those with an eye for boundaries between the two realms and those with an eye for integration. We can also draw on the foundational work of Viviana Zelizer (1994, 2005), which focuses on integration.

30.   See my book *The Outsourced Self* (Hochschild 2012).

31.   Tronto 1993.

32.   Simmel 1978.

33.   Marx and Engels 1887/1967.

34.   Hochschild 1983.

35.   A busy working mother living in an upscale neighborhood in which families have children's birthday planners may go with the trend or buck it. She might feel that "I'm not doing enough myself; I've bought myself out of a job," and so manage any feelings of guilt. Or she might displace her anxiety about not doing enough herself by anxiously monitoring the hired clown or the Chuck E. Cheese's waitress. Or she might envy those with enough money to commodify life more, but feel she should not envy them because, after all, they have become estranged from the important things in life. In doing this, she "works on" her envy.

36.   Pugh 2005.

CHAPTER TEN

This article is based on a talk given April 23, 2009, at the University of Frankfurt, Frankfurt, Germany.

1. Here I draw on research by Rhacel Parreñas (2001, 2003, 2005), S. Uma Devi (2003; Isaksen, Devi, and Hochschild 2008), and others as well as on my own interviews with Filipina nannies and Indian surrogate mothers.

2. Castles and Miller 1998; Zlotnik, 2003.

3. Farnam 2003.

4. United Nations, Department of Economic and Social Affairs 2011.

5. Gamburd 2000; Brochmann 1993.

6. Parreñas 2001, 2003, 2005.

7. Professor Francis Wilson, Economics Department, University of Cape Town, South Africa, personal communication with author, 1990.

8. Parreñas 2001, 2003, 2005; Isaksen, Devi, and Hochschild 2008; Cox 1990; Espiritu 2003.

9. The United States often recruits low-paid foreign workers to do industrial work. See Miraftab 2011.

10. Robles and Watkins 1993, cited in Foner and Dreby 2011, 555.

11. Parreñas 2001, 87. "Vicky" is the pseudonym provided by Parreñas.

12. Parreñas 2001, 87.

13. Parreñas 2001.

14. World Bank 2011. These figures are expected to increase significantly in the coming years (Mohapatra, Ratha, and Silwal 2011). Some economists dispute the economic benefits of remittances for the home countries' economies. Economists at the International Monetary Fund and Duke University argue, for example, that remittances are "wasted on big-screen TVs and faux-adobe mansions" instead of being invested in new businesses (Frank 2001, 2; Wheatley 2003).

15. Page and Plaza 2006.

16. World Bank 2013. In terms of the total value of remittances, however, the countries that received the greatest amount in 2010 were India, China, Mexico, the Philippines, and France (World Bank 2011, x).

17. DeParle 2008. According to the World Bank economist Dilip Ratha, in 2003 the amount of remittances sent by both male and female migrant workers worldwide was nearly three times greater than all the world's combined foreign aid (DeParle 2008).

18. DeParle 2008.

19. World Bank 2011.

20. Iliff 2008.

21. Confederation of Indian Industry, and McKinsey & Company 2012.

22. *Google Baby*, 2009, dir. Zippi Brand Frank.

23. This was the number of births and surrogates in residence as of 2011. Ditte Bjerg, Executive Producer and Director, Global Stories, Copenhagen, Denmark, personal communication with author.

24. Bjerg, personal communication.

25. For more on emotional labor, see Hochschild 1983.

26. Aditya Ghosh, a journalist with the *Hindustan Times*, translated for me from Gugarati to English.

27. Dr. Ghautam N. Allabadia, Director of the Rotunda Clinic, Mumbai, India, interview with author, 2010.

28. The regulatory bill drafted in 2010 is with the Indian Law Ministry, having not yet reached the parliament. N.B. Sarojini, SAMA Women's Health, Delhi, India, personal communication with author, 2010.

29. For a summary, see Pet 2011, and the letter posted there from the SAMA Resource Group for Women and Health to the Indian Health Ministry.

30. For N.B. Sarojini, director of the Delhi-based SAMA Resource Group for Women and Health, a nonprofit feminist research institute, the problem is one of distorted priorities. "The ART clinics are posing themselves as the answer to an illusory 'crisis' of infertility," she says. "Two decades back, a couple might consider themselves 'infertile' after trying for five years to conceive. Then it moved to four years. Now couples rush to ARTs after one or two. Why not put the cultural spotlight on *alternatives*? Why not urge childless women to adopt orphans? And what, after all, is wrong with remaining childless?" See Hochschild 2012.

31. Solid information on the size of the reproductive tourism sector is difficult to find. See Hochschild (2012), chapters 4 and 5, as well as Pande (2009a, 2009b, 2010) and Rudrappa (2012).

32. There are no official data comparing how much less Indian surrogates receive than their American counterparts, but published estimates range from between less than 10 percent to up to 50 percent (Smerdon 2008; Gentleman 2008; Arora 2012). Because of broker and institutional fees, the relationship between what clients pay and what surrogates receive varies between the countries as well. The clients of U.S. surrogates may pay anywhere from double (Rudrappa 2012), to three times (Gentleman 2008), five times (Fontanella-Khan 2010; Roy 2011), or nearly six times (Haworth 2007) what they would if they were contracting surrogacy in India.

33. Greider 1997. Right now international surrogacy is a confusing legal patchwork. Commercial surrogacy is banned in Canada, New Zealand, Australia, and much of Europe (such as Spain, Belgium, France, the Netherlands) and elsewhere (Davis 2012; Roy 2011; Anderson, Snelling, and Tomlins-Jahnke 2012; Ahmad 2011), though altruistic surrogacy is legal in some of these nations. Commercial surrogacy is unregulated or is permitted with few restrictions in some countries such as China (Davidson 2012), India, and Russia (Davis 2012; Svitnev 2010). It is legal, regulated, and paid for by the state in Israel for Israeli citizens (Teman 2010; Weisberg 2005). In the United Kingdom, one cannot hire a

commercial surrogate, but one can use foreign surrogates and, pending approval by the High Court, secure legal parenthood in the United Kingdom after birth (Davis 2012; Gamble 2012).

The handling of gestational surrogacy in the United States varies widely. According to Gugucheva (2010), "most states have unclear laws governing surrogacy agreements. Nevertheless, they can roughly be grouped into six categories, reflecting the degree of restriction they impose on surrogacy agreements. Ranging from most favorable to most restrictive, there are states that: (1) hold surrogacy agreements valid and enforceable, (2) have unclear statutes but favorable case law, (3) explicitly allow surrogacy agreements but regulate the market, (4) have unclear statutes and no case law, (5) hold surrogacy agreements void and unenforceable, and (6) prohibit and/or penalize individuals entering such agreements, sometimes under threat of heavy fines and jail time. Most states fall in the middle, and most do not have statutes that address the validity or legality of surrogacy contracts" (13). The Center for American Progress identified only seventeen states and the District of Columbia that had statutory laws on the books in 2007, including California, which allows commercial surrogacy, and New York, which bans it.

34. Orwell 1949; Bradbury 1981.

35. Huxley 1932.

36. Atwood 1985. Various films carry these themes further. *Amerika* (1987) was a television miniseries about a United States taken over by communism, with strict martial law enforced by a U.N.-appointed Russian general governing the United States from Moscow. To be sure, some recent films such as *Inside Job* (2010) have cast, as the villain, powerful corrupt companies.

37. Professor Kai Maiwald, Osnabruck University, Germany, personal communication with author, 2011.

CHAPTER ELEVEN

This essay is based on extensive original research conducted by the economist Professor S. Uma Devi in Kerala, India, funded by the Norwegian Research Council. All quotes from Keralan workers, caregivers, and children are from this research, first reported here. Many thanks to Bonnie Kwan for her excellent typing and editing assistance, to Adam Hochschild for his helpful critique of an early draft, and to Winnie Poster for helpful critique of a later draft. Also see Sheba George's fine 2005 study, which focuses on the relationship between Keralan migrant nurses and their follow-later husbands, and the stigma suffered by both.

1. United Nations, Department of Economic and Social Affairs 2011.

2. United Nations, Department of Economic and Social Affairs 2011; Castles and Miller 1998.

3. Zlotnik 2003.

4. Momsen 1999; Parreñas 2001; Hondagneu-Sotelo 2001; Ehrenreich and Hochschild 2003; Hochschild 2000b.

5. Scholars of female migration focus either on wives who joined their husbands in the North to reunify the family, or on female solo migrants who moved for work. But as Pierrette Hondagneu-Sotelo notes, women increasingly fit the "male model" of family provider. See Hondagneu-Sotelo 2003b, 1994; Anderson 2000; Khruemanee 2002.

6. Anderson 2000.

7. When Mother Comes Home for Christmas 1996.

8. Reyes 2008.

9. See García Zamora 2006 , table 13, "Niños y niñas que vivan sin padre y madre" [Children who live without mother or father]: Jalisco, 35%; Michoacan, 30%; Zacatecas, 33%.

10. Hondagneu-Sotelo 2003a, 267.

11. Parreñas 2001, 2003, 2005. Also see Erista et al. 2003; Morada 2001.

12. See Hochschild 2000a, 2000b.

13. Western scholars often focus on the two-person balancing act in the North, omitting the third, fourth, or more people involved in this act—the childcare worker, her children, and their caregivers living in the South. Curiously, the attention to "work-family balance"—and to care—that is so freely applied to families in the North is often missing from the more economically focused research on migrant women of the South.

14. Barbič and Miklavčič-Brezigar 1999, quoted in Momsen 1999, 169.

15. Yeates 2004.

16. Rowe 2002; Bollier 2003.

17. Mills 1967, 8.

18. Parreñas 2001.

19. Gamburd 2000; Brochmann 1993.

20. Devi 2003; Parreñas 2001.

21. And often the topic does not arise because it causes too much personal pain. Ana, a Thai nanny I interviewed, had worked for fifteen years in San Jose, California. When I asked her how many children she had, she answered that she had two. It was only when I asked her if she had left any children behind that she told me of a son she had had by her first husband, a child she had been forced to leave behind in Thailand with her mother and ex-husband. A photograph of this son was not among the dozen or so on her living room table.

When I asked about this child, she told me, "It's complicated. My son by my first marriage . . . I left him with my mother when I came here. And my husband wanted his son with him in the village. He wouldn't let me take him. Even at the hospital, I had my mother sign as the legal guardian. When I next went back to Thailand, my son was eight. I should never have gone back. Because then my son wanted to come with me. I tried to arrange for him to come here, but since I wasn't his legal guardian, I couldn't do it. My son *waited* and *waited*. But after he heard he couldn't come, he had a motorcycle accident. He died [weeps]."

22. Devi 2003; Ramji and Devi 2003.

23. Erista et al. 2003, 10.

24. Devi 2003; Ramji and Devi 2003. Many social problems have a "shame wrap-around." Many homeless people are ashamed of being homeless. Many poor people are ashamed of being poor. Many of the imprisoned are ashamed of being in prison. In each instance, to different degrees, the victim is led to violate some norm for which they experience shame. But erased from the picture is the larger pattern that led to that violation—that shame—in the first place.

25. For instance, Go and Postrado 1986; Abella and Atal 1986; Arnold and Shah 1986; Schmalzbauer 2004; Parreñas 2005; Aranda 2003; Artico 2003; Bryceson and Vuorela 2002.

26. Kandel and Kao 2001.

27. Battistella and Conaco 1998.

28. Battistella and Conaco 1998, 231.

29. Battistella and Conaco 1998, 231.

30. Schmalzbauer, 2004, 1328. Schmalzbauer also conducted focus groups and did some participant observation.

31. Parreñas 2005.

32. Dreby 2010. Also see George 2005.

33. Devi 2003; Ramji and Devi 2003.

34. Devi 2003; Ramji and Devi 2003. They interviewed the working mothers in the six Emirates of the United Arab Emirates (where nine of the twenty-two lived alone) and interviewed their children and the kin who cared for them in Kerala.

35. Kerala State Planning Board 2002.

36. The prevailing ideal in marriage also calls for coresidence and monogamy. Migration prevents the first and strains the second. Although this was not a focus of the Devi research, Parreñas found many husbands of long-absent Filipina migrant mothers set up house with other women in villages away from their own children (Parreñas 2005).

37. Isaksen, Devi, and Hochschild 2008, 412.

38. Ibid., 412.

39. Ibid., 413. In *Tahitians*, the social anthropologist Robert Levy (1973) speaks of whole realms of human feeling for which given cultures have few or no words. For feelings in the upper range of emotion such as joy, happiness, euphoria, he observed that the Tahitians had many words. But for the lower range—sadness, regret, longing, or depression, they had only one word: "sick." Where there are few words, Levi reasoned, there is a cultural underacknowledgment of feeling, an underarticulation of experience. In Malayalam, too, there is no special word for a feeling many children in Kerala experience— "mother-envy." In the context of a highly educated population and stagnant economy in which the desirability of migration goes largely unquestioned, such feelings clearly exist but with, so to speak, a cover over them.

40. Isaksen, Devi, and Hochschild 2008, 413.

41. Ibid., 413.

42. Ibid., 413.

43. Ibid., 413.

44. Rhacel Parreñas, for example, found that relatives who cared for migrants' children often came to resent their charges' negligent fathers, who had disengaged from their children's daily lives, sometimes accompanied by drinking, gambling, or carrying on extramarital affairs (Constable 2003; Parreñas 2005). Such male avoidance of care may express not simply a "traditional" reluctance to do women's work but also a backlash at lost privilege. Kin must then add to their caretaking responsibilities the task of dealing with a husband-father who feels he has lost "his place." Russian fathers who are separated or divorced from their wives are often replaced by their wives' mothers in caring for their children (see Utrata 2008).

45. In this sense, migrant parents and children are subject to the same materialization-doubts as absent or divorced fathers. An 18-year-old daughter of a divorced father interviewed for a previous study told Devi, "Every time I talk to my dad on the phone, the conversation begins, 'Do you need money?' It's as if he thinks that's all he could give me."

46. Isaksen, Devi, and Hochschild 2008, 415.

47. Devi 2003; Ramji and Devi 2003; Schmalzbauer 2004.

48. We need highly sophisticated research comparing the children of migrant mothers with those of non-migrant mothers and migrant fathers. We also need work comparing children who experience different kinds of nonparental care.

49. Habermas 1985.

50. People with many chits are high in social capital, and those with few are low. As Portes (1998) notes, "social capital [is] primarily the accumulation of obligations from others according to the norm of reciprocity" (7).

51. Isaksen, Devi, and Hochschild 2008, 416.

52. Lakoff 1980.

53. A brief word about "social capital": the concept draws on the work of Pierre Bourdieu (1986) and Bourdieu and Loïc Wacquant (1992), James Coleman (1988), and Robert Putnam (1993, 2000), and it has been applied to migration by Alejandro Portes (1998). Putnam (2000) defines social capital in a variety of ways—as the number of a person's social contacts, the sum of one's organizational memberships, and the norms of reciprocity and trustworthiness that arise from these contacts and memberships (19).

Actually, Putnam (2000) is confusing on just this point. He sometimes refers to "social capital" in the way the metaphor suggests—as the property of an individual; other times, he refers to social capital strictly as the attribute of a collectivity. Scholars applying the concept to the Third World tend to see social capital as the attribute of an individual (Harriss 2002).

As many social critics have noted, the concept of social capital is overly broad. Woolcock, a World Bank economist, observed: "Several critics, not without justification have voiced their concern that collapsing an entire discipline into a single variable (especially one with such economic overtones) is a travesty, but there are others who are pleased that mainstream sociological ideas are finally being given their due at the highest levels" (quoted in Harriss 2002, 82). In "Social Capital: The World Bank's Fungible Friend," the economist Ben Fine notes that the concept, initially applied to economic growth, school performance, and job placement, is now being applied to infant mortality, solid waste management, and communal violence (Fine 2003, 587).

The concept has also been critiqued for its woolliness, lack of empirical specificity, decontextualization (our concern), and depoliticizing implications. The more social capital a nation has, Harriss (2002) reasons, the more the World Bank feels it can press for reduced government aid in Third World countries and press for the liberalization of trade. "Is it a coincidence," Fine (2003) asks, "that social capital has come to the fore just as the World Bank is proposing to reallocate billions of dollars for infrastructure funding from the IDA (International Development Assistance), which makes concessional loans to governments, to the IFC (International Financial Corporation), which lends exclusively to the private sector?" (600).

54. Dalton 1969, 65–66.

55. The concept of social capital, let us hasten to add, was not originally designed to obscure the human cost of global migration. Those who first added social capital to the conversation about Third World development and care did so, rather, with the idea of adding a human touch to the economic discussions of money, bridges, factories, and the like. But "the human side" was paradoxically used in such a way as to obscure it. The market metaphor has been making its

way through social science via what we might call the "capital series." The series begins with material capital and extends to human capital (Coleman 1988), social capital (Putnam 1995, 2000), emotional capital (Illouz 2007; Hochschild 2012), and pugilistic capital (Wacquant 2004).

Theorists of the commons, for their part, offer us two pictures of social capital. One is a positive picture—a set of resources or relationships that are common and shared for mutual benefit, such as the trust and copresence of mother and child. Here the emphasis is on sharing a sense of in-commonness. The second is negative—a similarly shared set of resources that people, each thinking of their private good, ultimately abuse (Harden 1995). In this chapter, we extend the first picture. See also Tronto 1993; Rowe 2002; Polanyi 1944.

56. Some commons are temporary and emergency based (as in response to a natural disaster); others establish expectations of long-term reciprocity.

57. Solari 2006a, 2010.

58. Cinzia Solari, e-mail communication with author, 2011. Also see Solari 2006b, 2010, 2011.

59. To World Bank economists, indicators of social capital are seen as a sign of "good prospects" for foreign investment in the Third World. But little analysis is devoted to how immigration erodes the very community and family life—the social capital—they see as the "missing link" in economic development. (Harriss 2002; Fine 2003; Woolcock 2001).

60. Durkheim 1893/1984; Polanyi 1944.

61. Durkheim 1893/1984.

62. Fevre 2003, 3–7.

63. Polanyi 1944, 134–35.

CHAPTER TWELVE

1. All names in this article are pseudonyms. Hochschild 2009, 2012; Garey and Hansen 2011.

2. Kuttner 1997.

3. Friedman 1962.

4. Marx 1844/1986. Using different terms, a number of sociologists have dealt with this question. In Granovetter's seminal 1985 paper, he proposes that we think of markets as embedded in society and think of society as a set of social networks. Since then, some network theorists have talked about such social networks in increasingly threadbare terms. Uzzi (1997), for example, writes that "a network structure rich in structural holes is virtually all that is needed to induce information and resources to flow through the network like electric

current through a circuit board" (63). Zukin and DiMaggio (1990) propose that we distinguish between structural, political, cognitive, and cultural forms of embeddedness. Zelizer (2010), a pioneer in this field, warns that "embeddedness" as a concept can lead us to avert our eyes from the "relational work" through which actors fit money (or other media of exchange) to the needs of self-differentiating individuals.

5. Hochschild 1983, 2003.

6. Zelizer (2005) gives us the idea that money penetrates our everyday lives. We give and receive allowances, pin money, gifts, payment for chores, alimony, all within the realm of "intimate life." Individual will and culture matter a great deal, she argues. Arjun Appadurai (1986) adds to Zelizer the intriguing idea that things—religious relics, stones, artifacts—have a social life. That is, they get valued and devalued in the eye of the beholder depending on what they represent. In the same way, the value of personal services can rise and fall in the eyes of clients, depending on the cultural eyes through which we see them.

7. Although the concept of a gift economy was first applied by Mauss (1954/2000) to preliterate societies, Hyde (1983) points out that in modern life the rules of the gift economy apply to relations between lovers, family, friends, and other forms of community.

8. If a person were to donate a kidney to an ill child, one would detach the idea of "me" from the organ and conceive of it as a gift-for-my-child. But what if one has a child for money, and the money is intended for one's existing child? Is a person detached from the baby but attached to the money? How, I wondered, does this work?

9. And, of course, this perspective denies the myriad ways that the surrogate and fetus are strongly connected. The surrogate feels the baby's presence in many other parts of her body—her digestive system, ankles, hips, and breasts, not to mention her fantasies and dreams. And psychologists have found that babies respond with faster heartbeats to their (gestational) mother's voices in utero (for example, see Kisilevsky et al. 2003).

10. Government of India, Ministry of Health and Family Welfare, and Indian Council of Medical Research 2010; Roy 2011; SAMA Resource Group for Women and Health 2012.

11. Pande 2009a, 2009b, 2010.

12. Left out of the usual story, however, is good government. Anjali credited the market for her good fortune and thought nothing about government services. But were she to live in Canada—the country of her clients—she would not be forced to earn money to pay for a good education for her children or medical care for her husband, nor would she herself lack an education. Given an

honest, well-functioning government, these would be hers as a citizen. With better resulting options, she would have freer choices.

13.   Indeed, at this writing, a large new dormitory called "The Nest" is being constructed at the Akanksha Clinic to house some sixty more surrogates. Ditte Bjerg, Director of Global Stories, Copenhagen, Denmark, personal communication with author, 2012.

Bibliography

Abella, Manolo I., and Yogesh Atal, eds. 1986. *Middle East Interlude: Asian Workers Abroad*. Bangkok: United Nations Educational, Scientific and Cultural Organization.

Ahmad, Nehaluddin. 2011. "An International View of Surgically Assisted Conception and Surrogacy Tourism." *Medico-Legal Journal* 79, no. 4: 135–45.

Ainsworth, Mary D. Salter. 1978. *Patterns of Attachment: A Psychological Study of the Strange Situation*. Hillsdale, NJ: Lawrence Erlbaum Associates.

American Association of University Professors. 2012. "Background Facts on Contingent Faculty." AAUP.org, www.aaup.org/issues/contingency/background-facts.

Anderson, Bridget. 2000. *Doing the Dirty Work? The Global Politics of Domestic Labour*. London: Zed Books.

Anderson, Lynley, Jeanne Snelling, and Huia Tomlins-Jahnke. 2012. "The Practice of Surrogacy in New Zealand." *Australian and New Zealand Journal of Obstetrics and Gynaecology* 52, no. 3: 253–57.

Anthony, Mitch. 2003. *Selling with Emotional Intelligence: 5 Skills for Building Stronger Client Relationships*. Chicago: Dearborn Trade.

Appadurai, Arjun. 1986. *The Social Life of Things: Commodities in Cultural Perspective*. Cambridge: Cambridge University Press.

Aranda, E. 2003. "Global Care Work and Gendered Constraints: The Case of Puerto Rican Transmigrants." *Gender and Society* 17, no. 4: 609–26.

Arnold, Fred, and Nasra M. Shah, eds. 1986. *Asian Labor Migration: Pipeline to the Middle East*. Boulder, CO: Westview Press.

Arora, Ishika. 2012. "Wombs for Rent: Outsourcing Surrogacy to India." *Prospect: Journal of International Affairs at UCSD*, January 10, http://prospect journal.org/2012/01/10/wombs-for-rent-outsourcing-surrogacy-to-india-2/.

Artico, Ceres I. 2003. *Latino Families Broken by Immigration: The Adolescents' Perceptions*. New York: LFB Scholarly Publications.

Association for Diplomatic Studies and Training. 2012. "A More Representative Foreign Service," *U.S. Diplomacy: An Online Exploration of Diplomatic History and Foreign Affairs*, www.usdiplomacy.org/history/service/representative.php.

Atwood, Margaret. 1985. *The Handmaid's Tale*. New York: Fawcett Crest.

Barbič, Ana, and Inga Miklavčič-Brezigar. 1999. "Domestic Work Abroad: A Necessity and an Opportunity of Rural Women from the Goriška Borderland Region of Slovenia." In *Gender, Migration and Domestic Service*, edited by Janet Henshall Momsen, 161–73. London: Routledge.

Barnett, Rosalind C., Lois Biener, and Grace K. Baruch. 1987. *Gender and Stress*. New York: Free Press.

Barnett, Rosalind C., and N. L. Marshall. 1992. "Worker and Mother Roles; Spillover Effects and Psychological Distress." *Women and Health* 18, no. 2: 9–40.

Barnett, Rosalind C., N. L. Marshall, and A. Sayer. 1992. "Positive-Spillover Effects from Job to Home: A Closer Look." *Women and Health* 19, nos. 2–3: 13–41.

Bartholomew, Kim, and Leonard M. Horowitz. 1991. "Attachment Styles Among Young Adults: A Test of a Four-Category Model." *Journal of Personality and Social Psychology* 61, no. 2: 226–44.

Battistella, Graziano, and Cecilia Conaco. 1998. "The Impact of Labour Migration on the Children Left Behind: A Study of Elementary School Children in the Philippines." *SOJURN: Journal of Social Issues in Southeast Asia* 13, no. 2: 220–41.

Baugher, John. 2012. "Caring for Dying Strangers." Unpublished manuscript. Department of Sociology, University of Southern Maine.

Bellah, Robert Neelly, Richard Madsen, William M. Sullivan, Ann Swidler, and Steven M. Tipton. 1996. *Habits of the Heart: Individualism and Commitment in American Life*. Berkeley: University of California Press.

Bernard, Jessie. 1981. *The Female World*. New York: Free Press.

Bloch, Julia Chang. 2004. "Women and Diplomacy." Speech given at the Council of American Ambassadors, Washington, DC. *Ambassadors Review*,

Fall, www.americanambassadors.org/index.cfm?fuseaction=publications .article&articleid=69.

———. 2010. "Women and Diplomacy." Speech given at China Foreign Affairs University, May 2010, Beijing, China.

Bohlen, Mrs. Charles. 1962. "Young Foreign Service Officers' Wives." Speech given March 20, 1962; published in *Department of State Newsletter*.

Bollier, David. 2003. *Silent Theft: The Private Plunder of Our Common Wealth*. New York: Routledge.

Boltanski, Luc, and Laurent Thévenot. 2006. *On Justification: Economies of Worth*. Translated by Catherine Porter. Princeton, NJ: Princeton University Press.

Bolton, Sharon C., and Carol Boyd. 2003. "Trolley Dolly or Skilled Emotion Manager: Moving on from Hochschild's *Managed Heart*." *Work, Employment and Society* 17, no. 2: 289–308.

Borges, Jorge Luis. 1998. *Brodie's Report*. Translated by Andrew Hurley. New York: Penguin Books.

Bornstein, David. 2012. "The Power of Nursing." *New York Times Opinionator*, May 16, http://opinionator.blogs.nytimes.com/2012/05/16/the-power-of -nursing/.

Borzekowski, D. L., and T. N. Robinson. 2001. "The 30-Second Effect: An Experiment Revealing the Impact of Television Commercials on Food Preferences of Preschoolers." *Journal of the American Dietetic Association* 101, no. 1: 42–46.

Bourdieu, Pierre. 1986. "The Forms of Capital." Translated by Richard Nice. In *Handbook of Theory and Research for the Sociology of Education*, edited by John G. Richardson, 241–58. Westport, CT: Greenwood Press.

Bourdieu, Pierre, and Loïc J. D. Wacquant. 1992. *An Invitation to Reflexive Sociology*. Cambridge, UK: Polity Press.

Bowlby, John. 1969–80. *Attachment and Loss*. 3 vols. New York: Basic Books.

Bradberry, Travis, and Jean Greaves. 2005. *The Emotional Intelligence Quick Book: Everything You Need to Know to Put Your EQ to Work*. New York: Simon & Schuster.

Bradbury, Ray. 1981. *Fahrenheit 451*. New York: Ballantine Books. (Orig. pub. 1953.)

Brochmann, Grete. 1993. *Middle East Avenue: Female Migration from Sri Lanka to the Gulf*. Boulder, CO: Westview Press.

Bryceson, Deborah, and Ulla Vuorela. 2002. "Transnational Families in the Twenty-First Century." In *The Transnational Family: New European Frontiers and Global Networks*, edited by Deborah Bryceson and Ulla Vuorela, 3–30. New York: Berg.

Burleson, B. R., and Kunkel, A. W. 2006. "Revisiting the Different Cultures Thesis: An Assessment of Sex Differences and Similarities in Supportive Communication." In *Sex Differences and Similarities in Communication*, 2nd ed., edited by K. Dindia and D. J. Canary, 137–59. Mahwah, NJ: Lawrence Erlbaum Associates.

Burley, K. A. 1991. "Family-Work Spillover in Dual-Career Couples: A Comparison of Two Time Perspectives." *Psychological Reports* 68, no. 2: 471–80.

Burroughs, James E., and Aric Rindfleisch. 1997. "Materialism as a Coping Mechanism: An Inquiry into Family Disruption." *Advances in Consumer Research* 24: 89–97.

Cacioppo, John. 2011. "Social Isolation." Lecture given at the International Society for Research on Emotion, Kyoto, Japan, July 28.

Cacioppo, John, and William Patrick. 2009. *Loneliness: Human Nature and the Need for Social Connection.* New York: W. W. Norton.

Cairnes, Margot. 2003. *Approaching the Corporate Heart: New Horizons of Personal and Professional Success.* East Roseville, Australia: Simon & Schuster.

Campaign for a Commercial-Free Childhood. 2012. "2012 School Bus Ad Action Center," http://commercialfreechildhood.org/action/2012-school-bus-ad-action-center.

Carroll, James B. 1991. "Career Paths of Department Chairs: A National Perspective." *Research in Higher Education* 32, no. 6: 669–88.

Carroll, James B., and Mimi Wolverton. 2004. "Who Becomes a Chair?" *New Directions for Higher Education* 126: 3–10.

Castles, Stephen, and Mark J. Miller. 1998. *The Age of Migration.* New York: Guilford Press.

Central Intelligence Agency. 2012. "Total Fertility Rate." In *The World Factbook.* Washington, DC: CIA, www.cia.gov/library/publications/the-world-factbook/fields/2127.html.

Cheaper by the Dozen. 1950. Directed by Walter Lang. Los Angeles: Twentieth Century-Fox.

———. 2003. Directed by Shawn Levy. Los Angeles: Twentieth-Century Fox.

Cheaper by the Dozen 2. 2005. Directed by Adam Shankman. Los Angeles: Twentieth-Century Fox.

Cherlin, Andrew J. 2009. *The Marriage-Go-Round: The State of Marriage and the Family in America Today.* New York: Alfred A. Knopf.

Cherry, John. 2006. "The Impact of Normative Influence and Locus of Control on Ethical Judgments and Intentions: a Cross-Cultural Comparison." *Journal of Business Ethics* 68, no. 2: 113–32.

Child Trends. 2007. "Head Start." Child Trends' Lifecourse Interventions to Nurture Kids Successfully (LINKS) database summary, www.childtrends.org/Lifecourse/programs/headstart.htm.

Christensen, Perry M., and Ben Porter. 2004. *Family 360: A Proven Way to Get Your Family to Talk, Solve Problems, and Improve Relationships.* New York: McGraw-Hill.

Clark, Nicola. 2011. "Government of France Proposes Austerity Cuts." *New York Times*, November 8, A12, www.nytimes.com/2011/11/08/world/europe /french-austerity-measures-aimed-at-new-reality.html.

Coalition for Evidence-Based Policy. 2012a. "Top Tier Evidence: Career Academies." Coalition for Evidence-Based Policy, http://toptierevidence.org /wordpress/?page_id=176.

————. 2012b. "Top Tier Evidence: Nurse-Family Partnership." Coalition for Evidence-Based Policy, http://toptierevidence.org/wordpress/?page _id=168.

————. 2012c. " Top Tier Evidence: Success for All for Grades K–2." Coalition for Evidence-Based Policy, http://toptierevidence.org/wordpress/?page _id=178.

Cohen, Lizabeth. 2003. *A Consumers' Republic: The Politics of Mass Consumption in Postwar America*. New York: Alfred A. Knopf.

Cohen, Rick. 2011. "Corporate Commercialism Running Wild in America's Schools." National Education Policy Center, *Non Profit Quarterly Newswire*, November 8, www.nonprofitquarterly.org/index.php?option=com_content& view=article&id=17431.

Coleman, James. 1988. "Social Capital and the Creation of Human Capital." *American Journal of Sociology* 94, Suppl.: S95–120.

Confederation of Indian Industry, and McKinsey & Company. 2012. "Healthcare." *Building Business Leadership*, www.cii.in/Sectors.aspx?enc=prvePUj2bd MtgTmvPwvisYH+5EnGjyGXO9hLECvTuNu2yMtqEr4D4o8mSsgiIyM/.

Constable, Nicole. 2003. "Filipina Workers in Hong Kong Homes: Household Rules and Relations." In *Global Woman: Nannies, Maids, and Sex Workers in the New Economy*, edited by Barbara Ehrenreich and Arlie Russell Hochschild, 115–41. New York: Metropolitan Books/Henry Holt.

Consumers International. 1996. *Television Advertising Aimed at Children: An International Comparative Survey*. London: Consumers International.

Cook, Karen S., Russell Harden, and Margaret Levi. 2007. *Cooperation without Trust*. New York: Russell Sage Foundation.

Cooper, Marianne. 2013. *Cut Adrift: Families in Insecure Times*. Berkeley: University of California Press.

Cox, D. 1990. "Children of Migrant Workers: A Family Relationship Issue." In *Children and Migration: A New Challenge for World-Wide Social Services*. Hong Kong: International Social Service.

Cruz, Manny. 2003. "Daily Business Report." *San Diego Metropolitan Magazine*, May 23, http://sandiegometro.com/2012/05/daily-business-report-%E2%80 %94-may-23-2012/.

Csikszentmihalyi, Mihaly. 1996. *Creativity: Flow and the Psychology of Discovery and Invention*. New York: HarperCollins.

———. 1997. *Finding Flow: The Psychology of Engagement with Everyday Life.* New York: Basic Books.

Dalton, George. 1969. "Theoretical Issues in Economic Anthropology." *Current Anthropology* 10, no. 1: 63–102.

Davidson, Nicola. 2012. "China's Surrogate Mothers See Business Boom in Year of the Dragon." *The Guardian*, February 8, www.guardian.co.uk/world/2012 /feb/08/china-surrogate-mothers-year-dragon.

Davis, Erica. 2012. "Rise of Gestational Surrogacy and the Pressing Need for International Regulation." *Minnesota Journal of International Law* 21: 120–44.

Deam, Jenny. 2003. "What Brand Is Your Baby?" *Denver Post*, October 16.

Dearen, Jason. 2011. "California Parks Closure: State Parks Closing Has Unlikely Consequences." *Huffington Post*, July 17, www.huffingtonpost.com /2011/07/17/california-parks-closure-unlikely-consequences_n_901156 .html.

De Callières, François. 1716/2000. *On the Manner of Negotiating with Princes: On the Uses of Diplomacy, the Choice of Ministers and Envoys, and the Personal Qualities Necessary for Success in Missions Abroad.* Translated by Alexander Frederick Whyte. Boston: Houghton Mifflin.

Decision Information Resources, Inc. 2007. "Youth Opportunity Grant Initiative: Impact and Synthesis Report." Houston: Decision Information Resources, http://wdr.doleta.gov/research/FullText_Documents/YO%20Im pact%20and%20Synthesis%20Report.pdf.

DeParle, Jason. 2008. "World Banker and His Cash Return Home." *New York Times*, March 17.

Devi, Sambasivan Uma. 2003. "Care across Borders: The Case of Migrant Female Health Workers from Kerala in the Middle East." Unpublished manuscript. Part of the project Gender and Globalization: Care across Borders, University of Bergen.

DeWall, C. Nathan, Richard S. Pond Jr., W. Keith Campbell, and Jean M. Twenge. 2011. "Tuning in to Psychological Change: Linguistic Markers of Psychological Traits and Emotions over Time in Popular U.S. Song Lyrics." *Psychology of Aesthetics, Creativity, and the Arts* 5, no. 3: 200–7.

Dewey, John. 1976. *The Middle Works, 1899–1924.* Carbondale: Southern Illinois University Press.

———. 1981. *The Later Works, 1925–1953.* Carbondale: Southern Illinois University Press.

Dizon, Nicole Ziegler. 2000. "Many Chicago-Area Nursing Homes Fall Short of Federal Standards." *Associated Press*, March 28, B1.

Dougherty, Rebecca. 2011. "2010 Maryland State Parks Economic Impact and Visitor Study." Baltimore, MD: Maryland Office of Tourism Development/ Department of Natural Resources.

Dreby, Joanna. 2010. *Divided by Borders: Mexican Migrants and their Children.* Berkeley: University of California Press.

Durkheim, Émile. 1893/1984. *The Division of Labor in Society.* Translated by W. D. Halls. New York: Free Press.

———. 1912/1995. *The Elementary Forms of Religious Life.* New York: Free Press.

Eagly, Alice H. 2009. "The His and Hers of Prosocial Behavior: An Examination of the Social Psychology of Gender." *American Psychologist* 64, no. 8: 644–58.

Ehrenreich, Barbara. 2001. *Nickel and Dimed: On (Not) Getting by in America.* New York: Metropolitan Books/Henry Holt.

Ehrenreich, Barbara, and Arlie Russell Hochschild, eds. 2003. *Global Woman: Nannies, Maids, and Sex Workers in the New Economy.* New York: Metropolitan Books/Henry Holt.

Elder, Sara, and Dorothea Schmidt. 2004. "Global Employment Trends for Women, 2004." International Labour Organization Employment Strategy Papers series, August 2004, www.ilo.org/wcmsp5/groups/public/@ed_emp /@emp_elm/documents/publication/wcms_114325.pdf.

Elias, Norbert. 1978. *The Civilizing Process.* New York: Urizen Books.

———. 1982. *The History of Manners.* New York: Pantheon Books.

Elliott, Stuart. 2006. "Letting Consumers Control Marketing: Priceless." *New York Times,* October 9, www.nytimes.com/2006/10/09/business/media /09adcol.html.

Erista, Carmelita N., Mercedita E. Tia, Amalia S. Sevilla, and Teodeoro M. Orteza. 2003. "Profile of Filipino Overseas Workers." Paper presented at the Statistical Research and Training Center (SRTC) Annual Conference; Quezon City, Manila, Philippines.

Esping-Andersen, Gosta. 1990. *The Three Worlds of Welfare Capitalism.* Cambridge, UK: Polity Press.

Espiritu, Yen Le. 2003. *Homebound: Filipino American Lives Across Cultures, Communities and Countries.* Berkeley: University of California Press.

Family360/LeaderWorks. 2012. "Family360." LeaderWorks, www.family360 .net/.

Farnam, Arie. 2003. "Children Left Parentless as Migrants Flee Poor Ukraine." *Christian Science Monitor,* June 10.

Fevre, Ralph. 2003. *The New Sociology of Economic Behaviour.* London: Sage.

Fey, Tina. 2011. "Confessions of a Juggler." *New Yorker,* February 14, 64.

Fildes, Valerie A. 1988. *Wet Nursing: A History from Antiquity to the Present.* Oxford: Basil Blackwell.

Fine, Ben. 2003. "Social Capital: The World Bank's Fungible Friend." *Journal of Agrarian Change* 3, no. 4: 586–603.

Fischer, Claude S. 1982. *To Dwell among Friends: Personal Networks in Town and City.* Chicago: University of Chicago Press.

———. 2010. "Mind the Gap." *Boston Review* 35, no. 4: 30.

———. 2011. *Still Connected: Family and Friends in America since 1970.* New York: Russell Sage.

Fischer, Claude S., and Michael Hout. 2006. *Century of Difference: How America Changed in the Last One Hundred Years.* New York: Russell Sage Foundation.

Fisher, Glen H. 1966. "The Foreign Service Officer." *Annals of the American Academy of Political and Social Science* 368, no. 1: 71–82.

Foner, Nancy, and Joanna Dreby. 2011. "Relations Between the Generations in Immigrant Families." *Annual Review of Sociology* 37: 545–64.

Fontanella-Khan, Amana. 2010. "India, the Rent-a-Womb Capital of the World: The Country's Booming Market for Surrogacy." *Slate,* August 23, www.slate .com/articles/double_x/doublex/2010/08/india_the_rentawomb_capital_of _the_world.html.

Foster, John W. 1906. *The Practice of Diplomacy as Illustrated in the Foreign Relations of the United States.* Boston: Houghton Mifflin.

Fowler, Geoffrey A. 2011. "The Perk Bubble Is Growing as Tech Booms Again." *Wall Street Journal,* July 6, http://online.wsj.com/article/SB10001424052702303 76340457641980399742369o.html.

Frank, Robert. 2001. "Checks in the Mail." *Wall Street Journal,* May 22.

Freud, Sigmund. 1960. *The Ego and the Id: The Standard Edition of the Complete Psychological Works of Sigmund Freud.* Edited by James Strachey. New York: W. W. Norton.

Friedman, M. 1962. *Capitalism and Freedom.* Chicago: University of Chicago Press.

Gamble, Natalie. 2012. "International Surrogacy Law Conference in Las Vegas, October 2011." *Family Law* (February): 198–201.

Gamburd, Michele Ruth. 2000. *The Kitchen Spoon's Handle: Transnationalism and Sri Lanka's Migrant Housemaids.* Ithaca, NY: Cornell University Press.

García Zamora, Rodolfo. 2006. "Un pasivo: Mujeres y niños en comunidades de alta migración internacional en Michoacan, Jalisco y Zacatecas, México" [A debt: Women and children in communities of high international migration from Michoacan, Jalisco, and Zacatecas]. In *Las remesas de los migrantes Mexicanos en Estados Unidos y su impacto sobre las condiciones de vida de los infantes en México* [Remittances of Mexican migrants in the United States and their impact on the living conditions of their children in Mexico]. Unpublished UNESCO field report.

Garey, A. I., and K. V. Hansen, eds. 2011. *At the Heart of Work and Family: Engaging the Ideas of Arlie Hochschild.* New Brunswick, NJ: Rutgers University Press.

Gat, Azar. 2012. "Is War Declining—and Why?" *Journal of Peace Research* (published online before print, December 21).

Gentleman, Amelia. 2008. "India Nurtures Business of Surrogate Motherhood." *New York Times*, March 10, www.nytimes.com/2008/03/10/world/asia /10surrogate.html.

George, Sheba Mariam. 2005. *When Women Come First: Gender and Class in Transnational Migration*. Berkeley: University of California Press.

Gilbreth, Frank B., and Ernestine Gilbreth Carey. 1950/2005. *Cheaper by the Dozen*. New York: HarperCollins.

Gillis, John R. 1996. *A World of Their Own Making: Myth, Ritual, and the Quest for Family Values*. Cambridge, MA: Harvard University Press.

Gilson, Dave, and Carolyn Perot. 2011. "It's the Inequality, Stupid." *Mother Jones* (March/April), http://motherjones.com/politics/2011/02/income-inequality -in-america-chart-graph.

Gipple, Emily, and Ben Gose. 2012. "America's Generosity Divide," *Chronicle of Philanthropy*, August 19, http://philanthropy.com/article/America's-Generosity -Divide/133775/.

Glass, Jennifer. 2013. "Its About the Work, Not the Office." *New York Times*, March 7, Op-Ed.

Go, Stella P. and Leticia T. Postrado. 1986. "Filipino Overseas Contract Workers: Their Families and Communities." In *Asian Labor Migration: Pipeline to the Middle East*, edited by Fred Arnold and Nasra Shah, 125–44. Boulder, CO: Westview Press.

Gobé, Marc. 2001. *Emotional Branding: The New Paradigm for Connecting Brands to People*. New York: Allworth Press.

Goffman, Erving. 1959. *Presentation of Self in Everyday Life*. Garden City, NY: Doubleday.

———. 1961. *Asylums: Essays on the Social Situation of Mental Patients and Other Inmates*. Garden City, NY: Anchor Books.

Goldthorpe, John H. 2010. "Analysing Social Inequality: A Critique of Two Recent Contributions from Economics and Epidemiology." *European Sociological Review* 26, no. 6: 731–44.

Goleman, Daniel. 1995. *Emotional Intelligence*. New York: Bantam Books.

Google Baby. 2009. Directed by Zippi Brand Frank. Israel: Brandcom, Ltd., 75 min.

Gopnik, Adam. 2002. "Bumping into Mr. Ravioli." *New Yorker*, September 30, 80–84.

Gove, Walter R. 1972. "The Relationship Between Sex Roles, Marital Status, and Mental Illness." *Social Forces* 51, no. 1: 34–44.

Gove, Walter R., Michael Hughes, and Omer R. Galle. 1983. *Overcrowding in the Household: An Analysis of Determinants and Effects*. New York: Academic Press.

Government of India, Ministry of Health and Family Welfare, and Indian Council of Medical Research. 2010. "The Assisted Reproductive

Technologies (Regulation) Bill—2010." New Delhi: Indian Council of Medical Research, www.icmr.nic.in/guide/ART%20REGULATION%20Draft%20Bill1.pdf.

Grandey, Alicia, Jim Diefendorff, and Deborah Rupp. 2013. *Emotional Labor in the 21st Century: Diverse Perspectives on Emotion Regulation at Work.* New York: Routledge Academic.

Granovetter, Mark. 1985. "Economic Action and Social Structure: The Problems of Embeddedness." *American Journal of Sociology* 91: 481–510.

Greenwald, Rachel. 2003. *Find a Husband after 35 Using What I Learned at Harvard Business School: A Simple 15-Step Action Program.* New York: Ballantine Books.

Greider, William. 1997. *One World, Ready or Not: The Manic Logic of Global Capitalism.* New York: Simon & Schuster.

Gugucheva, Magdalina. 2010. "Surrogacy in America." Cambridge, MA: Council for Responsible Genetics, www.councilforresponsiblegenetics.org/pageDocuments/KAEVEJ0A1M.pdf.

Guynn, Jessica. 2012. "Facebook Settles into New Home Just Days before Expected IPO Filing." *Los Angeles Times*, January 31, http://articles.latimes.com/2012/jan/31/business/la-fi-facebook-campus-20120131.

Habermas, Jürgen. 1985. *The Theory of Communicative Action.* Boston: Beacon Press.

Hacker, Helen Mayer. 1993. *Women as a Minority Group.* New York: Irvington.

Hall, Edward T. 1959. *The Silent Language.* Greenwich, CT: Fawcett Premier Books.

Halpern, Jodi, and Harvey M. Weinstein. 2004. "Rehumanizing the Other: Empathy and Reconciliation," *Human Rights Quarterly* 26: 561–81.

Harden, Garrett. 1995. "The Tragedy of the Commons." *Science* 162: 1243–48.

Harrington, Charlene. 2010. "Nursing Home Staffing Standards in State Statutes and Regulations." San Francisco: University of California, www.theconsumervoice.org/sites/default/files/advocate/action-center/Harrington-state-staffing-table-2010.pdf.

Harrington, Charlene, Helen Carrillo, and Brandee Woleslagle Blank. 2009. "Latest Data: Nursing Facilities, Staffing, Residents and Facility Deficiencies 2003 through 2008." San Francisco: University of California. Available at www.theconsumervoice.org/node/227.

Harriss, John. 2002. *Depoliticizing Development: The World Bank and Social Capital.* London: Anthem Press.

Hausmann, Ricardo, Laura D. Tyson, and Saadia Zahidi. 2010. *The Global Gender Gap Report 2010.* Geneva: World Economic Forum, www3.weforum.org/docs/WEF_GenderGap_Report_2010.pdf.

———. 2012. *The Global Gender Gap Report 2012.* Cologny/Geneva, Switzerland: World Economic Forum, www3.weforum.org/docs/WEF_GenderGap_Report_2012.pdf.

Hawkes, C., T. Lobstein, and Consortium for the Polmark. 2011. "Regulating the Commercial Promotion of Food to Children: A Survey of Actions Worldwide." *International Journal of Pediatric Obesity* 6, no. 2: 83–94.

Haworth, Abigail. 2007. "Surrogate Mothers: Womb for Rent." *Marie Claire*, July 29, www.marieclaire.com/world-reports/news/surrogate-mothers -india.

Hazan, Cindy, and Phillip Shaver. 1987. "Romantic Love Conceptualized as an Attachment Process." *Journal of Personality and Social Psychology* 52, no. 3: 511–24.

Heidmarsdottir, R. 2002. "Retirement Fantasies and Other Coping Strategies of Employees Experiencing Work-Life Conflicts." Ph.D. diss., University of Texas at Austin.

Hiestand, Bev. 2001. "For-Profit Nursing Care in Crisis." *Workers World*, December 27, www.workers.org/ww/2001/buffalo1227.php.

Hochschild, Arlie Russell. 1975. "The Sociology of Feeling and Emotion: Selected Possibilities." *Sociological Inquiry* 45, nos. 2–3: 280–307.

———. 1983. *The Managed Heart: The Commercialization of Human Feeling.* Berkeley: University of California Press.

———. 1997. *The Time Bind: When Work Becomes Home and Home Becomes Work.* New York: Metropolitan Books.

———. 2000a. "Global Care Chains and Emotional Surplus Value." In *On the Edge: Globalization and the New Millennium*, edited by Tony Giddens and Will Hutton, 130–46. London: Sage.

———. 2000b. "The Nanny Chain." *American Prospect*, January 3, 32–36.

———. 2003. *The Commercialization of Intimate Life: Notes from Work and Home.* Berkeley: University of California Press.

———. 2005. "The Chauffeur's Dilemma." *American Prospect*, June 19, http://prospect.org/article/chauffeurs-dilemma.

———. 2009. "Childbirth at the Global Crossroads." *American Prospect*, October: 25–28.

———. 2012. *The Outsourced Self: Intimate Life in Market Times.* New York: Metropolitan Press/Henry Holt.

Hochschild, Arlie Russell, and Anne Machung. 1989. *The Second Shift: Working Parents and the Revolution at Home.* New York: Viking Press.

Hondagneu-Sotelo, Pierrette. 1994. *Gendered Transitions: Mexican Experiences of Immigration.* Berkeley: University of California Press.

———. 2001. *Domestica: Immigrant Workers Cleaning and Caring in the Shadow of Affluence.* Berkeley: University of California Press.

———. 2003a. "Families on the Frontier: From Braceros in the Fields to Braceras in the Home." In *Latinos: Remaking America*, edited by Marcelo M. Suarez-Orozco and Mariela M. Paed. Berkeley: University of California Press.

———. 2003b. *Gender and U.S. Immigration: Contemporary Trends.* Berkeley: University of California Press.

Hood, Grace. 2011. "School Budget ABCs: Ads Plus Bus Equal Cash." KUNC report for National Public Radio, March 4. www.npr.org/2011/03/04 /134253858/School-Budget-ABCs-Ads-Plus-Bus-Equal-Cash.

Hoover, J. Edgar. 1962. *A Study of Communism.* New York: Holt, Rinehart and Winston.

Hout, Michael, and Claude S. Fischer. 2002. "Why More Americans Have No Religious Preference: Politics and Generations." *American Sociological Review* 67, no. 2: 165–90.

Huxley, Aldous. 1932. *Brave New World.* London: Chatto & Windus.

Hyde, Lewis. 1983. *The Gift: Imagination and the Erotic Life of Property.* New York: Vintage.

Iliff, Laurence. 2008. "U.S. Seniors Find They Can Get More—for Less: Retirees Enjoy Low-Cost Amenities, Family-Style TLC in Growing Market." *Dallas Morning News,* November 16, 1A.

Illouz, Eva. 2007. *Cold Intimacies: The Making of Emotional Capitalism.* Malden, MA: Polity.

Inglehart, Ronald, and Pippa Norris. 2007. "Uneven Secularization in Europe and the United States." In *Democracy and the New Religious Pluralism,* edited by Thomas Banchoff, 31–58. Oxford: Oxford University Press.

International Labour Office. 2011. "Economically Active Population, Estimates and Projections: Harmonised Datasets (1990–2020) with Selected Metadata." International Labour Office, Department of Statistics, http://laborsta.ilo.org /applv8/data/EAPEP/eapep_E.html.

Isaksen, Lise, Sambasivan Uma Devi, and Arlie R. Hochschild. 2008. "Global Care Crisis: A Problem of Capital, Care Chain or Commons?" *American Behavioral Scientist* 52, no. 3: 405–25.

Jaumotte, Florence. 2005. "Women and Work: Resolving the Riddle." *OECD Observer,* no. 248 (March), www.oecdobserver.org/news/fullstory.php/aid /1573/Women_and_work.html.

Kandel, William, and Grace Kao. 2001. "The Impact of Temporary Labor Migration on Mexican Children's Educational Aspirations and Performance." *International Migration Review* 35, no. 4: 1205–33.

Kantor, Jodi. 2011. "At Harvard, a Master's in Problem Solving." *New York Times,* December 25, A1.

Kaputa, Catherine. 2005. *U R a Brand: How Smart People Brand Themselves for Business Success.* Mountain View, CA: Davies-Black.

Kasser, Tim. 2002. *The High Price of Materialism.* Cambridge, MA: MIT Press.

———. 2011. "Cultural Values and the Well-Being of Future Generations: A Cross-National Study." *Journal of Cross-Cultural Psychology* 42, no. 2: 206–15.

Kelly, Marjorie. 2001. *The Divine Right of Capital: Dethroning the Corporate Aristocracy.* San Francisco: Berrett-Koehler.

Kenworthy, Lane, and Leslie McCall. 2008. "Inequality, Public Opinion and Redistribution." *Socio-Economic Review* 6: 35–68.

Kerala State Planning Board. 2002. *Economic Review.* Thiruvananthapuram: Government of Kerala.

Kessler, Ronald C., and Jane D. McLeod. 1984. "Sex Differences in Vulnerability to Undesirable Life Events." *American Sociological Review* 49, no. 5: 620–31.

Keys, Tracey, and Thomas W. Malnight. 2012. "Corporate Clout: The Influence of the World's Largest 100 Economic Entities." Strategy Dynamics Global Limited, www.globaltrends.com/knowledge-center/features/shapers-and -influencers/66-corporate-clout-the-influence-of-the-worlds-largest-100 -economic-entities#_edn2.

Khruemanee, Maliwan. 2002. "All Work, No Play: An Evaluation of Health and Employment Rights of Female Burmese Migrants Working as Domestic Workers in Bangkok." Paper presented at the Conference on Gender, Migration and Governance in Asia, Australian National University; Canberra; December 5–6.

Kisilevsky, Barbara S., Sylvia M. J. Hains, Kang Lee, Xing Xie, Hefeng Huang, Hai Hui Ye, Ke Zhang, and Zengping Wang. 2003. "Effects of Experience on Fetal Voice Recognition." *Psychological Science* 14, no. 3: 220–24.

Klinenberg, Eric. 2012. *Going Solo: The Extraordinary Rise and Surprising Appeal of Living Alone.* New York: Penguin Press.

Kohut, Andrew, and Bruce Stokes. 2006. *America against the World: How We Are Different and Why We Are Disliked.* New York: Times Books.

Konrath, Sara H., Edward H. O'Brien, and Courtney Hsing. 2011. "Changes in Dispositional Empathy in American College Students Over Time: A Meta-Analysis." *Personality and Social Psychology Review* 15, no. 2: 180–98.

Kundera, Milan. 1992. *The Book of Laughter and Forgetting.* London: Faber and Faber.

Kuttner, Robert. 1997. *Everything for Sale: The Virtues and Limits of Markets.* New York: Albert Knopf.

Lakoff, George. 1980. *Metaphors We Live By.* Chicago: University of Chicago Press.

Lasch, Christopher. 1977. *Haven in a Heartless World.* New York: Basic Books.

Levy, Robert. 1973. *Tahitians: Mind and Experience in the Society Islands.* Chicago: University of Chicago Press.

Lewin, Tamar. 2011. "Coal Curriculum Called Unfit for 4th Graders." *New York Times,* May 12, A18, www.nytimes.com/2011/05/12/education/12coal.html.

Leyens, Jacques-Philippe, Stephanie Demoulin, Jeroin Vaes, Ruth Gaunt, and Marie Paula Paladino. 2007. "Infra-humanization: The Wall of Group Differences," *Social Issues and Policy Review* 1, no. 1: 139–72.

Linn, Susan. Forthcoming. "Too Many Screens, Too Much Stuff," *2012 Yearbook for the International Clearinghouse on Children, Youth and Media*. Göteborg, Sweden: Nordicom, University of Gothenburg.

Livingston, Gretchen. 2011. "In a Down Economy, Fewer Births." Washington, DC: Pew Research Center; Pew Social and Demographic Trends, www.pewsocialtrends.org/files/2011/10/REVISITING-FERTILITY-AND-THE-RECESSION-FINAL.pdf.

Lomax, Eric. 1995. *The Railway Man*. New York: Norton Books.

Lopez, Steven H. 2006. "Emotional Labor and Organized Emotional Care: Conceptualizing Nursing Home Care Work." *Work and Occupations* 33, no. 2: 133–60.

Mahler, Irwin. 1974. "A Comparative Study of Locus of Control." *Psychologia: An International Journal of Psychology in the Orient* 17, no. 3: 135–39.

Marcuse, Herbert. 1955. *Eros and Civilization*. New York: Vintage.

Martin, Joyce A., Brady E. Hamilton, Stephanie J. Ventura, Michelle J. K. Osterman, Sharon Kirmeyer, T. J. Mathews, and Elizabeth C. Wilson. 2011. "Births: Final Data for 2009." Hyattsville, MD: National Center for Health Statistics.

Marx, Karl. 1844/1986. *The Economic and Philosophic Manuscripts*. New York: International.

Marx, Karl, and Friedrich Engels. 1887/1967. *Capital: A Critique of Political Economy*. New York: International.

Mattera, Philip, and Anna Purinton. 2004. "Shopping for Subsidies: How Wal-Mart Uses Taxpayer Money to Finance Its Never-Ending Growth." Washington, DC: Good Jobs First, www.goodjobsfirst.org/sites/default/files/docs/pdf/wmtstudy.pdf.

Mauss, M. 1954/2000. *The Gift: The Form and Reason for Exchange in Archaic Societies*. New York: W. W. Norton.

McCall, Leslie. 2005. "Do They Know and Do They Care? Americans' Awareness of Rising Inequality." Paper presented at the Russell Sage Foundation Social Inequality Conference; University of California–Berkeley; May 2005, www.russellsage.org/sites/all/files/u4/McCall.pdf.

McNally, David, and Karl D. Speak. 2011. *Be your Own Brand: Achieve More of What You Want by Being More of Who You Are*. San Francisco: Berrett-Koehler.

Merton, Robert K. 1965. "Bureaucratic Structure and Personality." In *Social Theory and Social Structure*, 195–206. New York: Free Press.

Milkie, M. A., S. B. Raley, and S. M. Bianchi. 2009. "Taking on the Second Shift: Time Allocations and Time Pressures of U.S. Parents with Preschoolers." *Social Forces* 88, no. 2: 487–518.

Mills, C. Wright. 1963. *Power, Politics and People: The Collected Essays of C. Wright Mills*. New York: Oxford University Press.

————. 1967. *The Sociological Imagination*. New York: Oxford University Press.

Minder, Raphael. 2011. "Spain to Raise Retirement Age to 67." *New York Times,* January 27, www.nytimes.com/2011/01/28/world/europe/28iht-spain28.html.

Miraftab, Faranak. 2011. "Faraway Intimate Development: Global Restructuring of Social Reproduction." *Journal of Planning Education and Research* 31, no. 4: 392–405.

Mohapatra, Sanket, Dilip Ratha, and Ani Silwal. 2011. "Outlook for Remittance Flows 2012–14." *World Bank Migration and Development Brief* 17, http://siteresources.worldbank.org/INTPROSPECTS/Resources/334934-1110315015165/MigrationandDevelopmentBrief17.pdf.

Mokros, Janice R., Sumru Erkut, Lynne Spichiger, and Spencer Foundation. 1981. *Mentoring and Being Mentored: Sex-Related Patterns among College Professors*. Wellesley, MA: Wellesley College, Center for Research on Women.

Molnar, Alex, Faith Boninger, and Joseph Fogarty. 2011. "The Educational Cost of Schoolhouse Commercialism." Boulder, CO: National Education Policy Center.

Momsen, Janet Henshall. 1999. *Gender, Migration and Domestic Service*. London: Routledge.

Morada, Hector. 2001. "Left-Behind Households of Filipino Overseas Filipino Workers." Paper presented at the Asian Population Network Workshop on Migration and the Asian Family in a Globalising World; Singapore; April 16–18.

More, Thomas, and Thomas Stevens. 2000. "Do User Fees Exclude Low-Income People from Resource-Based Recreation? New Hampshire, Vermont Area." *Journal of Leisure Research* 32, no. 3: 341–57.

Morgan, Mrs. George A. 1965a. "Language and the Foreign Service Wife." *Department of State Newsletter*, no. 45 (January).

————. 1965b. "Language and the Foreign Service Wife." *Department of State Newsletter*, no. 47 (March).

Morin, Richard. 1998. "Keeping the Faith." *Washington Post,* January 12, www.washingtonpost.com/wp-srv/politics/polls/wat/archive/wat011298.htm.

Mueller, Stephen L., and Anisya S. Thomas. 2001. "Culture and Entrepreneurial Potential: A Nine Country Study of Locus of Control and Innovativeness." *Journal of Business Venturing* 16, no. 1: 51–75.

Murray, Charles. 2012. *Coming Apart: The State of White America, 1960–2010*. New York: Crown Forum.

Nafstad, Hilde Eileen, Rolv Mikkel Blakar, Erik Carlquist, Joshua Marvle Phelps, and Kim Rand-Hendriksen. 2007. "Ideology and Power: The Influence of Current Neo-Liberalism in Society." *Journal of Community and Applied Social Psychology* 17, no. 4: 313–27.

————. 2009. "Globalization, Neo-Liberalism and Community Psychology." *American Journal of Community Psychology* 43, no. 1–2: 162–75.

Newman, Martyn. 2008. *Emotional Capitalists: The New Leaders*. Chichester, UK: John Wiley & Sons.

Nicolson, Harold. 1952. *Diplomacy*. London: Oxford University Press.

Niemeier, Debbie A., and Cristina González. 2004. "Breaking into the Guildmasters' Club: What We Know about Women Science and Engineering Department Chairs at AAU Universities." *NWSA Journal* 16, no. 1: 157–71.

Nippert-Eng, Christena E. 1996. *Home and Work: Negotiating Boundaries through Everyday Life*. Chicago: University of Chicago Press.

Nolen-Hoeksema, Susan. 1987. "Sex Differences in Unipolar Depression: Evidence and Theory." *Psychological Bulletin* 101, no. 2: 259–82.

Norris, Floyd. 2011. "As Corporate Profits Rise, Workers' Income Declines." *New York Times*, August 6, B3, www.nytimes.com/2011/08/06/business/workers-wages-chasing-corporate-profits-off-the-charts.html.

Ogden, Cynthia, and Bill Dietz. 2010. "The Childhood Obesity Epidemic: Threats and Opportunities." Online presentation for Public Health Grand Rounds, Centers for Disease Control and Prevention, www.cdc.gov/about/grand-rounds/archives/2010/06-June.htm.

Organisation for Economic Co-operation and Development (OECD). 2011. "Table B. Employment/Population Ratios, Activity and Unemployment Rates: Women Aged 15–64 Years (Percentages)." In *Employment Outlook 2011 Statistical Annex*, edited by Directorate for Employment, Labour and Social Affairs, www.oecd.org/document/2/0,3746,en_2649_33729_48614146_1_1_1_1,00.html.

Orwell, George. 1949. *Nineteen Eighty-Four*. London: Secker and Warberg.

Ostergren, David, Frederic I. Solop, and Kristi K. Hagen. 2005. "National Park Service Fees: Value for the Money or a Barrier to Visitation?" *Journal of Park and Recreation Administration* 23, no. 1: 18–36.

Page, John, and Sonia Plaza. 2006. "Migration Remittances and Development: A Review of Global Evidence." *Journal of African Economies* 15, Suppl. 2: 245–336.

Pande, A. 2009a. "'It May Be Her Eggs But It's My Blood': Surrogates and Everyday Forms of Kinship in India." *Qualitative Sociology* 32: 379–97.

———. 2009b. "Not an 'Angel,' Not a 'Whore': Commercial Surrogacy as 'Dirty' Workers in India." *Indian Journal of Gender Studies* 16: 141–73.

———. 2010. "'At Least I Am Not Sleeping with Anyone': Resisting the Stigma of Commercial Surrogacy in India." *Feminist Studies* 36: 292–312.

Papanek, Hanna. 1973. "Men, Women, and Work: Reflections on the Two-Person Career," *American Journal of Sociology* 78, no. 4: 852–72.

Parreñas, Rhacel Salazar. 2001. *Servants of Globalization: Women, Migration, and Domestic Work*. Stanford, CA: Stanford University Press.

————. 2003. "The Care Crisis in the Philippines: Children and Transnational Families in the New Global Economy." In *Global Woman: Nannies, Maids and Sex Workers in the New Economy*, edited by Barbara Ehrenreich and Arlie Russell Hochschild, 39–55. New York: Metropolitan Books/Henry Holt.

————. 2005. *Children of Global Migration: Transnational Families and Gendered Woes*. Palo Alto, CA: Stanford University Press.

Parsons, T., and R. F. Bales. 1955. *Family, Interaction and Socialization Process*. Glencoe, IL: Free Press.

Paules, G. 1991. *Dishing It Out: Power and Resistance among Waitresses in a New Jersey Restaurant*. Philadelphia: Temple University Press.

Pear, Robert. 2008. "Violations Reported at 94% of Nursing Homes." *New York Times*, September 30, A20.

Penfield, Anne. 1963. "The Ambassador's Wife." *Foreign Service Journal* (August).

Pet, Doug. 2011. "India Moves Toward Regulation of Assisted Reproduction and Surrogacy." *Biopolitical Times*, February 10, www.biopoliticaltimes.org /article.php?id=5591.

Peters, Tom. 1997. "The Brand Called You." *Fast Company*, August 31, www .fastcompany.com/magazine/10/brandyou.html.

Peterson, Esther. 1965. "Esther Peterson Discusses the Foreign Service Wife." *Department of State Newsletter*, No. 48 (April): 20.

Pew Research Center. 2012. "'Nones' on the Rise: One-in-Five Adults Have No Religious Affiliation." Washington, DC: Pew Research Center's Forum on Religious & Public Life, www.pewforum.org/uploadedFiles/Topics /Religious_Affiliation/Unaffiliated/NonesontheRise-full.pdf.

Pew Research Center for the People and the Press. 2010. *The People and Their Government: Distrust, Discontent, Anger and Partisan Rancor*. Washington, DC: Author.

Piccalo, Gina. 2004. "The Pitch That You Won't See Coming." *Los Angeles Times*, August 22, http://articles.latimes.com/2004/aug/22/entertainment/ca -piccalo22.

Piccinelli, Marco, and Greg Wilkinson. 2000. "Gender Differences in Depression." *British Journal of Psychiatry* 177, no. 6: 486–92.

Piff, Paul K., Michael W. Kraus, Stéphane Côté, Bonnie Hayden Cheng, and Dacher Keltner. 2010. "Having Less, Giving More: The Influence of Social Class on Prosocial Behavior." *Journal of Personality and Social Psychology* 99, no. 5: 771–84.

Pinker, Steven. 2011. *The Better Angels of Our Nature: Why Violence Has Declined*. New York: Viking.

Pissarides, Christopher, Pietro Garibaldi, Claudia Olivetti, Barbara Petrongolo, and Etienne Wasmer. 2003. "Women in the Labour Force: How Well

Is Europe Doing?" Presented at the 5th European Conference of the Fondazione Debenedetti: "European Women at Work"; Alghero, Italy; June 21.

Polanyi, Karl. 1944. *The Great Transformation: The Political and Economic Origins of Our Time.* Boston: Beacon Press.

Portes, Alejandro. 1998. "Social Capital: Its Origins and Applications in Modern Sociology." *Annual Review of Sociology* 24: 1–24.

Post, Emily. 1960. *Etiquette: The Blue Book of Social Usage.* 10th ed. New York: Funk & Wagnalls.

Pugh, Allison J. 2005. "Selling Compromise: Toys, Motherhood, and the Cultural Deal." *Gender and Society* 19, no. 6: 729–49.

———. Forthcoming. *The Tumbleweed Society: Working and Caring in an Age of Insecurity.* New York: Oxford University Press.

Putnam, Robert. 1993. *Making Democracy Work: Civic Traditions in Modern Italy.* Princeton, NJ: Princeton University Press.

———. 1995. "Bowling Alone: America's Declining Social Capital." *Journal of Democracy* 6, no. 1: 65–78.

———. 2000. *Bowling Alone: The Collapse and Revival of American Community.* New York: Simon and Schuster.

Ramji, Vidya, and S. Uma Devi. 2003 "Caring across Borders: Voices from the South." Paper presented at the 44th ISA Annual International Convention on the Construction and Cumulation of Knowledge; Portland, OR; February–March 1.

Ratha, Dilip, and Zhimei Xu. 2008. *Migration and Remittances Factbook 2008.* Washington, DC: World Bank.

Reyes, Melanie M. 2008. "Migration and Filipino Children Left-Behind: A Literature Review." Quezon City, Philippines: Miriam College/UNICEF.

Reyes, Sonia. 2004. "Brand Builders: Putting the Bite Back into Ruffles." *Brandweek* 45, no. 11: 18.

Rifkin, Jeremy. 2000. *The Age of Access: The New Culture of Hypercapitalism, Where All of Life Is a Paid-For Experience.* New York: Jeremy P. Tarcher/Penguin.

———. 2009. *The Empathic Civilization: The Race to Global Consciousness in a World in Crisis.* New York: Jeremy P. Tarcher/Penguin.

Robles, Arodys, and Susan Cotts Watkins. 1993. "Immigration and Family Separation in the U.S. at the Turn of the Twentieth Century," *Journal of Family History* 18, no. 3: 191–211.

Roetter, Charles. 1963. *The Diplomatic Art: An Informal History of World Diplomacy.* Philadelphia: Macrae Smith.

Roos, Patricia A., and Mary L. Gatta. 2009. "Gender (In)equity in the Academy: Subtle Mechanisms and the Production of Inequality." *Research in Social Stratification and Mobility* 27, no. 3: 177–200.

Rowe, Jonathan. 2002. "The Promise of Commons." *Earth Island Journal,* Autumn: 28–30.

Roy, Nilanjana S. 2011. "Protecting the Rights of Surrogate Mothers in India." *New York Times,* October 4, www.nytimes.com/2011/10/05/world/asia/05iht -letter05.html.

Rudrappa, Sharmila. 2012. "India's Reproductive Assembly Line." *Contexts* 11, no. 2: 22–27.

Salcedo, Luis Moreno. 1959. *A Guide to Protocol.* Rev. ed. Manila, Philippines: University Book Supply.

Salmon, J. 1996. "For Hire: Helpers for Harried Parenting." *Washington Post,* September 17, A1.

Saltmarsh, Matthew. 2010. "France and Spain Act to Rein in Budgets." *New York Times,* June 17, B7, www.nytimes.com/2010/06/17/business/global/17euro.html.

SAMA Resource Group for Women and Health. 2012. "The Regulation of Surrogacy in India: Questions and Concerns." *Kafila,* http://kafila.org/2012 /01/10/the-regulation-of-surrogacy-in-india-questions-and-concerns-sama/

Sandholtz, Kurt, Brooklyn Derr, Kathy Buckner, and Dawn Carlson. 2002. *Beyond Juggling: Rebalancing Your Busy Life.* San Francisco: Berrett-Koehler.

———. 2004. "Beyond Juggling: Outsourcing—Having It All, but Not Doing It All." Business Know-How.Com, www.businessknowhow.com/growth/ beyondjuggling4.htm.

Satow, Ernest Mason. 1917. *A Guide to Diplomatic Practice.* London: Longmans.

Scheler, Max. 1912/1961. *Ressentiment.* Edited by Lewis A. Coser. Translated by William W. Holdheim. New York: Free Press of Glencoe.

Schmalzbauer, Leah. 2004. "Searching for Wages and Mothering from Afar: The Case of Honduran Transnational Families." *Journal of Marriage and Family* 66, no. 5: 1317–31.

Schor, Juliet B. 1992. *The Overworked American: The Unexpected Decline of Leisure.* New York: Basic Books.

———. 2004. *Born to Buy: The Commercialized Child and the New Consumer Culture.* New York: Scribner.

———. 2010. *Plenitude: The New Economics of True Wealth.* New York: Penguin Press.

Schor, Juliet B., and Margaret Ford. 2007. "From Tastes Great to Cool: Children's Food Marketing and the Rise of the Symbolic." *Journal of Law, Medicine and Ethics* 35, no. 1: 10–21.

Schor, Juliet B., and D. B. Holt, eds. 2000. *The Consumer Society Reader.* New York: New Press.

Schwab, Klaus, and Saadia Zahidi. 2010. "Preface." In *The Global Gender Gap Report,* edited by Ricardo Hausmann, Laura D. Tyson, and Saadia Zahidi, v. Geneva: World Economic Forum.

Shorto, Russell. 2008. "No Babies?" *New York Times Magazine,* June 29, www
.nytimes.com/2008/06/29/magazine/29Birth-t.html.

Simmel, Georg. 1978. *The Philosophy of Money.* London: Routledge/Kegan Paul.

Smelser, Neil J. 2002. *The Social Edges of Psychoanalysis.* New York: Oxford
University Press.

Smerdon, Usha Rengachary. 2008. "Crossing Bodies, Crossing Borders:
International Surrogacy between the United States and India." *Cumberland
Law Review* 39, no. 1: 15–85.

Smith, Adam. 1759/1976. *The Theory of Moral Sentiments.* Oxford: Clarendon
Press.

———. 1776/1875. *An Inquiry into the Nature and Causes of the Wealth of Nations.*
London: Ward, Lock and Tyler.

Smith, Bridie. 2005. "Making Your Bundle of Joy™ Stand Out." *The Age,*
February 12, www.theage.com.au/news/National/Making-your-Bundle-of
-Joy153-stand-out/2005/02/11/1108061875050.html.

Smith, T. W. 2003. "Altruism in Contemporary America: A Report from the
National Altruism Study." Report prepared for the Fetzer Institute. University of Chicago: National Opinion Research Center.

Snowdon, Christopher. 2010. *The Spirit Level Delusion: Fact-Checking the Left's
New Theory of Everything.* Ripton, UK: Little Dice/Democracy Institute.

Social Security Administration. 2009. "Normal Retirement Age." Baltimore:
Social Security Association, www.ssa.gov/OACT/ProgData/nra.html.

Solari, Cinzia. 2006a. "Professionals and Saints: How Immigrant Careworkers
Negotiate Gendered Identities at Work." *Gender and Society* 20: 301–31.

———. 2006b. "Survival and Status Migration Patterns: Constructions of
Poverty, Motherhood, and the Ukrainian Nation." Presented at the 101st
Annual Meeting of the American Sociological Association; Montreal,
Canada; August 11–14.

———. 2010. "Exile vs. Exodus: Nationalism and Gendered Migration from
Ukraine to Italy and California." Ph.D. diss., University of California,
Berkeley.

———. 2011. "Between 'Europe' and 'Africa': Building the New Ukraine on the
Shoulders of Migrant Women." In *Mapping Difference: The Many Faces of Women
in Ukraine,* edited by Marian J. Rubchak, 23–40. New York: Berghahn Books.

Spector, Paul E., Cary L. Cooper, Juan I. Sanchez, Michael O'Driscoll, Kate
Sparks, Peggy Bernin, Andre Büssing, et al. 2001. "Do National Levels of
Individualism and Internal Locus of Control Relate to Well-Being?: An
Ecological Level International Study." *Journal of Organizational Behavior* 22,
no. 8: 815–32.

Stack, Carol B. 1974. *All Our Kin: Strategies for Survival in a Black Community.*
New York: Harper & Row.

Stets, Jan E. 2010. "Future Directions in the Sociology of Emotions." *Emotion Review* 2, no. 3: 265–68.

Stolberg, Sheryl. 2012. "Political Lessons, from a Mother's Losing Run." *New York Times*, February 24, www.nytimes.com/2012/02/24/us/politics/political -lessons-from-a-mothers-losing-run.html.

Streitfeld, David. 2010. "Anger as a Private Company Takes Over Libraries." *New York Times*, September 27, A1, www.nytimes.com/2010/09/27/business /27libraries.html.

Svitnev, Konstantin. 2010. "Legal Regulation of Assisted Reproduction Treatment in Russia." *Reproductive Biomedicine Online* 20, no. 7: 892–94.

Taylor, Shelley E. 2003. *The Tending Instinct: Women, Men and the Biology of Relationships.* New York: Henry Holt.

Taylor, Tiffany, Christine Mallinson, and Katrina Bloch. 2008. "'Looking for a Few Good Women': Volunteerism as an Interaction in Two Organizations." *Nonprofit and Voluntary Sector Quarterly* 37: 389–410.

Teinowitz, Ira. 2006. "Army Rolls Out 'Strong' New Campaign," *Advertising Age*, October 9, http://adage.com/article/news/army-rolls-strong-campaign /112420/.

Teman, Elly. 2010. "The Last Outpost of the Nuclear Family: A Cultural Critique of Israeli Surrogacy Policy." In *Kin, Gene, Community: Reproductive Technology among Jewish Israelis,* edited by Daphna Birenbaum-Carmeli and Yoram Carmeli, 107–26. Oxford: Berghahn Books.

Themnér, Lotta, and Peter Wallensteen. 2012. "Armed Conflicts, 1946–2011." *Journal of Peace Research* 49, no. 4: 565–75.

Thomas, Amelia. 2005. "Israeli and Palestinian Children Participate in Peace Camps," *Middle East Times*, August 2, www.commongroundnews.org/article .php?id=967.

Thompson, James Westfall, and Saul K. Padover. 1963. *Secret Diplomacy, Espionage, and Cryptography, 1500–1815.* New York: Frederick Ungar.

Thomson, Kevin M. 1998. *Emotional Capital: Capturing Hearts and Minds to Create Lasting Business Success.* Oxford, UK: Capstone.

Tocqueville, Alexis de. 1840/1945. *Democracy in America.* Translated by Henry Reeve. Vol. 2, book 2. New York: Knopf.

Tolich, Martin B. 1993. "Alienating and Liberating Emotions at Work: Supermarket Clerks' Performance of Customer Service." *Journal of Contemporary Ethnography* 22: 361–81.

Tough, Paul. 2002. "The Year in Ideas; Dad's Performance Review." *New York Times Magazine*, December 15, 80–82, www.nytimes.com/2002/12/15 /magazine/the-year-in-ideas-dad-s-performance-review.html.

Tronto, Joan C. 1993. *Moral Boundaries: A Political Argument for an Ethic of Care.* New York: Routledge.

Twain, Mark. 1885/1992. *The Adventures of Tom Sawyer & The Adventures of Huckleberry Finn*. Ware, UK: Wordsworth Classics.

Twenge Jean M., W. Keith Campbell, and Elise C. Freeman. 2012. "Generational Differences in Young Adults' Life Goals, Concern for Others, and Civic Orientation, 1966–2009." *Journal of Personality and Social Psychology* 102, no. 5: 1045–62.

UNICEF. 2007. "Child Poverty in Perspective: An Overview of Child Well-Being in Rich Countries." *Innocenti Report Card 7*. Florence: Innocenti Research Centre.

———. 2010. "The Children Left Behind: A League Table of Inequality in Child Well-Being in the World's Rich Countries." *Innocenti Report Card 9*. Florence: Innocenti Research Centre.

United Nations, Department of Economic and Social Affairs. 2009. *International Migration 2009*. New York: Population Division, United Nations Department of Economic and Social Affairs, www.un.org/esa/population/publications /2009Migration_Chart/ittmig_wallchart09.pdf.

———. 2011. *Trends in International Migrant Stock: Migrants by Age and Sex*. United Nations database, POP/DB/MIG/Stock/Rev.2011. New York: Population Division, U.N. Department of Economic and Social Affairs.

U.S. Department of State. 1963. *Social Usage Abroad: A Guide for American Officials and Their Families*. Washington, DC: Office of Operations, U.S. Department of State.

———. 1964. "Anatomy of the Ambassador." *Department of State Newsletter*, no. 33 (January), 18.

———. 1967. *The Country Team*. Department of State Publication, no. 8193. Department and Foreign Service Series 136. Washington, DC: U.S. Government Printing Office.

———. 2009. "Protocol, Precedence and Formalities." *Foreign Affairs Manual*. Vol. 2, Chapter 300. Data.gov, http://explore.data.gov/d/2hbe-wycu.

Uppsala Conflict Data Program. 2012. "Definitions." Department of Peace and Conflict Research, Uppsala University, Sweden. www.pcr.uu.se/research /ucdp/definitions.

Useem, Jerry. 2000. "Welcome to the New Company Town." *Fortune*, January 10, 62–70.

Utrata, Jennifer. 2008. "*Babushki* as Surrogate Wives: How Single Mothers and Grandmothers Negotiate the Division of Labor in Russia." Institute of Slavic, East European and Eurasian Studies, BPS Working Paper Series, http://escholarship.org/uc/item/3b18d2p8.

Uzzi, B. 1997. "Social Structure and Competition in Interfirm Networks: The Paradox of Embeddedness." *Administrative Science Quarterly* 42: 35–67.

Veblen, Thorstein. 1899/1912. *The Theory of the Leisure Class*. New York: B. W. Huebsch.

Wacquant, Loïc. 2004. *Body and Soul: Notebooks of an Apprentice Boxer*. New York: Oxford University Press.

Walkerdine, Valerie, and Luis Jimenez. 2012. *Gender, Work and Community after De-Industrialization: A Psychosocial Approach to Affect*. London: Palgrave MacMillan.

Wallulis, Jerald. 1998. *The New Insecurity: The End of the Standard Job and Family*. Albany: State University of New York Press.

Warner, Judith. 2010. "The Charitable-Giving Divide." *New York Times Sunday Magazine*, August 22, MM11, www.nytimes.com/2010/08/22/magazine /22FOB-wwln-t.html.

Weber, Max. 1930/2001. *The Protestant Ethic and the Spirit of Capitalism*. London: Routledge.

Weisberg, D. Kelly. 2005. *The Birth of Surrogacy in Israel*. Gainesville: University of Florida Press.

Weissman, Myrna M., and Gerald L. Klerman. 1977. "Sex Differences and the Epidemiology of Depression." *Archives of General Psychiatry* 34, no. 1: 98–111.

Wellman, Barry, and Stephen D. Berkowitz. 1988. *Social Structures: A Network Approach*. Cambridge: Cambridge University Press.

Wellman, Barry, and Scot Wortley. 1990. "Different Strokes from Different Folks: Community Ties and Social Support." *American Journal of Sociology* 96, no. 3: 558–88.

Wheatley, Alan. 2003. "Remittances: An Economic Lifeline or a Liability?" *Reuters News Agency*, December 18, http://web.archive.org/web /20070808144649/http://in.news.yahoo.com/031218/137/2afq3.html.

When Mother Comes Home for Christmas/Otan erthei i mama gia ta Hristougenna. 1996. Written and directed by Nilita Vachani. Greece/Germany: FilmSixteen, ZDF, Greek Film Centre, 16mm, 109 min.

Wilkinson, Richard, and Kate Pickett. 2009. *The Spirit Level: Why Greater Equality Makes Societies Stronger*. London: Bloomsbury Press.

Winfield, Louise. 1962. *Living Overseas*. Washington, DC: Public Affairs Press.

Winnicott, D. W. 1965. *The Maturational Processes and the Facilitating Environment: Studies in the Theory of Emotional Development*. New York: International Universities Press.

Wolff, Kurt. 1951. *The Sociology of George Simmel*. New York: Free Press.

Woolcock, Michael. 2001. "The Place of Social Capital in Understanding Social and Economic Outcomes." *Isuma Canadian Journal of Policy Research* 2, no. 1: 11–17.

World Bank. 2011. *Migration and Remittances Factbook 2011*. 2nd ed. Washington, DC: International Bank for Reconstruction and Development/World Bank,

http://siteresources.worldbank.org/INTLAC/Resources/Factbook2011
-Ebook.pdf.

———. 2013. Annual remittances data: Inflows. Washington, DC: International
Bank for Reconstruction and Development/World Bank, http://
go.worldbank.org/092X1CHHDo.

World Health Organization. 2012. "Prevalence of Alcohol Use Disorders (%),
Adults Males and Females (15 Years and Above), 2004." World Health
Organization, Resources for the Treatment and Prevention of Substance Use
Disorders, http://gamapserver.who.int/gho/interactive_charts/substance
_abuse/bod_alcohol_prevalence/atlas.html.

Yeates, Nicola. 2004. "Global Care Chains: Critical Reflections and Lines of
Inquiry." *International Feminist Journal of Politics* 6, no. 3: 369–91.

Zelizer, Viviana A. 1994. *The Social Meaning of Money: Pin Money, Paychecks, Poor
Relief and Other Currencies.* New York: Basic Books.

———. 2005. *The Purchase of Intimacy.* Princeton, NJ: Princeton University Press.

———. 2010. "How I Became a Relational Economic Sociologist and What Does
That Mean?" Paper presented at the Relational Work Conference; University
of California–Davis; May 1.

Zimmerman, Frederick J., and Janice F. Bell. 2010. "Associations of Television
Content Type and Obesity in Children." *American Journal of Public Health* 100,
no. 2: 334–40.

Zlotnik, Hania. 2003. "The Global Dimensions of Female Migration." *MPI
Migration Information Source,* March, www.migrationinformation.org/feature
/display.cfm?ID=109.

Zukin, Sharon, and Paul DiMaggio. 1990. *Structures of Capital: The Social
Organization of the Economy.* New York: Cambridge University Press.

Credits

Earlier versions of the essays in this book were previously published as listed below.

Can Emotional Labor Be Fun? "Invited Commentary: Can Emotional Labour Be Fun?" *International Journal of Work Organisation and Emotion* 3, no. 2 (July 2009): 112–19.

Time Strategies. "On the Edge of the Time Bind: Time and Market Culture," *Social Research* 72, no. 2 (2005): 339–54, www.socres.org.

The Diplomat's Wife. "The Role of the Ambassador's Wife: An Exploratory Study," *Journal of Marriage and Family* 31, no. 1 (February 1969): 73–87.

The Personalized Market and the Marketized Self. "Beyond Tocqueville's Telescope: The Personalized Brand and the Branded Self" (with Sarah Garrett), *Hedgehog Review* 13, no. 3 (2011): 82–95.

At Home in the Office. "Feeling at Home at Work: Life in Academic Departments" (with Barrie Thorne), *Qualitative Sociology* 20, no. 4 (July 1997): 517–20.

Rent-a-Mom. " 'Rent a Mom' and Other Services: Markets, Meanings and Emotions," *International Journal of Work Organisation and Emotion* 1, no. 1 (July 2005): 74–86.

Two-Way Global Traffic in Care. Based on a talk given at the University of Frankfurt, Germany, April 23, 2009.

Children Left Behind. "Global Care Crisis: A Problem of Capital, Care Chain, or Commons?" (with Lise Widding Isaksen and Sambasivan Uma Devi), *American Behavioral Scientist* 52, no. 3 (November 2008): 405–25.

The Surrogate's Womb. "Childbirth at the Global Crossroads," *American Prospect* 20, no. 8 (October 2009): 25–28.

Index